The Traveler's Gun & Knife Law Book

The Essential Resource For Travelers, Hunters and Concealed-Carry Permit Holders

Covering All Fifty States And the District of Columbia

First Edition

David Wong, Esq.

The Traveler's Gun and Knife Law Book:
The Essential Resource for Travelers, Hunters and Concealed-Carry Permit Holders
by David Wong, Esq.

Published by Spartan Press, L.L.C.
Post Office Box 1598
Nashua, New Hampshire 03061-1598

On the Web: SpartanPressOnline.com

ISBN-13: [Print Edition] 978-0-9826840-0-9

Gun stores, clubs, organizations, libraries, firearms instructors and educators: Quantity discounts are available! Contact Spartan Press at the website above for information.

Booksellers and Distributors: Quantity discounts and wholesale pricing available. Visit **SpartanPressOnline.com** for the quantity discount schedule and more information.

Cover design by Ralph Richardson.

Printed in the United States of America.

Table of Contents

Important Notice

This book is not "the law", does not purport to offer legal advice, and is not a substitute for such advice. The information in this book is of a general nature and is presented for informational purposes only, and should not be used as a substitute for competent legal advice regarding specific situations from a lawyer licensed to practice in the jurisdiction you are in, or traveling to or through.

The author is a licensed attorney and has researched and consulted with a variety of sources in preparing this book, and the information is believed to be generally accurate as of the date of publication. However, no guarantee of accuracy is expressed or implied, and the reader should not consider any information in this book (including, but not limited to, any explanatory or summary text) as legal advice, or a restatement of the law. The author and publisher of this book expressly disclaim any and all liability whatsoever arising out of any reliance on the information contained in this book, or due to any errors or omissions therein.

Laws and regulations concerning weapons, and specifically such items as guns and knives, are constantly changing. What's legal today may not be legal tomorrow. In addition, court decisions (case law) can, and often do, change the law and/or affect the meaning and interpretation of statutory law. Also, a great number of cities, towns, county governments and governmental agencies have enacted their own rules, regulations, and ordinances concerning weapons within their respective jurisdictions. The author and publisher make no representation that the information in this book includes all such laws, rules, regulations, ordinances, or other legal requirements, restrictions or prohibitions.

You are responsible for complying with all of the laws and other legal requirements of any jurisdiction that you are in, or traveling to or through, and are strongly urged to consult with a competent, qualified attorney and/or local authorities in advance to determine the current status and applicability of such laws or other legal requirements to specific situations or circumstances you may face.

1 Introduction

A well regulated Militia, being necessary to the security of a free State, the right of the people to keep and bear Arms, shall not be infringed.

United States Constitution, Amendment II.

In a perfect world, there would be no need for this book.

In a perfect world, the twenty seven words of the Second Amendment quoted above, incorporated against the states via the Fourteenth Amendment, would be all the law a peaceable citizen needed to know to determine what's legal or not when it comes to carrying guns or knives, or any other type of arms, for that matter.

Unfortunately, in case you haven't noticed, we live in a world that is far, far from perfect. How else to explain the bewildering and massive collection of laws that regulate what, how, when and where peaceable citizens can carry arms?

To give you some idea of the scale of how utterly vast and intrusive the law has become, consider that the United States Code, the body of federal statutory law, is over 50,000 pages long. Single spaced, in small type. The Code of Federal Regulations, the body of federal administrative rules, is over 161,000 pages long. Both keep getting more voluminous every year. And that's just federal statutory law. Add to that the many hundreds of thousands of pages of federal appellate case law *interpreting* those laws and regulations, and it's safe to say that no single human being – no lawyer, no judge, no one – knows all of what federal law requires or prohibits.

Include the many tens of thousands of pages of state statutory law, administrative rules, and local ordinances for each state, along with state appellate court case law, and simply finding the law becomes a challenge. What a far cry from the handful of handwritten parchment pages that comprise the U.S. Constitution and the Bill of Rights.

Indeed, one has only to look at the thousands of laws at the local, state, and federal levels pertaining to arms – weapons – to realize just how far we've strayed from the Republic of armed citizens that the founders envisioned:

George Washington: "The very atmosphere of firearms anywhere and everywhere restrains evil interference – they deserve a place of honor with all that is good."

Thomas Jefferson: "No free man shall ever be debarred the use of arms."

Patrick Henry: "The great object is, that every man be armed ... Everyone who is able may have a gun."

George Mason: "To disarm the people ... [is] the best and most effectual way to enslave them."

Thomas Jefferson: "The strongest reason for the people to retain the right to keep and bear arms is, as a last resort, to protect themselves against tyranny in government."

Our nation's founders and other early commentators knew how important the right to keep and bear arms was to the preservation of ordered liberty. Can there be any doubt that the wise, brave men who founded this nation would be horrified at the infringements we have allowed our elected servants to impose upon us? Yet that is the sad situation we find ourselves in today. Thus, as we work to roll back those infringements, we, as peaceful, law-abiding armed citizens, must nevertheless know and understand the law.

This book was born of the author's extensive cross-country travels, and the need to determine the legalities of carrying a firearm and knife, typically a folding pocket knife, in a particular state the author was visiting. If you're going to be traveling to another state, you will be subject to that state's law.

The gun or knife that you carry today may be legal to carry in your home state, but that very same gun or knife may not be legal in the state you're visiting.

For example, in some states, open carry is legal. In others, it's not. Or only with a government-issued permit. In some states, carrying a handgun in a restaurant that serves alcohol is perfectly legal. In others, doing so even with a carry permit, is a felony.

When it comes to knives, that most useful of tools, a folding knife with a five inch blade may be legal to carry in one state. In others, the maximum blade length may be four inches. Or three and a half. In some, three inches is the maximum legal blade length for carry.

These aren't mere distinctions without a difference. People do get arrested for violating gun and knife carry laws. They get prosecuted, convicted, and they go to jail. After conviction, they will have a criminal record that may adversely affect them for the rest of their lives, whether via adverse employment, hiring or professional licensure decisions, the inability to possess firearms or other weapons, or the denial or revocation of certain types of business licenses. If they're lucky, they avoid a criminal conviction, usually after spending many thousands of dollars of their own money on a good defense attorney.

Unfortunately, finding out what's legal to carry, and where, is often not an easy thing to do, even (maybe especially!) in the age of the Internet. In fact, Internet message boards are filled with innumerable "Is this legal?" type discussion threads, where someone, usually after searching in vain, is trying to figure out what's legal in a particular state. Sometimes, such online forums provide useful and accurate information. But more often than not, the accurate information is mixed in with inaccurate, incomplete, outdated, or just flat out wrong information.

My goal in writing this book is to provide you, the peaceable, law-abiding traveler with a better understanding of, and a way to successfully navigate, the gun and knife laws of each state. In particular, the laws related to what's legal to carry, and where, so that you may abide by the laws of the state(s) you visit and not have any unpleasant and unwanted encounters with our criminal-justice system. In reading this book, you will discover that gun and knife laws often vary widely from state to state, and (particularly in the case of knives) even within a state, from city to city, or town to town!

My hope is that you will not only be able to use the information in this book to have a safe and legally uneventful trip or vacation, but will gain a greater appreciation of the diversity and complexity of gun and knife regulation throughout our great nation.

2   How this Book is Organized

The first few chapters discuss matters of interest to law-abiding travelers that are common to firearms and knife carry throughout the country. I suggest you read them all, and then select the specific state chapters that interest you. Such topics include explanations of common terminology, such as the difference between "shall issue" states and "may issue" states, reciprocity and recognition, preemption laws and the like.

Other topics of interest to travelers and non-travelers alike include the law of self-defense, the Castle Doctrine and so-called "Stand Your Ground" laws. Carrying and transporting firearms on federal lands like national parks and national forests, and via public transportation is also covered. Additionally, I also include important information on handling traffic stops and your rights during such stops, as well as federal laws generally applicable throughout the country concerning firearm and knife carry.

Each state has its own chapter, which includes state-specific summary tables and discussion of firearm and knife-related carry considerations, permit reciprocity and recognition lists, off-limits locations, as well as local jurisdictions in that state with differing regulations (mostly applicable to knife carry).

3   A Guide to the Fascinating World of Firearms and Knife Law Terminology

Okay, perhaps fascinating isn't quite the right word, but "mind numbingly boring" didn't seem like a good choice to encourage you to read this section. The purpose of this section is to explain some of the common terms and terminology you will encounter in the chapters describing each state's weapons law. Most of these terms will be familiar to those readers who are long-time permit holders and who follow firearms legislation or are active in gun rights advocacy. Those new to firearms carry should find the descriptions and explanations below helpful in understanding some of the more important terms used in the laws applying to the carrying of weapons.

3.1   To issue, or not to issue: "Shall Issue" vs. "May Issue"

The terms "shall issue" and "may issue" describe the two different types of permit-issuance laws that exist in this country. In a state with a "shall issue" system, the law requires that the permit-issuing authority – typically a state or local law enforcement agency – to issue a permit to any person who meets the objective criteria set forth in the statute authorizing the issuance of permits. The permit-issuing authority "shall issue" a permit to such person is the typical language used in such statutes, and that is where the term comes from. The statute takes away discretion from the issuing authority, and bases issuance solely on satisfying such objective criteria as having never been convicted of a felony crime or a misdemeanor crime of domestic violence, having never been institutionalized for a mental disorder, etc. Shall issue permit systems now constitute the vast majority of firearms carry licensing laws in effect today.

In contrast, in a state with a "may issue" system, the permit-issuing authority has discretion, often broad discretion, whether or not to issue a permit to any individual. Basically, some bureaucrat gets to decide whether you may legally carry the tools to defend your life or the lives of your loved ones. Not surprisingly, "may issue" permit systems are ripe for abuse. In addition to the problem of arbitrary and varying standards for issuance, in which different towns and counties in the same state have different criteria for issuing permits, in many "may issue" jurisdictions only those persons who are famous, or wealthy, or well-connected politically are able to obtain permits. Indeed, in many "may issue" states there often exist some localities – often the large urban locations – that are essentially "no issue" to ordinary citizens.

Fortunately, the number of "may issue" states has consistently declined over the past two decades, with a corresponding increase in the number of "shall issue" states as those former "may issue" and "no issue" states have changed their laws to treat ordinary citizens the same as the famous, wealthy, or well-connected when it comes to obtaining a carry permit. Unfortunately, however, the remaining "may issue" and "no issue" holdouts represent the hard-core anti-gun, anti-self-defense states.

3.2 Please allow me to reciprocate: Reciprocity and Recognition

Central to the traveler's ability to carry personal protection tools such as firearms when visiting another state is the issue of permit recognition. That is, the issue of whether the traveler's home state carry permit will be valid for carry in the state he or she is visiting.

The terms "reciprocity" and "recognition", in the context of firearms carry, typically refer to the ability to lawfully carry in a state that's not your home state. Technically, reciprocity refers to a legal agreement between states to honor each other's permits, while recognition refers to one state's unilateral decision to honor another state's permits even if that other state doesn't honor permits from the first state.

So what's the difference? As a practical matter, not much, and the terms are often used interchangeably. It's critically important to note, however, that even if a state recognizes your home state's permit, you will be subject to the same permit restrictions as residents of the state you happen to be visiting. For example, if your home state does not restrict your ability to carry in restaurants that serve alcohol, but the state that you're visiting does, you will not be able to legally carry in restaurants that serve alcohol when in the state that you're visiting. Basically, you're subject to the same restrictions that apply to citizens of the state you're visiting. Makes sense, right? After all, why should a visitor to a state enjoy greater legal rights than residents of that state? They don't.

Every state's chapter lists which permits that state recognizes, as well as which other states recognize that state's permits. Readers should be aware, however, that permit recognition lists do tend to change over time, as states either modify their carry permit statutes, which may include changing their criteria for permit recognition, or enter into reciprocity agreements with other states.

An increasing number of states recognize the carry permits of all other states, and the general trend in recent years has been to increase recognition of other states' permits, although occasionally some states have made changes that resulted in a decrease in the number of states whose permits they recognize. In addition to the lists in this book, travelers may further confirm whether their particular permit is recognized by a state they plan on visiting by contacting the official state agencies listed under each state's chapter. Most states have placed this information online on their official websites.

Travelers should be aware that most states carry permits cover handguns only. A small number of states issue a true concealed weapons permit, allowing the holder of such a permit him to carry not only handguns, but weapons like tasers, large fixed-bladed knives, swords canes, etc. Travelers should limit their carry to handguns and the specific types of knives and carry modes allowed under the particular state's law, unless the state they are visiting allows other weapons to be carried with a permit.

3.3 Now you see it, now you don't: Open versus Concealed Carry

Ok, this isn't about the advantages and disadvantages of open versus concealed carry. Each has its pluses and minuses, and I support both (quite the diplomat, aren't I?).

Rather, this section discusses the general legal definitions of what constitutes "open" weapon carry or carry "in plain view", and when the law considers a weapon concealed. In general, the legal definitions, while they may vary somewhat from state to state, do for the most part follow the common sense, ordinary meanings of those terms.

In general, the term "concealed" refers to weapons that are readily accessible and which are hidden from ordinary observation. Thus, a firearm or other weapon concealed under one's clothing or in a bag or purse carried by the person would likely meet the definition of "concealed" in all states. In addition, for a traveler in a vehicle, many states also consider a firearm located with arm's reach, such as stored in a vehicle glove compartment or center console storage box, to be concealed.

Some states require that a firearm be carried openly, or in plain view, if the carrier does not possess a recognized permit. The definition of what is considered "plain view" does vary from state to state. In general, however, if the firearm and holster are clearly visible and immediately recognizable as such, then such a firearm would be considered openly carried, or carried in plain view. Inside a vehicle, the term plain view typically refers to a firearm that is visible to a person from outside the vehicle. Carry of long guns in visible window-mounted gun racks would qualify. A handgun in a holster uncovered on the dashboard or uncovered on the passenger seat would generally qualify.

3.4   McClure who? Federal law on interstate firearms transportation

Travelers should be aware that there exist a few jurisdictions that are anti-gun to their very core. Those jurisdictions prohibit even mere possession of unloaded firearms without permits issued by those jurisdictions (which are difficult or often impossible for non-residents to obtain). In some cases, the prohibition applies to any firearm. In others, it applies to so-called "assault weapons" and associated "assault accessories" such as normal capacity magazines ("high-capacity ammunition feeding devices" in the anti-gun parlance).

Normally, such prohibitions would be fatal to the ability of a law-abiding traveler to enter such a jurisdiction even if the traveler was merely passing through, with no desire or intention to remain in a place so hostile to his constitutionally protected rights. Fortunately, federal law since 1986 has provided a limited remedy for this intolerable situation. In that year, Congress passed, and President Reagan signed into law the McClure-Volkmer Act, also known as the Firearms Owners Protection Act of 1986. One provision of that law provides a "safe passage" for those travelers who are merely transiting (passing through) the offensive jurisdiction.

Here's what the interstate transportation statute, codified at 18 U.S.C. § 926A, actually says:

§ 926A. Interstate transportation of firearms

Notwithstanding any other provision of any law or any rule or regulation of a State or any political subdivision thereof, any person who is not otherwise prohibited by this chapter from transporting, shipping, or receiving a firearm shall be entitled to transport a firearm for any lawful purpose from any place where he may lawfully possess and carry such firearm to any other place where he may lawfully possess and carry such firearm if, during such transportation the firearm is unloaded, and neither the firearm nor any ammunition being transported is readily accessible or is directly accessible from the passenger compartment of such transporting vehicle: Provided, That in the case of a vehicle without a compartment separate from the driver's compartment the firearm or ammunition shall be contained in a locked container other than the glove compartment or console.

In order to fall within the McClure-Volkmer safe passage protections, the traveler must be on a continuous, uninterrupted journey with no intention to remain in the offending jurisdiction, and the traveler's firearms must be transported in a completely unloaded and securely cased condition, and either locked in the trunk of the vehicle, or, if the vehicle has no trunk, then the cases containing the firearms must be locked. To be on the safe side, any ammunition should be stored apart from the firearms in separate, locked containers. In addition, the traveler's possession of the firearms in question must be legal at both the origin and destination of his trip.

For example, a traveler in lawful possession of a machine gun in New Hampshire traveling by car to visit relatives in Pennsylvania must pass through the anti-rights state of New York. There's no way around it, unfortunately. New York, naturally, prohibits possession of machine guns by "mere" citizens. Thus, the law-abiding traveler must rely on the interstate transport provisions of federal law, namely, the McClure-Volkmer safe passage provisions in order to legally drive through New York State, and must maintain steady, uninterrupted travel through the state. The traveler's firearms must be completely unloaded, securely cased in a commercial gun case, and either stored in the locked trunk of the vehicle or, if the vehicle has no separate trunk compartment, then the gun case must be locked and stored in the vehicle's cargo area.

Note that the federal law protections cease to exist if the traveler does not maintain a continuous, uninterrupted journey through the offending jurisdiction. If the traveler stops to sightsee or visit friends in New York, the interstate transport protections of federal law no longer apply, and the traveler is subject to arrest for possession of firearms that are highly illegal under New York state law.

A traveler relying on federal law to legally transit states with restrictive gun laws may wish to consider having with him or her documentation such as hotel or campground reservations for a hotel or campground in their destination state to help demonstrate that they are indeed merely passing through the restrictive state, with no intention of remaining within that restrictive state.

3.5 The Preemption Issue: Can cities and towns separately regulate carry?

One of the more important concerns of travelers who carry firearms and knives is the issue of whether weapons laws are uniform throughout a given state. That is, whether local governments such as those of towns and cities or other regulatory bodies can each separately regulate firearms possession, carry or transportation, thereby creating a patchwork of differing rules depending on where in the state – which city, town, or county – you are in. Fortunately, the vast majority of state legislatures have enacted so-called preemption statutes that, to varying degrees, prohibit local governments and other regulatory bodies in their states from enacting their own separate ordinances or regulations regarding firearms. Such statutes help ensure that most firearms regulation is uniform throughout the state.

Many states completely preempt their political subdivisions from regulating firearms possession, carry or transportation. Others states allow limited regulation, such as the ability to ban the carry of firearms in local government buildings, or unlicensed open carry in public parks. In addition, some states have grandfathered certain types of local ordinances and allowed them to remain in effect. The preemption status of each state is noted in that state's chapter.

Travelers should be aware, however, that virtually all states allow municipal governments to regulate the *discharge* of firearms within their jurisdictions. That is, cities and towns can prohibit or otherwise restrict the discharge of firearms within city or town limits (with either an explicit or implied statutory or case law exception for self-defense).

Travelers should also be aware that unfortunately very few states preempt their political subdivisions from separately regulating knife possession or carry, and many towns and cities have indeed enacted their own knife regulations, often resulting in a patchwork of differing rules for what's legal with regard to knives. Indeed, only one state, Arizona, has explicitly preempted knife regulation by its political subdivisions, and only very recently. I have summarized knife ordinances for selected cities and towns in each state's chapter.

3.6   A loaded question: Loaded vs. Unloaded

In general, the term "loaded" when used in connection with firearms means a firearm containing live ammunition in either the chamber, cylinder, or any integral or attached magazine.

The term "unloaded" typically refers to a firearm containing no live ammunition whatsoever, whether in the chamber, cylinder, or in any integral or attached magazine.

So far, so good, right? Sure, and the above definitions jive with commonsense definitions of those terms and will serve you in good stead in all fifty states.

In a handful of states, however, the term "loaded" is specifically defined as a firearm containing a live round in the firing chamber. In such states, ammunition may be contained in, e.g., integral or attached magazines and the gun would still be considered unloaded under state law, provided no live round was in the firing chamber.

In other states like Utah, a firearm is not considered "loaded" if the firing chamber is empty *and* firing the gun requires *at least two* separate physical actions.

Those states with such definitional differences are noted in the relevant state chapters. Following the general and more common definitions for "loaded" and "unloaded" given at the start of this section, however, will allow you to be compliant in all fifty states.

3.7 That's Off-Limits: Commonly Restricted Areas and Areas Restricted under Federal Law

Readers should be aware that most states commonly restrict firearms carry in a variety of "sensitive" areas, regardless of whether the carrier has a recognized permit or not. For example, most states explicitly prohibit firearms carry in schools and on school premises, even for those with carry permits. Exceptions typically exist for approved and school sanctioned activities related to firearms. Some states also make exceptions for possession and storage of firearms in a private vehicle on school property, typically requiring that the firearms be unloaded and secured in a locked vehicle. Other states allow those with carry permits to enter onto school property with loaded firearms temporarily for the purpose of picking up or dropping off students.

Many states also prohibit firearms carry in colleges and universities or on college or university property.

In addition, readers should be aware that the current federal Gun Free School Zones Act prohibits firearms possession on or within 1000 feet of the premises of primary or secondary schools unless the person possessing the firearms holds a valid permit from the state in which the school is located, or the firearms are unloaded and secured in locked containers, or a locked firearms rack that is on a motor vehicle. Exceptions also exist for possession of firearms for use in approved firearms-related school activities, and for possession of unloaded firearms while traversing school property with the permission of school authorities to gain access to public or private lands open to hunting.[1]

Many states also prohibit carrying of firearms into law enforcement facilities, prisons and other detention or correctional facilities, and in court houses and court facilities.

Most states also prohibit firearms carry, even with a recognized permit, in establishments such as bars and taverns that are primarily devoted to the sale and serving of alcoholic beverages for on-

---

[1] See, 18 U.S.C. § 922(q) (2009).

premises consumption. Many states extend that prohibition to include all establishments, such as restaurants, licensed to sell or serve alcoholic beverages for on premises consumption, although a number of states have relaxed or removed the restaurant restriction for those with recognized permits.

A fair number of states also explicitly prohibit firearms carry out public sporting and athletic events, polling places, and government offices and buildings. Some states provide an exception to such prohibitions for those with recognized permits.

Readers should be aware that federal law restricts the carry of firearms, even by those with recognized carry permits, in a number of locations. Anyone who travels by air probably knows that firearms carry is prohibited in the secure areas of airports. In addition, federal law prohibits the carry of firearms in federal buildings and facilities, and in federal courts and courthouses.

Military bases and reservations generally prohibit firearms carry, and may restrict or regulate possession of firearms in vehicles. Visitors to such military installations should check with base officials prior to their visit to ascertain the applicable rules regarding firearms possession or carry.

Note that in practically every state private property owners and private employers have broad discretion to permit or deny firearms possession and/or carry on their property. Due to some perceived and well-publicized abuses by big company employers, however, some states have limited the ability of private employers to prohibit the storage of firearms in employees' private vehicles that are parked in company parking lots.

Travelers should be sure to check the "places off-limits" section located in each state chapter for the states they plan on visiting.

3.8 Guns and Bikes: Motorcycle Issues

Travelers with firearms exploring the open road on motorcycle should be aware that while most states address carry of firearms in "motor vehicles", the definition of which includes motorcycles, most such statutes envision carry in automobiles, and thus employed such terms as "glove compartment", "trunk", and the like. Thus, travelers on motorcycles are forced to translate those terms to their vehicle's configuration.

In general, a lockable storage compartment on a motorcycle will likely qualify as a trunk when locked. Transport of an unloaded handgun in such a locked compartment should be acceptable in most states that prohibit the possession of loaded firearms in a vehicle. If the traveler possesses a recognized permit, then the firearm may be carried concealed on the person. In states where open carry of a loaded firearm in a vehicle is lawful, that carry mode would also be an option. The traveler should be aware, however, that such carry may result in adverse and unwanted attention from the local constabulary.

3.9 Rolling Home: RVs and Motor Homes

Travelers who choose to see the country via recreational vehicle (RV) or motor home should be aware of some important quirks in the legal status of such vehicles depending on their usage and mobility. While motoring on the roadways in such a vehicle, a traveler is using the conveyance as a motor vehicle, and thus the traveler and vehicle is subject to all traffic laws as well as firearms laws pertaining to vehicular transport.

When that RV or motor home is off the roadways and in a fixed and immobile state, such as in a campground hooked up to utilities (electric, water, sewer, etc.), courts have typically ruled that such a condition is sufficient to transform the RV or motor home into a dwelling. One notable result of such a change in legal status is that the firearm laws pertaining to possession and carry in the home or dwelling would now apply. Travelers should be cautious, however, as the exact contours and requirements for an RV or motor home to be considered a dwelling vary from state to state.

In the context of an RV or motor home, statutory references to a vehicle's trunk compartment can typically be translated to legitimately refer to lockable external storage compartments, as such compartments are separate from the passenger compartment, and typically require motorists to exit the vehicle in order to access the compartment's contents. Such a configuration is thus functionally equivalent to a traditional trunk compartment on an automobile. As such, the same rationales for any statutory automobile trunk transport requirements would likely apply to such external compartments on an RV or motor home.

4   The Law of Self-Defense, in a Nutshell

If you carry a firearm or other deadly weapon such as a knife for personal protection, you must be familiar with the laws governing the use of deadly force for self-defense, or defense of another person such as a loved one.

Self-defense cases are typically highly fact and circumstance-specific, but the basic black letter law governing the use of force in self-defense is actually quite easy to state:

> A person may use deadly force in self-defense only when he or she reasonably believes that doing so is necessary to prevent an imminent, unlawful, and otherwise unavoidable threat of death or grave bodily harm to an innocent person.

> A person may use <u>less than</u> deadly force in self-defense to the extent that he or she reasonably believes that doing so is necessary to prevent the imminent and unlawful use of force against an innocent person.

The above definition is one that is generally applicable in every state. Different states may express their law of self-defense slightly differently, but all embody the elements of the above definition, either explicitly or implicitly.   Note that you must satisfy every single element of the definition in order to successfully assert a claim of justifiable self-defense.

In order to be legally justified in using deadly force in self-defense, your use of force must be reasonable, and the danger you face must be (a) unlawful, (b) deadly or grave, (c) immediate, and (d) otherwise unavoidable.

The term "unlawful" means that you must be the innocent party -- e.g., the armed robber cannot claim self-defense for shooting his noncompliant victim. "Grave" means that the danger you face is life-threatening, i.e., one that has the likelihood of inflicting or resulting in death or serious bodily injury. Forcible rape is also considered a crime of such heinous violation of a person's bodily integrity that it would qualify as grave bodily harm.

The danger being faced must also be an immediate one, as in *right now*. Finally, the danger must be "otherwise unavoidable", which simply means no reasonable options existed to avoid the danger, such as the option to retreat. Note that in most states there is no duty to retreat in one's own home or dwelling. In addition, in an increasing number of states there is no duty to retreat if you are in any place where you have a legal right to be. Note that generally, even in states where a legal duty to retreat prior to using defensive force exists, such duty typically only applies if the actor can retreat *safely*.

You are thus only justified (authorized) in using deadly force when facing grave, immediate, otherwise unavoidable danger of death or serious bodily harm to the innocent. In addition, any force you employ will be judged by the standard of that mythical creation so beloved in the law, namely, the "Reasonable and Prudent Person": that is, what would a reasonable person, in the same circumstances, and knowing what the defender knew at the time, have done.

The legal defense of self-defense is what is known in the law as an affirmative defense, one that must be raised by the defendant. That is, a person asserting a claim of self-defense must raise sufficient facts at trial to show that his or her actions were legally justified. Once raised, the prosecution must convince the jury (or the judge in a bench trial) to reject the affirmative defense. A successful claim of self-defense provides a legal justification for conduct that would otherwise be unlawful.

Obviously, I'm simplifying here for the sake of brevity. I could spend a good chunk of the book on all the nuances and intricacies of the law of self-defense, from the role that specialized knowledge may play in the determination of reasonableness, to the ways courts in different states have approached the issues involving reputation evidence involving the attacker's propensity for violence, to more obscure issues such as the evidentiary role that things like prior domestic violence may play in asserting a successful claim of self-defense. Such a discussion might also cover issues of excessive force and the differing approaches courts (and states) have taken with regard to such force and its effect on the legal defense of self-defense.

Indeed, I teach a course on self-defense law and threat management that delves into all these various nuances and wrinkles in the law of self-defense, in addition to exploring many of the possible physical, psychological, and legal consequences of a violent physical encounter and ways to mitigate or avoid those adverse consequences. In that course, I use real life examples culled from news reports and quotes from actual court decisions, along with excerpts of statutes from around the country to explore the contours of this important area of the criminal law.

While we won't get into such detail here, the gentle reader can take solace in the fact that the basic black letter law noted above at the start of this chapter will serve him or her well as a concise distillation of what is needed to assert a successful claim of self-defense. Learn it, understand it, and live by it, because it's mostly common sense distilled over many centuries of Anglo-American civilization into a pithy legal rule.

4.1 Retreat! Of Doctrines, and Castles, and Standing Your Ground

The term "Castle Doctrine" derives from the old English saying that the home is a man's castle, and within his castle he is king. A corollary to this axiom is that no man should be required to abandon his castle when attacked, but should be able to meet force with force. In its modern appellation and application in the context of self-defense, the Castle Doctrine refers to the lack of any legal duty to retreat when threatened in one's own home or dwelling prior to resorting to force to protect one's life or the life of some other innocent person.

In recent years a number of states have passed statutes loosely, and in some cases imprecisely, referred to as "Castle Doctrine" statutes. These statutes have variously done *some combination* of the following: (a) removed any legal duty to retreat before resorting to defensive force if attacked in one's own home, dwelling, or place of employment; (b) created a legal (but rebuttable) presumption that a person attacked in his or her own home who defends himself or herself acted in lawful self-defense; (c) limited or eliminated the ability of unlawful attackers to sue for damages in civil court any person who used lawful defensive force in self-defense or defense of other innocent life; and/or (d) removed the legal duty to retreat so long as the person using defensive force was in *any* place (including outside the home) where he or she had the legal right to be.

Statutes that abrogate the duty to retreat outside one's own home are more properly referred to as "Stand Your Ground" statutes, rather than "Castle Doctrine" statutes. The Castle Doctrine more correctly refers to the lack of a legal duty to retreat when in one's own home or dwelling.

Readers should also be aware that some states have adopted the Castle Doctrine or have delineated their retreat requirements via judicial decisions in case law, rather than via statute. So just because a search through the statute books doesn't turn up a statute(s) that addresses the retreat requirement, doesn't necessarily mean that state hasn't adopted essentially the same position via court decisions.

Castle Doctrine laws that provide a legal presumption that a homeowner who uses force against an intruder did so lawfully go a long way towards reining in frivolous prosecutions by overzealous prosecutors. Such prosecutions are often costly to defend against, requiring the homeowner to expend scarce funds to pay for lawyers, expert witnesses, etc. Not to mention the stress of knowing that his freedom and the economic security of his family hang in the balance. Castle Doctrine laws serve the salutary purpose of reaffirming that peaceful citizens have a right to be safe in their own homes.

In addition, many of the recent Castle Doctrine or Stand Your Ground statutes enacted within the last few years also protect an individual who uses lawful defensive force from frivolous civil lawsuits. As is the case with frivolous criminal prosecutions, this is important because defending against such suits can often bankrupt the person who merely acted in lawful self-defense. If your state doesn't have the statutory protections afforded by the recent crop of Castle Doctrine and/or Stand Your Ground laws, you might want to consider contacting your elected representatives to voice your support for such laws. The bankruptcy you prevent might be your own.

Finally, readers should always remember that just because you are in a location where you don't have a legal duty to retreat before resorting to force, doesn't mean you can't retreat if you choose to do so or if doing so would likely avoid the necessity of defensive force. To state the obvious, just because you *can* do something, doesn't necessarily mean you *should*. For example, you may consider it your moral duty to retreat if that course of action can be accomplished safely and if it is likely to allow you to avoid bloodshed, particularly if the confrontation occurs outside your home. Unlike in the movies, taking another human life is a difficult and momentous decision, and one with long lasting and potentially life-altering consequences for the taker.

In addition, bear in mind that in order to be justified in using deadly force in self-defense, you must be facing an imminent and unlawful threat of death or grave bodily injury. There is no guarantee that you will prevail, or even survive, a violent physical confrontation resulting from such a threat. Thus, if retreat is an option that might allow you to avoid such a confrontation from occurring, it ought to be one that you consider seriously. In states without a legal requirement to retreat, the choice is yours and yours alone, as it should be in a nation of free men and women. In such states, the law will support your choice either way, provided you meet all the other requirements for justifiable use of force. Choose wisely.

5 Traffic Stops: Interacting with Law Enforcement

In the event that you are stopped, say, for speeding, you should be aware of your rights and consider handling the interaction with the officer as follows. First, remain calm, cool and collected. You may wish to place your hands in a relaxed position on the steering wheel as the officer approaches your vehicle to show him or her that you aren't holding any weapons. Avoid making any sudden movements during the stop. The officer has the right to inquire about your operation of the vehicle, and can generally require that you produce your driver's license[2] and registration. In most cases, the officer will issue you a warning or ticket and you will be on your way.

If you are carrying a concealed firearm on a recognized permit, you should be aware that some states require that you immediately and affirmatively (that is, without the officer asking) inform the officer that you are carrying a concealed firearm. In such states, you should present your carry permit along with your driver's license, while informing the officer that you are currently carrying a firearm.

To avoid a potentially tense situation or misunderstanding, you might want to consider wording your communication to specifically mention that you have a carry permit (or license to carry), and that you are currently carrying. Using words like "permit" or "license" helps put you in the "law-abiding citizen" category as the officer sizes you up. Avoid the word "gun" if you can – use the less emotionally-charged term "firearm". Don't blurt out, for example, "I have a gun!" as the officer approaches, lest the officer misunderstand your intent and proceed to show you that he too, has a gun, while proceeding to give you a free close-up view of the barrel end of his.

---

[2] *See*, Hiibel v. Nevada, 542 U.S. 177 (2004) (affirming conviction under Nevada's "stop and identify" statute for failure to produce driver's license upon request by law enforcement officer). In *Hiibel*, a divided United States Supreme Court upheld Larry Hiibel's conviction for failure to produce identification upon request by a deputy sheriff investigating a reported assault, and held that such request (and subsequent conviction) did not violate his Fourth or Fifth Amendment Constitutional protections. *See, id.* Note that many states have similar "stop and identify" statutes.

In the event that the officer decides to question you about, e.g., possible contraband in your vehicle, you have the right to refuse to answer questions that would be self-incriminating, and may inform the officer that you would prefer to consult with counsel before answering such questions. Sometimes, the officer will be interested in searching your vehicle. You should be aware that, in order for a search for contraband to be legal, the officer will generally need either probable cause, or your consent. In general, most stops for routine traffic violations do not provide sufficient probable cause for an officer to search your vehicle. As such, the officer will often politely ask for your consent to search, often at the end of the traffic stop, after the officer has handed you back your license and papers and told you that you're free to go. You have the right to say no, and in almost all cases, probably should.

Simply tell the officer that you will not consent to such a search, and that if he wants to search he will have to do so without your consent. You might say the following: "I know that you're just doing your job, officer (or trooper, deputy, etc.), but I don't consent to searches." Then ask the officer whether you are being detained, or whether you are free to go. Without your consent, most officers will not search unless they believe they have enough probable cause to withstand judicial scrutiny.

Note, however, that during the traffic stop the officer generally can require that you exit the vehicle, and if he has concern for his safety can perform a limited search of your person and the areas of the vehicle that you would have immediate access to, for weapons. The search, however, must be limited to weapons that might pose a danger to the officer's safety, and may not be extended to a general search for contraband without probable cause or your consent, which you should generally refuse.

Should the officer continue to press his request that you allow him to search your vehicle, you should simply repeat the refusal of your consent, and ask whether you are being detained, and whether you're free to leave. A simple query to the officer, such as "Excuse me, officer, am I being detained, or am I free to go?" should be sufficient to put the officer on notice that you are aware of your rights and wish to end the encounter. At all times, however, remain calm and courteous. And learn to say "no" with a smile. These are *your* Constitutionally-protected rights that our forefathers fought and died to bequeath you, and you ought not to give them up lightly.

6   Other Interactions with Law Enforcement

With regard to carry of your knife in public, particularly open carry of large fixed blades in urban areas, you should understand that even if such carry is technically legal in that particular state and municipality, in many cases you may still potentially be arrested and charged under other statutes or ordinances. For example, the circumstances of such carry ("sir, why are you carrying that machete / dagger / Bowie / big evil knife in downtown Sheepsville?") may support a charge under a disturbing the peace, disorderly conduct, or brandishing statute or ordinance, depending on the state or municipality involved.   Thus, the savvy traveler would be wise to carefully consider the nature and circumstances of his or her knife carry, in order to minimize the likelihood of presenting a threatening or intimidating appearance to the typical persons the traveler is likely to encounter under those circumstances, and possible unwanted law enforcement attention as a result.   For example, if you're carrying a hunting knife while lawfully hunting, you are not likely to raise any eyebrows or cause alarm among the other hunters you meet in the field doing the same, but carrying that same knife in a densely populated urban area will likely generate considerable concern (and a possible 9-1-1 emergency call) from the many city-dwellers who don't carry a knife, have never hunted, and who associate the carrying of any knife with unlawful criminal activity.

Finally, if you use a firearm or knife to defend yourself against a violent, unlawful criminal attack, you should realize that such use will almost certainly be considered deadly force. As such, you had better be sure that the circumstances warrant use of deadly force, typically defined as the level of force likely to result in death or serious bodily injury. As previously discussed, in general, you are authorized to use deadly force in defense of your life or the lives of your loved ones if you are not the initial aggressor and are facing grave, immediate, and otherwise unavoidable danger of death or serious bodily injury. All of those factors must be present for your use of deadly force to be legally justified.   As noted previously, in some states if the attack occurs outside your home, state law requires you to retreat from the attack if you can do so safely. In states with so-called "stand your ground" laws, the law does not require you to retreat if you are attacked outside your home, so long as you are in a place where you have a legal right to be, and were not the initial aggressor.

In the event that you have to use a firearm, knife or other deadly weapon in defense of your life or the lives of your loved ones, you should understand your rights, and should consider using the following protocol in dealing with responding law enforcement officers. Your first priority is obviously your safety and the safety of your loved ones – once the fight is over, and if needed, emergency medical services have been called and first aid efforts are underway, then worry about dealing with the responding officers. You need to convey the following information to the 9-1-1 operator and to responding officers: you were attacked; you feared for your life or the lives of your loved ones; you acted in self-defense. If your attacker(s) has fled the scene, you should be prepared to give a description to responding officers. You may or may not get arrested. Identify any potential witnesses who might be able to corroborate your story that you were the one attacked. Point out any potential evidence that your attacker(s) may have left – spent cartridge casings, the probable locations of bullet holes from the shots the assailant(s) fired at you, the baseball bat your attacker tried to smash your brains out with, etc., etc.

At this point, you should inform the officers that while you fully intend to cooperate with their investigation, having just used deadly force in defense of your life, you understand the gravity of the situation, and need to speak with your attorney before answering any questions concerning the details of the event. At this point, you should also consider explicitly stating that you wish to exercise your constitutional right to remain silent pending consultation with your lawyer. Exercising your right to have your attorney present during questioning will give you time to collect your thoughts, and will help you avoid making unwise statements during the extremely agitated mental and emotional state you will likely be in, having just been in a life or death struggle.

7   Some Notes on Knives and Knife Carry

First, this book assumes that you, the reader, possess a certain key characteristic, namely, that you are a law-abiding adult citizen. State law in virtually every state prohibits convicted felons from possessing and carrying deadly or dangerous weapons. (Of course, if you're a convicted felon, you're probably not reading this book anyway.) In addition, many states prohibit minors from possessing deadly or dangerous weapons, without the permission and/or supervision of their parents or legal guardians.

Second, the book generally assumes that you are carrying a knife primarily for use as a utility tool, e.g., for opening packages, peeling fruit, etc., and *not* specifically as a weapon. While knives make excellent weapons, this is an important distinction. Many states have laws that prohibit persons from possessing or carrying deadly or dangerous weapons with the specific intent to use such weapons unlawfully against others. Prosecution under such statutes generally requires the government to prove (1) the knife was a deadly or dangerous weapon, and (2) that you knowingly carried the weapon with (3) the intent to use unlawfully against another. Therefore, if you carry a knife primarily as a weapon, or a knife designed as, or particularly well-suited for use as, a weapon, you should realize that this fact will be used against you if you're prosecuted under these statutes, regardless of whether, for example, your knife met all the criteria for blade length, type, etc., and may otherwise have been legal to carry if carried as a non-weapon tool.

Additionally, you should get used to thinking of your knife primarily as a tool, even if you also carry the knife as a weapon. You will no doubt use your knife for everyday utility purposes and chores a lot more than you will ever use it as a weapon. Consider this: If you're stopped, and the officer asks whether you have any weapons on you, and you say "yes, officer, I have a pocket knife", you have indicated to that officer that you consider the knife to be a weapon. In some states, carrying such a weapon may be illegal, and you may be cited or arrested. If you instead think of your knife as a tool (and use it as such), and in response to "do you have any weapons on you?" you answer "no officer, but I do have a pocket knife, although I don't consider that a weapon", your legal situation is much enhanced, and it will be much more difficult to use your statement against you should you be charged with unlawful carry of a deadly weapon or similar crime.

Obviously, the decision to carry a knife, whether primarily as a tool, or primarily as a weapon, is ultimately yours alone. My purpose in writing this book is simply to provide information on the laws of the various states that impose legal restrictions, prohibitions or other limitations on such carry. As the saying goes, knowledge is power, and knowing the law will enable you to make an informed decision on whether to carry a particular knife, given your particular situation.

7.1 Selecting a Legally "Friendly" Knife

So, what characteristics should you consider when selecting a knife for everyday carry and use that will minimize the chances of inadvertently running afoul of knife carry laws or ordinances? First off, let me say that I have nothing against buying and collecting any of the many fine, quality knives available today. We are truly blessed in this country to have a vast range of great, high quality knives and knife-makers to choose from, and nothing I say here should stop you or anyone else from purchasing, using, appreciating, or otherwise indulging in your passion for knives. Having said that, there are knives you collect, and then there are knives you carry. Of the knives you carry, some are more legally "friendly" than others, regardless of whether you carry the knife primarily as a utility tool, or as a weapon.

For example, let's assume you're in a state (or traveling to, or through, such a state) where you may not legally carry a knife as a concealed deadly weapon, but an "ordinary pocket knife", as that term is used in many statutes, may be carried as a utility tool. Which knife do you think would look more like a utility tool, versus a weapon, should it come before a jury – a simple pocket knife with a stainless, common spearpoint blade marked "Woodsman Model" or "Camper's Friend", or your Ninja Masters folder with the "tactical" black tanto-style blade, emblazoned with a skull and crossbones and "Special Tactical Assault Blade"? If, heaven forbid, you had to use a knife as a weapon to defend your life, think about which bloody knife you'd rather have a police investigator, prosecutor, grand juror, judge, or petit (trial) juror examine. In a clear-cut case of self-defense, it may not matter. But in a close case, or in a jurisdiction or with a prosecutor hostile to citizens defending themselves with deadly force, perception can make all the difference between being prosecuted, or not, or between a conviction, and an acquittal.

Even if you aren't criminally prosecuted, or are prosecuted but acquitted on self-defense grounds, in many jurisdictions (not all) you can still be sued in civil court by your attacker, his family, or his estate, as the case may be. Which bloody knife would you rather those civil trial jurors, none of whom will likely be "knife" enthusiasts, have to examine in the jury room as they decide, by the lower proof standard of a civil trial, whether or not you should be liable to the attacker or his family or estate for money damages? The appearance of your knife can make a lot of difference in a close case.

Indeed, you should realize that jurors are drawn from the general population, and as a practical matter are free to draw upon their own life experiences and subjective cultural preconceptions regarding knives and knife usage in weighing the evidence and arriving at their verdict. If you used an automatic knife (which the prosecutor or plaintiff's attorney will describe as an evil "switchblade", possibly along with a dramatic in-court demonstration by a suitable witness) or boot knife, for example, you run the risk of invoking a negative image in the minds of the average juror due to the portrayal of such knives by Hollywood and the media as weapons often used by violent criminals for criminal purposes. Regardless of whether this portrayal is accurate or not, such will often be the stereotype in the mind of the typical, non-knife carrying juror, especially one from an urban area. Couple that with photos of your attacker's injuries (presented as the "victim's" injuries), inflicted with that knife, and that negative image may work against you. In general, you want the jury to identify with you and what you did, especially in a close case; the more you appear as an honest, upstanding citizen defending himself and his loved ones with an uncontroversial, familiar defensive tool, the better.

Now, some people say "it's better to be judged by twelve, than carried by six," that is to say, it's better to be alive and tried by a jury of twelve, than to be dead, carried by six pallbearers at your funeral. No doubt this is true, and I wholeheartedly agree. Most of the people who say such things, however, have never been through the criminal justice system, with their freedom hanging in the balance, or survived a multi-million dollar civil lawsuit, with every penny they own or will earn in the next twenty years at stake. Obviously, you need to survive and prevail against your attacker(s), but the reality is that you also want every possible advantage to survive and prevail in the legal struggle that will almost inevitably follow. Although only one small factor, in general, the more innocuous and commonplace your knife looks, the better your chances of surviving and prevailing in that legal struggle.

So my recommendation for an everyday carry knife is to get and carry a knife that obviously meets all of the technical legal requirements of the jurisdictions you plan on carrying it in, i.e., one that meets any blade length restrictions, if any, and isn't of a proscribed type, such as a dagger, or bowie knife, and so forth. Avoid knives with names that include words like "combat", "assault", or "fighting", or knives specifically marketed or touted as being designed or suitable for combat or fighting. Does the name of the knife really matter? Having read literally hundreds upon hundreds of cases involving knives, I can tell you that there are cases where the name of the knife is specifically mentioned and discussed as providing insight into the knife's designed purpose or the intent of the person carrying the knife, i.e., as a tool, or as a prohibited weapon.

Even if you carry your knife as both a utility tool and self-defense tool or weapon, you should actually use your knife for those utility or work tasks, so that you can honestly say, and the knife's physical appearance and forensic evidence will support, that you in fact used and considered your knife a utility tool, rather than a weapon. Obviously, you should keep your knife sharp, as a sharp knife is a safe knife. If you don't know how to sharpen your knives, learn.

Knife sharpening is a valuable skill, and worth putting in your toolbox of life skills.

As an aside, if you train, or plan to train with a knife as a self-defense tool, you should consider selecting an instructor who teaches tactics and techniques that work with the types and sizes of knife that you can legally carry, and who has at least researched the laws pertaining to knife carry and the use of deadly force in the state(s) where he or she teaches. For instance, tactics and techniques that may work well with a large bowie knife, may not work well at all with the three inch blade folding knife you actually carry. I am not saying don't learn how to use a large blade; for the serious student of the martial arts and self-defense, such training serves to advance your knowledge and skills by helping you understand the various methods of employment of such large bladed weapons, and helps prepare you to counter an attacker(s) using such weapons. What I am suggesting, however, is that your instructor should be conversant with, and the tactics and techniques he or she teaches should reflect, both the tactical *and* legal realities you will face in a real-life defensive situation.

Finally, you should realize that if you carry more than one or two knives, the chances that at least one of your knives will be considered a weapon increases with each additional knife you carry. If a police officer finds four concealed knives on you, and you're in a state with an unlawful use or carry of weapons statute and you don't otherwise have a permit that would cover such carry, you may be getting a first-hand look at that state's criminal justice system. I'm not saying don't carry more than one knife; I'm saying you should have a reasonable, and believable, explanation for why you carry more than one, especially if you're in a state that prohibits carry of concealed weapons.

7.2 A Note on Blade Length Measurement

Many knife statutes list specific blade length restrictions. But what exactly does a folding knife with, for example, a "four inch" blade mean? More precisely, how is such blade length measured? Does it include the entire blade, or only the sharpened edge? Do you measure in a straight line, or along the edge? What about blades types with different shapes – spear point, drop point, tanto, clip point, etc? Depending on the measurement method used, a blade may measure 3.8 inches, or 4.2 inches. In a state with a four inch blade length restriction, how you measure can mean the difference between a legal and illegal blade length.

Don't think it matters? People have been arrested, prosecuted, and convicted for carrying knives with blades that exceeded the statutory maximum by literally a fraction of an inch. Their convictions have been upheld on appeal.

Unfortunately, most statutes and municipal ordinances are silent on exactly how blade length is measured. A few statutes and ordinances do explicitly specify how blade length is to be measured, but these are the exception, not the rule. When in doubt, the safe route is to include the entire blade, including any unsharpened portion, in your blade length measurement, as this represents the worst-case measurement scenario. In fact, appellate courts in several states with statutory blade length limits have held that the blade measurement includes both the sharpened and unsharpened portions of the blade, as measured from the tip of the blade to the point where the blade enters the handle.

The American Knife and Tool Institute, a knife-maker's industry association, has proposed a standard protocol for measuring blade length that appears to incorporate the results of such case law, where the blade is measured in a straight line from the tip to the "forward-most aspect of the hilt or handle."[3] Of course, such a protocol has no binding legal effect on any law enforcement entity, but may serve as persuasive authority on such entities in considering whether the blade in question exceeds a particular jurisdiction's specified regulatory maximum.

7.3   Before you travel

Before traveling, I suggest you read the specific sections for each state you intend to travel to or through. Just because you may legally carry a particular knife in your home state and in your destination state, does not mean that you may legally do so in the states you may simply be traveling through. As an example, in Oregon, a switchblade with a three inch blade is legal to carry openly under state law. Right next door in our most populous state, California, that same knife is illegal to carry. Or, how about a folding pocket knife with a four inch blade? In Texas, such as knife may legally be carried concealed. A short trip through the Oklahoma panhandle into Colorado, however, and such concealed carry is illegal, as Colorado has a statutory three and a half inch blade length limit for concealed

---

[3] *See*, AMER. KNIFE & TOOL INST., PROTOCOL FOR MEASURING KNIFE BLADE LENGTH, in AKTI NEWS & UPDATE, VOL. 6, ISSUE 1 (2004)

carry. As a general rule, you are responsible for complying with the laws of any state you happen to be in, even if you are merely traveling through that state.

In addition, you should be aware that in most states, individual cities and towns have enacted their own ordinances and regulations concerning knife carry. For example, in Massachusetts, a number of cities, including Boston, prohibit carry of knives with blade lengths exceeding two and a half inches, even though state law does not impose a maximum blade length limit. In a few states, violations of such ordinances are considered infractions, with the penalty "only" a hefty fine, but no criminal record. In most states, however, violations of weapons-related ordinances are criminal offenses, either misdemeanors or felonies, depending on the offense and the particular state and city/town/county.

In the few states where violation of the municipal ordinance is only an infraction, some may argue that failure to observe such city ordinances may often "only" result in a violation punished with a hefty fine and no criminal misdemeanor or felony conviction. Readers should be aware, however, that even in such cases the ordinances often specifically authorize law enforcement to arrest you. So now you have an arrest record. Try explaining why your arrest for unlawful weapon possession, even if it only resulted in a fine and no criminal conviction, is "no big deal" on your next concealed carry permit renewal, if the renewal application requires disclosure of your arrest record.

A word of caution: as stated previously, a lot of information exists online, on websites, message boards, online forums and the like regarding knives and what's legal or not. Some of the information is quite accurate, some is emphatically not. You should be aware that some of the information you will find on these sites will likely be incomplete, partially or wholly inaccurate, or in some cases, outdated. This is especially true when it comes to state laws regarding legal knife carry, as state legislatures repeal or amend existing laws, or pass new laws regulating knife carry. The older the information, the more likely that the law, statutory or judge made, will have changed. For example, I have come across online summaries for particular states' knife laws that may at one point have been accurate, but that today are inaccurate, due to changes in those states' laws.

In addition, courts interpreting statutes for issues of first impression, where the law is ambiguous whether a particular type of knife, not specifically listed in the statute, is legal or not, may declare certain types of knives legal, or illegal to carry. For example, in Alaska, prior to about 1990, the legal status of balisongs or butterfly knives was unclear. In 1990, the Court of Appeals of Alaska ruled that such knives did not fall under the statutory prohibition on switchblades or gravity knives, and thus, the persons arrested and criminally prosecuted for carrying balisongs were not convicted.[4] They now have arrest records, spent at least some time in lockup, and their lawyers are richer for the experience. My point: Don't be the test case.

7.4   Federal Knife Law

While knives and knife carry tend for the most part to be regulated at the state level, an understanding of some federal knife-related carry law is important for the law-abiding traveler.

Federal law prohibits carry of firearms and dangerous weapons in federal buildings and facilities (other than a Federal court facility).[5] The term "dangerous weapon" includes knives, but does not include a pocket knife with a blade less than two and a half inches in length. The law also provides an exemption for lawful carry of such weapons incident to hunting or other lawful purposes.

Federal law prohibits firearms in federal court facilities, and allows federal courts to regulate, restrict or prohibit possession of other weapons in their facilities.[6]

Federal law prohibits the mailing, via the U.S. Postal Service, of automatic knives, including switchblades, gravity knives, and ballistic knives, and prohibits the introduction or manufacture for introduction into interstate commerce, or the transport or distribution in interstate commerce, of switchblades and gravity knives, and possession of ballistic knives.[7] The law prohibits possession of automatic knives (switchblades, gravity knives, ballistic knives) in territories or U.S. possessions, and Indian Country, which includes all Indian reservations under the jurisdiction of the federal government.[8] A number of exceptions exist, most of which will not apply to the typical traveler, although federal law allows the possession and carry of a

---

[4] See, State v. Strange, 785 P.2d 563, 566 (Alaska Ct. App. 1990).
[5] See, 18 U.S.C. § 930 (2009).
[6] See, id.
[7] See, 18 U.S.C. § 1716 (mailing certain items prohibited); 15 U.S.C. § 1241-45 (switchblade and ballistic knife restrictions).
[8] See, 15 U.S.C. § 1241-45 (2009).

switchblade with a blade three inches or less by a person with only one arm.[9]

Finally, federal law prohibits carry of concealed dangerous weapons on, or attempting to get on, a passenger aircraft.[10] The law authorizes both felony criminal charges and hefty civil fines for violators, and in a post-9/11 world, prosecutions and fines for even inadvertent violations of these statutes are real possibilities. The Transportation Security Administration (TSA) is responsible for security screening at airports, and has published regulations concerning the specific types of items that may be carried on board with you.[11] In December 2005, TSA amended its rules to allow metal scissors with pointed tips and blades less than four inches in length, and tools such as screwdrivers seven inches or less in length. Knives and other edged instruments, other than plastic knives or round-bladed butter knives, remain prohibited as carry-on items.

8 For Current and Retired Law Enforcement – Carrying Under LEOSA

In 2004, Congress passed, and President Bush signed, the Law Enforcement Officers Safety Act (LEOSA). This federal law allows current or retired law enforcement officers who meet certain criteria to carry concealed firearms (other than machine guns, silencers, explosives and destructive devices as those terms are defined in federal law) in any state or political subdivision of a state without obtaining a separate carry permit recognized by that state. The definition of "state" includes the District of Columbia, Puerto Rico, and U.S. possessions. The LEOSA statute is codified at 18 U.S.C. § 926B (current law enforcement officers) and § 926C (retired law enforcement officers).

To benefit from LEOSA, a currently serving officer must be employed by a government agency, be authorized by the agency to carry a firearm and meet the agency's current firearms qualification standards, and not be subject to any current disciplinary action. The officer must also carry the official photographic identification issued by his or her agency while carrying.

---

[9] See, 15 U.S.C. § 1244.
[10] See, 49 U.S.C. § 46505 (2009) (criminal penalties); 49 U.S.C. § 46303 (civil penalties).
[11] See, Permitted and Prohibited Items, Trans. Sec. Admin., U.S. Dep't of Homeland Sec., available at http://www.tsa.gov/travelers/airtravel/prohibited/permitted-prohibited-items.shtm

A retired law enforcement officer must have retired in good standing from a government agency and for reasons other than mental instability, have been employed as an officer for at least fifteen years, and have a nonforfeitable right to retirement benefits under the agency's retirement plan. The retired officer must also annually meet the state's firearms qualification standards for law enforcement officers, and must carry the official photographic identification issued by their former agency to retired officers. A retired officer who no longer lives in the state he or she was employed in as a law enforcement officer may still be certified by the state he or she now resides in, and would carry this separate certification along with the official photo id issued by their former agency to retired officers.

Both current and retired law-enforcement officers carrying firearms should be aware that LEOSA does not authorize them to carry in or on any government or private property where firearms carry is prohibited under state law, or where state law allows private property owners to prohibit carry on their premises, and those private property owners have done so. In general, out-of-state current or retired officers are subject to the same restrictions that apply to recognized carry permit holders, although a few states have carved out additional exemptions for out-of-state current or retired officers. In addition, the LEOSA statute explicitly states that the officer cannot be intoxicated or under the influence of alcohol while carrying.

9 A Note about Open Carry

Open carry refers to the practice of carrying a firearm (or knife) such that the firearm or knife is openly visible and recognizable as such. In contrast concealed carry, as its name implies, refers to the practice of carrying a firearm or knife such that the item is not visible and/or recognizable as such.

Open carry is, and has historically been, the quintessential and honorable mode of exercising the right to bear arms for peaceful citizens. It is no coincidence that some state constitutions specifically allow the legislature to regulate only the concealed carry of arms. Concealed carry was historically the preferred carry mode of bandits and scoundrels; peaceful, law-abiding citizens carried their weapons openly.

In many states, open carry is legal (I indicate the legal status of open carry in each state's chapter). Indeed, in a good number of states no permit is required to openly carry a loaded firearm on your person. Unfortunately, and particularly with respect to firearms, open carry increases the chances that you will encounter unwanted attention from the local constabulary. This is especially true in urban areas. This is the sad reality of our time, and I mention it because as a traveler you probably desire to avoid such unwanted attention.

Thus, while I am an ardent supporter of open carry, and think that residents of states where such carry is lawful should absolutely, positively continue to exercise their right to bear arms via open carry, visitors and travelers may wish to consider concealed carry whenever possible and legal to do so, particularly if their travels take them to highly populated urban areas.

Should a traveler choose to carry openly, or need to do so due to the lack of a recognized concealed-carry permit in states where no permit is needed to carry openly, then he should be aware of the possibility of adverse law enforcement attention. A well-dressed and neatly groomed appearance, along with a handgun secured in a visible holster, preferably one with a retention device or devices will help identify you as a peaceful and law-abiding citizen to local law enforcement. In addition, a well-groomed and neatly dressed appearance will also put forward a positive image of the peaceful armed citizen, and will reduce the likelihood that some hoplophobic person will make a "man (or woman) with a gun" call to the local police.

10 Carrying in National Parks, National Forests, and on Native American Tribal Lands

This section discusses firearms carry in National Parks, National Forests, and on Native American tribal lands and reservations.

10.1 Carrying in National Parks

On February 22nd, 2010, it became legal for those visiting our National Parks to carry loaded guns in the same manner and to the same extent that such carry is legal in the state parks of the state in which the National Park is located.[12] For example, if a state allows

---

[12] The implementing federal regulations are codified at 36 C.F.R. §2.4 (2010), which states in relevant part: "(h) Notwithstanding any other provision in this Chapter, a person may possess, carry, and transport concealed, loaded, and operable firearms within a national park area in accordance with the laws of the state in which the national park area, or that portion thereof, is located, except as otherwise prohibited by applicable Federal law." See, id. at subsection (h).

open carry in its state parks, then open carry would also be legal in National Parks located in that state. Similarly, if concealed carry is permitted in state parks, then concealed carry would also be legal in National Parks located in that state.

This new law applies to National Parks and any of the hundreds of properties managed by either the National Park Service or the Fish and Wildlife Service.

Note, however, that even in National Parks where carry is permitted, the law continues to prohibit carry in federal facilities and buildings located in such Parks. Thus, carry is still banned in places like Park visitor centers, ranger stations and administrative buildings and officers regularly staffed by federal employees. In addition, the National Park Service will likely take a broad interpretation of "federal facility", although it has indicated that any areas it considers off-limits to firearms carry under federal law will be posted to that effect.

In addition, the law applies only to firearms possession and carry, not use. Restrictions on hunting, target shooting, and unlawful discharge remain in effect.

10.2 Carrying in National Forests

Unlike the case with National Parks, which are managed by the thoroughly anti-gun National Park Service, our National Forests come under the jurisdiction of the U.S. Department of Agriculture. The Department of Agriculture has more many years allowed lawful firearms carry in National Forests, provided that such carry in analogous state parks and forests is allowed under state law in the state where the National Forest is located in.

Basically, the Department of Agriculture defers to state law to determine whether firearms carry is legal or not. If state law of the state the National Forest is located in allows firearms carry in state parks and state forests, then such carry is legal in National Forests located in that state, and subject to the same conditions that state law imposes on carry in state parks and forests. For example, if state law requires a carry permit to carry in state parks and forests, then carry in National Forests located in that state would also require a carry permit.

Note, however, that even in National Forests where carry is permitted, the law continues to prohibit carry in federal facilities and buildings located on such federal lands. Thus, carry is still banned in places like Forest Service visitor centers, ranger stations or administrative buildings and other structures where federal employees normally work.

In addition, the law applies only to firearms possession and carry, not use. Any restrictions on hunting, target shooting, and unlawful discharge remain in effect.

10.3 Carrying on Native American Tribal Lands and Reservations

Travelers should be aware that American Indian and other Native American tribal lands and reservations that belong to federally recognized tribes (of which there are over five hundred, including some two hundred Native Alaska groups) are mostly autonomous, self-governing areas. There are about 310 Indian reservations, encompassing over 55 million acres of territory, or about 2.3% of the landmass of the United States.

Each tribe exists as a quasi-independent nation with limited tribal sovereignty, and can establish and operate its own tribal government, adjudicate cases within the borders of its lands, and levy taxes within its borders.

Thus, certain American Indian tribal lands and reservations may have stricter firearms and weapons carry laws within their borders than the states in which they are located. Travelers visiting casinos and other tourist attractions on tribal lands and reservations should contact the relevant tribal government to ascertain their carry laws. Cautious travelers would be well-advised to transport their firearms in accordance with the McClure-Volkmer interstate transport provisions of federal law in the event that definitive information on a particular tribe's laws or regulations cannot be obtained.

11 Traveling with Firearms on Commercial Passenger Aircraft

Federal law permits the transport of unloaded firearms in checked baggage on commercial passenger aircraft. Firearms must be unloaded and securely encased in locked, hard-side gun cases. Any ammunition should be stored in the factory ammo carton, or in commercial ammo boxes. Ammo should not be loaded into magazines.

Generally, ammo and the unloaded firearm(s) may be transported in the same locked case, unless a particular airline's policy requires separate cases. Individual airlines may also limit the number of firearms that may be transported in a single case, as well as the amount of ammunition. This is especially the case for international flights. Check with your airline prior to travel to ascertain its firearms policy.

A traveler must declare to the airline at the time of checking his baggage that he is traveling with unloaded firearms in his checked baggage. The airline will provide a firearms declaration tag (that is typically red) for the traveler to complete and sign. This tag should be placed with the firearm in the firearm case.

Airline and airport check-in procedures vary from airline to airline and airport to airport, but typically a TSA agent will be called over to verify the unloaded status of the firearm, following which the unloaded firearms declaration tag should be enclosed in the case with the firearm(s), and the case locked. Federal law requires the passenger (and only the passenger) to retain the key or combination to the locked case.

Depending on the airport, the checked bag containing the firearm may then go through the standard x-ray screening procedure. Cautious travelers should check with your airline and airport for their specific policies and procedures prior to arrival at the airport to avoid surprises.

Travelers should also be aware that airlines are prohibited by law from visibly marking or tagging baggage containing firearms with overt "firearms inside" tags.[13] Any attempt by airline personnel to mark the outside of a traveler's checked baggage with such tags or markings should be reported to an airline supervisor and to TSA.

---

[13] *See*, 18 U.S.C. § 922 (e), which states in relevant part: "No common or contract carrier shall require or cause any label, tag, or other written notice to be placed on the outside of any package, luggage, or other container that such package, luggage, or other container contains a firearm."

12 Traveling with Firearms on Trains, Ships, and Buses

Travelers should be aware that federal law requires that those engaged in interstate travel by train, cruise ship, or bus must temporarily surrender possession of their firearms and ammunition to the captain, conductor or operator for the duration of the trip.[14] Some carriers may make provisions for passengers traveling with firearms. For example, some cruise ship lines may allow vacationing travelers who are sworn law enforcement officers to retain possession of their firearms on board the vessel. Travelers should contact the carrier in advance to determine their firearms policy.

Some carriers, such as Amtrak, currently prohibit carry or transport of all firearms and ammunition, whether on the person, on in carry-on or checked baggage. A recent change to federal law, however, requires Amtrak to implement policies for the lawful transportation of firearms and ammunition in checked baggage by the end of 2010. Amtrak also prohibits transport of swords and other weapons in carry-on and checked baggage.

Travelers should note that a few states may restrict or prohibit carry or transport of firearms on trains under state law. I have noted several such restrictions in the relevant state chapters.

13 How to Use the State Summaries

The chapters that follow provide state-specific information. Each state has its own separate chapter. Each chapter is organized as follows: at the start of each chapter are some statistics and trivia about the state, such as area, population, and crime rate data.[15] Following this is a summary of key firearms transport and carry criteria, such as whether carry is permitted in restaurants that serve alcohol, in state parks and forests, etc.

The items in the table are as follows:

Restaurants and bars – indicates whether firearms carry is allowed in restaurants that serve alcohol, and/or in bars and taverns. Many states prohibit firearms carry, even with a recognized permit, in

---

[14] *See, id.*

[15] The violent crime rates and relative ranking for each state have been tabulated from crime rate data from 2008, the latest available, as published in the FBI's Uniform Crime Reports.

establishments that serve alcoholic beverages for on-premises consumption. Most prohibit carry in bars and taverns, i.e., in establishments primarily devoted to the selling or serving of alcoholic beverages for on-premises consumption. Others allow carry in restaurants only, i.e., in dining establishments whose primary purpose is the serving of food, rather than alcoholic drinks. Some states mandate open carry; others require concealed carry only. This section of the table summarizes the requirements and restrictions for the particular state.

Churches / Places of worship – indicates the status of lawful carry in churches, synagogues, and other places of religious worship.

State parks / forests – indicates whether firearms carry is allowed in state parks and forests.

Vehicle carry – summarizes the requirements for vehicle firearms carry or transport.

LE notification if stopped? – indicates whether state law requires a permit holder carrying concealed weapons to immediately inform any law enforcement officer who stops the permit holder for an official purpose of the permit holder's armed status.

Retreat requirement for self-defense – indicates whether state law imposes a duty to retreat prior to resorting to deadly force in self-defense.

Preemption law – indicates whether the state legislature has prohibited political subdivisions of the state such as cities and towns from separately regulating weapons (typically applies only to firearms regulation).

Open Carry – indicates whether open carry is legal in the state.

Military-pattern semi-auto restrictions – indicates whether the state restricts the ownership and possession of "assault style" cosmetically-impaired firearms.

NFA weapons – indicates the extent to which the state restricts possession of weapons subject to the National Firearms Act, such as machine guns, firearm silencers, short-barreled shotguns and rifles, and the like.

Note: Even if state law does not prohibit the carrying of firearms or other weapons in a particular location such as a restaurant or a church, travelers should be aware that private property owners can generally prohibit such carry on their premises. In some states they must post signage with particular wording specified by statute in order for such a ban to be given legal effect, although in most cases any notice, whether communicated via a written sign or verbally, is sufficient.

Following the firearms carry summary table are the permit reciprocity and recognition lists, showing which states' permits a given state recognizes, and which states recognize that state's permit. A table showing knife types and permissible carry modes follows.

Separate discussions of each state's firearms and knife carry legalities are provided, along with an overall assessment of the legal environment for weapons carry. This assessment is necessarily somewhat subjective, and includes this author's evaluation of both statutory and, particularly in the case of knives, case law, along with the state's general historical and cultural attitudes towards firearms and knife carry.

Each state's chapter provides a section detailing places off-limits to firearms and knife carry. Most typically this includes places like schools and courthouses, although some states have long, detailed lists of locations where carry is forbidden, sometimes with or without a permit. Note that these are places where specific statutory restrictions under state law exist. Locations such as the secure areas of commercial passenger airports, federal buildings, and federal courts already have their own restrictions under federal law (or regulatory authority to enact same) on weapon carry within their facilities. Also, locations which may not have specific statutory restrictions on weapon carry, such as state court facilities, state prisons, etc., typically restrict knife carry under their own regulatory powers as provided for in state law.

While most states have enacted at least limited preemption laws, those laws mostly apply to firearms. Very few states preempt their political subdivisions from regulating knives and knife carry, with the predictable result that many cities and towns have enacted their own knife-related ordinances. For each state with such areas of separate regulation, I have listed some selected cities and towns, along with a summary of their specific knife-related ordinances.

Finally, contact information – addresses, phone numbers, and websites – is provided for each state's primary agency for weapons permitting and related issues.

Additional information regarding the knife law-related sections:

As is the case with firearms, each state's knife law is listed in its own section. Within each section, a summary table listing various knife types and their carry status under that state's knife-related statutory and case law is provided, along with a short discussion of the state's general view of knife carry. In the summary tables and in the text I have used the term "automatic knife" to encompass switchblades, gravity knives, and ballistic knives, since state laws usually treat these sub-types similarly, and in many cases identically, as to prohibited conduct (penalties may differ in some states, with typically harsher treatment for illegal use or possession of ballistic knives). I have grouped daggers, dirks, and stilettos together, as these items are also often treated similarly under most state laws. In the rare case that one is treated substantially differently, I have noted this in the textual discussion that follows the summary table. In cases where a statute may be ambiguous or conflicting, I have generally taken the conservative approach and listed that carry mode as prohibited.

In most cases, I have tried to characterize the overall legal environment for knife carry, based on an assessment of both the statutory law, as well as the case law for that state, and have tried to describe the basic tenor of the state's historical or cultural perspective on knives and knife carry. I have used phrases like "moderately permissive", "fairly restrictive", and so forth to describe my subjective assessment of the state's "knife friendliness." As such, you may see two states with the same or similar summary tables, but different subjective assessments, reflecting differences in, for example, the types of prosecutions for knife offenses as evidenced through case law, the existence of restrictive municipal ordinances, etc.

In some states, a knife may be legally carried if the person possesses a valid CCW permit. In other states, however, CCW permits are really only concealed firearm or concealed handgun permits, and do not cover other types of deadly weapons. Where applicable, I have typically indicated whether the existence of a valid, recognized CCW permit would allow the otherwise unlawful possession or carry of certain types of knives.

I have endeavored to list prohibited places for carry where specific statutory restrictions under state law exist. As is the case with firearms, locations such as the secure areas of commercial passenger airports, federal buildings, and federal courts already have their own restrictions under federal law (or regulatory authority to enact same) on weapon, including knife, carry within their facilities. Also, locations which may not have specific statutory restrictions on weapon carry, such as state court facilities, state prisons, etc., typically restrict knife carry under their own regulatory powers as provided for in state law.

In addition, since most states do not preempt local municipal governments from enacting their own knife restrictions, most states have cities, towns, or counties with knife ordinances that are more stringent that those restrictions embodied in state law. As such, I have listed a few selected municipalities, typically the state's larger cities, with knife ordinances more restrictive than state law. Obviously, it would be impractical to list every such city, but typically the larger cities listed impose the most restrictive knife possession or carry restrictions. Thus, if your knife meets those restrictions, your knife will likely meet the less restrictive ordinances of most other towns or cities. As always, however, exceptions may exist.

Finally, you may want to check with the relevant state authorities if you have specific questions about the legality of your knife. I have included the contact information and website, if available, for each state's attorney general and primary state-wide law enforcement agency.

Good luck with your travels, stay sharp, and stay safe!

For further information, and to keep up to date with the latest changes in the law, you may wish to visit SpartanPressOnline.com

It will be of little avail to the people that the laws are made by men of their own choice, if the laws be so voluminous that they cannot be read, or so incoherent that they cannot be understood; if they be repealed or revised before they are promulgated, or undergo such incessant changes that no man who knows what the law is today can guess what it will be tomorrow.

James Madison, The Federalist Papers, #62

14 Alabama – The Heart of Dixie

Area: 50,744 sq.mi. (Rank: 28th)   Population: 4,661,900 (Rank: 23rd)
Violent Crime Rate (per 100,000 residents): 452.8 (Rank: 32nd Safest)
State Motto: *Audemus Iura Nostra Defendere (We Dare Defend Our Rights)*

Firearms Carry Summary:

Carry considerations	Status
Restaurants and bars	Allowed
Churches / Places of worship	Allowed
State parks / forests	Prohibited without written permission. *See*, ALA. ADMIN. CODE r. 220-5-.07 (state parks); 390-X-7-.08 (state forests)
Vehicle carry	Permit required for handguns, otherwise must be unloaded and cased; loaded long guns allowed in plain view or cased
LE notification if stopped	Not required
Retreat requirement for self-defense	Not required; *See*, CODE OF ALA. § 13A-3-23
Preemption law	Yes. *See*, CODE OF ALA. §11-45-1.1 (2009)
Open Carry	Allowed, no permit required, must be 18 or older
Military-pattern semi-auto restrictions	Not restricted
NFA weapons	NFA-friendly, compliance with federal law only

Reciprocity / Recognition

*Alabama **recognizes** permits from the following states:*

Alaska	Arkansas	Arizona	Colorado
Florida	Georgia	Idaho	Indiana
Kentucky	Louisiana	Michigan	Mississippi
Missouri	New Hampshire	North Carolina	North Dakota
Oklahoma	South Dakota	Tennessee	Texas
Utah	Wyoming		

*Alabama permits **are recognized by** the following states:*

Alaska	Arkansas	Arizona	Colorado*
Florida*	Georgia	Idaho	Indiana
Kentucky	Louisiana	Michigan*	Mississippi
Missouri	New Hampshire*	North Carolina	North Dakota

| Oklahoma | South Dakota | Tennessee | Texas |
| Utah | Vermont | Wyoming | |

Note: In the reciprocity / recognition tables above, states with an asterisk (*) require the permit holder to both have a permit from, and be a resident of, the recognized state in order for reciprocity / recognition of the permit.

Knife Carry Summary:

Note: Blade length limits, if any, in parentheses.

Knife Type	Open Carry	Concealed Carry	Notes
Folding	Yes	Yes	
Fixed Blade	Yes	No	See note[16]
Dirks, Daggers, Stilettos	Yes	No	See note[16]
Automatics	Yes	Yes	
Balisongs	Yes	Yes	

14.1 Discussion

Firearms Carry:

Visitors to Alabama will find the law generally favorable to those traveling with firearms. The state requires, however, that you possess a recognized permit in order to carry a loaded handgun either concealed or in a vehicle (whether openly visible or concealed). Even though such permits are issued on a discretionary "may issue" rather than a "shall issue" basis, as a practical matter, actual issuance does not appear to be biased against "ordinary" citizens, as is the case in most other discretionary issue states. Note, however, that due to the discretionary nature of permit issuance, sheriffs may (and some reportedly do) place arbitrary restrictions on the permit.

---

[16] Alabama law prohibits concealed carry of bowie knives or similar knives. *See*, ALA. CODE § 13A-11-50 (2009). Caution is advised in carrying any fixed bladed knife in a concealed mode, particularly large fixed bladed knives. The limited case law on the subject indicates that at least one Alabama appellate court has described a bowie knife as "a long knife shaped like a dagger but having only one edge," indicating the possibility that daggers and the like may be considered a knife "of like kind or description" under the statute. *See*, Smelley v. State, 472 So.2d 715, 717 (Ala. Crim. App. 1985) (quoting Tennessee Supreme Court's description of bowie knife (citation omitted)).

Open carry is legal in Alabama, and no permit is required for open carry of a loaded firearm (outside of a vehicle).

Loaded long guns may be carried in a vehicle in plain view, secured in gun cases, or in the trunk of the vehicle.

The state Legislature has preempted cities and towns from further regulating firearms (but not knife) possession or carry, and thus travelers can be assured of uniform firearms regulation throughout the state.

Knife Carry:

Visitors to Alabama will find a fairly permissive legal environment for knife carry, with a strong preference for open, versus concealed, carry. Ordinary folding pocket knives should pose no problem, and may be carried openly or concealed. There is no statutorily defined blade length limit. State law strictly prohibits concealed carry of bowies and similar knives. Unfortunately, the legal boundaries of what is considered a "bowie knife or knife or instrument of like kind or description" are fuzzy, and may very well include such knives as daggers, dirks, stilettos, and large fixed blades. Given the inherent difficulty of determining exactly what a court may consider a prohibited knife under the broad wording of the statute, the cautious traveler would do well to avoid concealed carry of fixed bladed knives, particularly large fixed bladed knives, as such knives may fall within the statutory prohibition described.

State law prohibits carry of deadly weapons on school property "with intent to do bodily harm[.]" The definition of "deadly weapon" includes a "switch-blade knife, gravity knife, stiletto, sword, or dagger[.]" Travelers should be aware that cities and towns may also pass their own ordinances restricting knife carry. Alabama does not preempt its cities and towns from regulating knife carry, unlike the case for firearms, where the state has prohibited cities and towns from enacting their own handgun carry restrictions, ensuring uniform state-wide handgun laws. For example, cities may restrict knife carry in bars and restaurants that serve alcohol, on school grounds, city parks, etc.

14.2 Places Off-Limits While Carrying

Alabama prohibits possession or carry of firearms by persons participating in or attending a demonstration in a "public place", defined as "[a]ny place to which the general public has access and a right to resort for business, entertainment or other lawful purpose, but does not necessarily mean a place devoted solely to the uses of the public. Such term shall include the front or immediate area or parking lot of any store, shop, restaurant, tavern, shopping center or other place of business. Such term shall also include any public building, the grounds of any public building, or within the curtilage of any public building, or in any public parking lot, public street, right-of-way, sidewalk right-of-way, or within any public park or other public grounds." CODE OF ALA. §13A-11-59 (2010).

Alabama law also prohibits possession or carry of a deadly weapon with the intent to do bodily harm on the premises of a public school (grade K-12 type school), or school bus used for same. The law, however, exempts law-enforcement officers and persons with pistol permits issued pursuant to §13A-11-75. *See*, CODE OF ALA. §13A-11-72 (2010).

State law prohibits carry or possession of firearms in any wildlife management area without a recognized permit. See, CODE OF ALA. §9-11-304 (2010).

The state administrative code also prohibits firearms possession or carry in state parks or state forests without written permission of the manager of the state park or forest visited. *See*, ALA. ADMIN. CODE Ch. 220-5-.08 (2010), .Ch. 390-X-7-.08 (2010).

14.3 Selected City Ordinances

The state legislature has preempted municipalities and other political subdivisions from regulating firearms to any extent greater than state law. Thus, firearms regulation is uniform throughout the state.

The city ordinances below relate to knife carry:

Decatur – Carry of "bowie knife or knife or instrument of like kind or description" prohibited in city-owned or city-controlled parks and places licensed to serve alcohol. See, DECATUR, ALA., CODE § 16-22.1 (2009).

Mobile – Unlawful to sell, or have in possession for sale, any switchblade within the city or its police jurisdiction. See, MOBILE, ALA., CODE OF ORDINANCES § 62-3 (2010).

Muscle Shoals – Concealed carry of bowie knives or "other knife or instrument of like kind or description," or razors, prohibited. *See*, MUSCLE SHOALS, ALA., CODE § 70-82 (2009). The ordinance appears to contain a provision exempting those with carry permits, but refers to a non-existent provision of Alabama law, so whether this exemption is outdated or currently applicable is questionable.

14.4 State Resources

Alabama Dept. of Public Safety
301 South Ripley St.
Montgomery, AL 36104
Phone: (334) 242-4371
Website: http://www.dps.state.al.us/

Attorney General of Alabama
500 Dexter Avenue
Montgomery, AL 36130
Phone: (334) 242-7300
Website: http://www.ago.state.al.us/

15 Alaska – The Last Frontier

Area: 571,951 sq.mi. (Rank: 1st)   Population: 683,293 (Rank: 47th)
Violent Crime Rate (per 100,000 residents): 651.9 (Rank: 44th Safest)
State Motto: *North to the Future*

Firearms Carry Summary:

Carry considerations	Status
Restaurants and bars	Allowed (must be concealed) in restaurants only, and no alcohol consumption permitted
Churches / Places of worship	Allowed
State parks / forests	Allowed
Vehicle carry	Loaded open/concealed firearms allowed, no permit required
LE notification if stopped	Required. *See*, ALASKA STAT. § 11.61.220 (2009)
Retreat requirement for self-defense	Required, except in home. *See*, ALASKA STAT. § 11.81.335 (2009)
Preemption law	Yes. *See*, ALASKA STAT. § 29.35.145 (2009)
Open Carry	Allowed, no permit required, must be 14 or older
Military-pattern semi-auto restrictions	Not restricted
NFA weapons	NFA-friendly: No state restriction, compliance with federal law only

Reciprocity / Recognition

Alaska **recognizes** permits from **all other states**. *In Alaska, anyone who is not a prohibited possessor, that is, anyone who can legally own a firearm, may carry that firearm concealed without a permit.*

Alaska permits **are recognized by** *the following states:*

Alabama	Arizona	Arkansas	Colorado*
Delaware	Florida*	Georgia	Idaho
Indiana	Kansas	Kentucky	Louisiana
Michigan*	Minnesota	Mississippi	Missouri
Montana	Nebraska	Nevada	New Hampshire*
New Mexico	North Carolina	North Dakota	Ohio
Oklahoma	Pennsylvania	South Carolina*	South Dakota
Tennessee	Texas	Utah	Vermont
Virginia	West Virginia	Wyoming	

Note: In the reciprocity / recognition tables above, states with an asterisk (*) require the permit holder to both have a permit from, and be a resident of, the recognized state in order for reciprocity / recognition of the permit.

Knife Carry Summary:

Note: Blade length limits, if any, in parentheses.

Knife Type	Open Carry	Concealed Carry	Notes
Folding	Yes	Yes	See notes[17,18]
Fixed Blade	Yes	Yes	See note[18]
Dirks, Daggers, Stilettos	Yes	Yes	See note[19]
Automatics	No	No	
Balisongs	Yes	Yes	See note[18]

15.1 Discussion

Firearms Carry:

The Nation's largest state by area, and more than twice as large as Texas, Alaska's over half a million square miles makes even large states like Texas and California look small by comparison. The state's rugged wilderness, vast distances, and few population centers foster a spirit of independence and self-sufficiency in its citizens. This spirit of self-sufficiency is notably reflected in Alaska's liberal firearms laws, Alaska being one of only two states that do not require its law-abiding citizens to obtain permits to carry concealed firearms.

Travelers to the Last Frontier will find a friendly legal environment for firearms carry. Alaska is one of two states that does not require a permit to carry a loaded firearm either openly or concealed. State law requires that those carrying concealed without a permit be at

---

[17] The careful traveler would be wise to avoid exceptionally large folders or those that appear particularly "weapon like". Ordinary pocket knives are excluded from the law enforcement notification requirement for concealed deadly weapons. *See*, ALASKA STAT. § 11.61.220 (2009).

[18] If carried concealed, and you are contacted by a law enforcement officer for an official purpose, state law requires you to immediately inform the officer of that fact, and allow the officer to secure the weapon. *See*, ALASKA STAT. § 11.61.220 (2009). In addition, you cannot carry a concealed deadly weapon into another person's residence without first obtaining permission to do so from an adult residing in that residence. *See*, *id*.

[19] While no explicit state law prohibition appears to exist, some municipalities specifically prohibit concealed carry of these types of knives.

least twenty-one years of age. Thus, any person twenty-one years of age or older who may legally possess a firearm, may carry it openly or concealed without a permit.

Alaska issues permits on a "shall issue" basis to qualified residents who wish to benefit from the reciprocity and permit recognition statutes and agreements when visiting other states.

State law requires that anyone carrying a concealed weapon must immediately inform any law enforcement officer who stops them for an official purpose of the fact that they are carrying a concealed weapon.

A traveler (who is 21 or older) in a vehicle may carry a loaded handgun either openly or concealed on his person, or stored in the glove compartment for center console, or other storage container. Similarly, long guns may be carry loaded in gun racks, or secured in commercial gun cases anywhere in the vehicle.

Knife Carry:

Visitors to Alaska will likewise find a generally permissive legal environment for knife carry. Ordinary folding pocket knives should pose no problem, and may be carried openly or concealed. There is no statutorily defined blade length limit. Carry or possession, however, of automatic knives in the form of switchblades and gravity knives is strictly prohibited. Fixed blades may be carried openly or concealed, but if carried concealed, state law requires the wearer to immediately disclose the presence of the weapon upon contact with any law enforcement officer acting in an official capacity, and to allow the officer to secure the weapon.

Case law indicates that balisongs, or butterfly knives, do not fall within the statutory prohibition on switchblade or gravity knives. While no explicit statutory prohibition on dirks, daggers, or stilettos appears to exist, the wise traveler would be well-advised to avoid carrying these types of knives, as some municipalities, notably Anchorage, specifically prohibit concealed carry of dirks and daggers.

No state-wide statutory prohibitions on off-limits locations for otherwise legal knife carry exist, although travelers should be aware that cities and towns may pass their own ordinances restricting knife carry. Alaska does not preempt its cities and towns from regulating knife carry, unlike the case for firearms, where the state has prohibited cities and towns from enacting their own handgun carry restrictions, ensuring uniform state-wide laws. As such, towns and cities may regulate knife carry in or on such areas as school property.

15.2 Places Off-Limits While Carrying

Firearms Carry:

Alaska prohibits the carry of firearms in schools, school buses, and on school grounds, including school parking lots, without permission of the chief administrative officer of the school or district. Those twenty-one years or older may possess unloaded firearms stored in the trunk of the vehicle or securely encased in commercial gun cases. *See,* ALASKA STAT. § 11.61.210 (2009).

State law also prohibits possession of firearms on the grounds or parking lots of licensed childcare facilities. A person twenty-one years or older may possess an unloaded firearm stored in the trunk of the vehicle were securely encased in a commercial gun case. *See id.* at § 11.61.220.

Firearms possession is also prohibited in court rooms and courthouses, and in state-funded domestic violence and sexual assault shelters. *See, id.*

Carry of firearms is forbidden in establishments that serve alcoholic beverages for on premises consumption. An exception exists for the carry of concealed handguns in restaurants only (not bars), provided the carrier does not consume any alcohol. *See, id.*

State law requires that those carrying concealed deadly weapons, prior to entering another's private residence, must obtain express permission from the person(s) residing there. *See, id.*

Knife Carry:

No state law limitation. Towns and cities, however, may pass their own local ordinances prohibiting carry.

15.3 Selected City Ordinances

The state legislature has preempted municipalities and other political subdivisions from regulating firearms to any extent greater than state law. Thus, firearms regulation is uniform throughout the state.

The city ordinances below relate to knife carry:

Anchorage – Concealed carry of knives other than ordinary pocket knives prohibited. *See*, ANCHORAGE, ALASKA, MUNICIPAL CODE § 8.25.020 (2009). Carry of switchblades or gravity knives prohibited. *See, id.* at § 8.75.130 (2009).

Fairbanks – Possession of "dangerous weapons" on school grounds prohibited. The definition of "dangerous weapons" specifically includes knives other than ordinary pocket knives of blade length not more than 3½ inches. *See*, FAIRBANKS, ALASKA, CODE OF ORDINANCES § 46-294 (2010)

15.4 State Resources

Alaska Department of Public Safety
5700 East Tudor Road
Anchorage, Alaska 99507
Phone: (907) 269-5086
Fax: (907) 269-4543
Website: http://www.dps.state.ak.us/

Attorney General of Alaska
P.O. Box 110300
Juneau, AK 99811-0300
Phone: (907) 465-2133
Fax: (907) 465-2075
Website: http://www.law.state.ak.us/

16 Arizona – The Grand Canyon State

Area: 113,635 sq.mi. (Rank: 6th) Population: 6,500,180 (Rank: 14th) Violent Crime Rate (per 100,000 residents): 447.0 (Rank: 30th Safest) State Motto: *Ditat Deus (God Enriches)*	

Firearms Carry Summary:

Carry considerations	Status
Restaurants and bars	Concealed carry allowed with permit, unless posted otherwise; *See*, ARIZ. REV. STAT. § 4-229 (2010)
Churches / Places of worship	Allowed
State parks / forests	Generally allowed; municipalities may prohibit carry without permit if so posted; allowed with permit[20]
Vehicle carry	Loaded handguns allowed, in plain view without permit, or concealed with permit; long guns must be in plain view or securely cased
LE notification if stopped?	Not required, but must inform LE of the presence of concealed weapon if asked (effective July 29, 2010)
Retreat requirement for self-defense	Not required in the home or occupied vehicle; *See*, ARIZ. REV. STAT. §13-418 (2009)
Preemption law	Yes. *See*, ARIZ. REV. STAT. §13-3108 (2009). Note: For preemption of knife regulation see §13-3120 (2010), effective date July 29, 2010.
Open Carry	Allowed, no permit required, and generally accepted, must be 18 or older
Military-pattern semi-auto restrictions	Not restricted
NFA weapons	NFA-friendly: No state restriction, compliance with federal law only

Reciprocity / Recognition

*Arizona **recognizes** permits from **all other states**.*

---

[20] Note that in April 2010 the state amended its preemption law to restrict the ability of local governments to ban firearms carry without a permit in public parks. This new legislation is slated to take effect July 29, 2010.

*Arizona permits **are recognized by** the following states:*

Alabama	Alaska	Arkansas	Colorado*
Delaware	Florida*	Georgia	Idaho
Indiana	Kansas	Kentucky	Louisiana
Michigan*	Mississippi	Missouri	Montana
Nebraska	New Hampshire*	New Mexico	North Carolina
North Dakota	Ohio	Oklahoma	Pennsylvania
South Carolina*	South Dakota	Tennessee	Texas
Utah	Vermont	Virginia	West Virginia
Wyoming			

Note: In the reciprocity / recognition tables above, states with an asterisk (*) require the permit holder to both have a permit from, and be a resident of, the recognized state in order for reciprocity / recognition of the permit.

Knife Carry Summary:

Note: Blade length limits, if any, in parentheses.

Knife Type	Open Carry	Concealed Carry	Notes
Folding	Yes	Yes	See notes[21,24]
Fixed Blade	Yes	No	See note[22]
Dirks, Daggers, Stilettos	Yes	No	See note[22]
Automatics	Yes	No	See note[22]
Balisongs	Yes	No	See note[22]

16.1 Discussion

Firearms Carry:

In April 2010, Arizona passed a law eliminating the permit requirement for concealed carry, and statewide preemption of knife regulation (see Knife Carry section below). This law is scheduled to take effect at the end of July 2010. In addition to eliminating the need for a permit to carry a concealed weapon, travelers should be aware that the law requires that a person carrying a concealed

---

[21] State law permits concealed carry of pocket knives without a permit. *See*, ARIZ. REV. STAT. § 13-3102 (2009). Note, however, that the term "pocket knife" is not defined in the statute. Travelers should avoid carry of folding knives with large blades without a recognized concealed weapons permit.
[22] May be carried concealed with a valid, recognized concealed weapons permit.

weapon(s) inform a law enforcement officer of the presence of the concealed weapon(s) if asked, and the statute allows the law enforcement officer to take temporary possession of a concealed firearm during the encounter. Note that carry in restaurants that serve alcohol, however, still requires a concealed carry permit.

The law-abiding traveler to the Grand Canyon State will find a generally favorable environment for firearms and knife carry, especially outside the state's major cities. Open carry of holstered handguns is both legal and generally accepted. No permit is required for open carry of either firearms or knives. In addition, Arizona recognizes concealed carry permits from all other states (provided the permit holder is at least 21 years or age), one of a growing number of states that do so. Unlike many other states, the Arizona permit is a true concealed weapons permit, covering not just firearms, but knives and other deadly weapons as well.

Travelers should note, however, that tribal governments may impose their own restrictions on the carrying of firearms and knives on tribal reservations.

A traveler in a vehicle may carry a loaded handgun without a permit provided the handgun is openly carried in plain view. In addition, handguns in a case, holster, or scabbard may be stored in a glove compartment or other vehicle storage compartment without a permit.

Travelers with permits may of course carry their handguns concealed when in a vehicle. Long guns must be visible from outside the vehicle, such as stored in a gun rack, or securely encased in commercial gun cases.

Arizona's preemption statute prohibits local governments from regulating most aspects of firearms possession and carry to any extent greater than state law. Cities and towns, however, may regulate and/or prohibit those without permits from carrying firearms openly in public parks within their jurisdictions. Notice of any such prohibition or restriction must be conspicuously posted, and state law prohibits local governments from imposing any such prohibitions on those with recognized permits. Travelers should be aware that in April 2010 the state updated its preemption law to remove the ability of local governments to ban firearms carry without a permit in public parks. This new law is expected to take effect July 29, 2010.

Knife Carry:

In April 2010, Arizona enacted the nation's first knife-specific preemption law, which prohibits local governments from regulating knives to any extent greater than state law. Any local ordinance or regulation that is more restrictive than state law becomes null and void upon the effective date of this new law. Schools, however, are still allowed to prohibit knife carry on their property, unless the carrier is a peace officer of has specific permission from the school administrator.[23]

With respect to knives, ordinary folding pocket knives should pose no problem, and may be carried either openly visible or concealed, although pocket knives with large blades should be carried openly, unless the wearer possesses a recognized concealed weapons permit.[24] There is no statutorily defined blade length limit. Note, however, that some cities may have ordinances requiring a shorter blade length.

There also appears to be no explicit statutory prohibition on dirks, daggers, stilettos, and automatic knives, although such knives may fall under the statutory definition of "deadly weapons", and therefore concealed carry would require a valid concealed carry weapons permit. In addition, since Arizona's preemption law only relates to firearms, cities and towns are free to regulate carry of other weapons such as knives, and several do just that. For knives other than ordinary pocket knives, open carry is legal, provided that such knives are carried in a visible scabbard.

Balisongs should be carried openly, or concealed with a recognized permit, as such knives are likely to be deemed weapons, due to their association with the martial arts, and public perception as martial arts weapons.

---

[23] *See*, ARIZ. REV. STAT. § 13-3120 (2010) (preempting knife ordinances or regulations more restrictive than state law); § 15-341 (2010) (allowing schools to restrict knife carry without school permission).
[24] Some (erroneous) information available online has indicated that, ostensibly pursuant to an opinion of the state's Attorney General, a pocket knife with a blade less than four inches may be carried concealed without a recognized concealed weapons permit. A search of the state's Attorney General formal opinions from 1999 through March 2006, however, has revealed no such public opinion. Furthermore, in response to an inquiry from the author, the Arizona Attorney General's office has indicated that they "did not find any opinions specifically discussing pocket knives with blades under four inches." *See*, Email from Ariz. Att'y Gen. Office (Jun. 5, 2006) (on file with author).

State law prohibits carry of deadly weapons on school grounds. Apart from schools, however, no state-wide statutory prohibitions on off-limits locations for otherwise legal knife carry exist, although travelers should be aware that cities and towns may pass their own ordinances restricting knife carry. Court buildings and other secured government buildings may also restrict or prohibit knife carry of any kind within their facilities.

16.2 Places Off-Limits While Carrying

Firearms Carry:
Arizona prohibits the carry of firearms into state or local government buildings if the entity operating the public building prohibits firearms therein. Such entity must provide for temporary and secure storage of firearms for those entering the building. *See*, ARIZ. REV. STAT. § 13-3102 (2009).

Carry of firearms is also prohibited in polling places on election day, or in nuclear or hydroelectric generating stations. *See, id.*

Carry of loaded firearms and other deadly weapons on school grounds is prohibited. Firearms may be kept in a locked vehicle if unloaded and not visible from the outside. *See, id.*

Carry of firearms in correctional facilities is also prohibited.

Knife Carry:

Carry of deadly weapons are prohibited in the same places as those for firearms (see above).

Towns and cities may pass their own local ordinances prohibiting carry in specified areas. In addition, courts and other secured state buildings may restrict and/or prohibit a broad range of weapons, including knives, on their premises. *See, e.g.*, POLICIES AND PROCEDURES MANUAL § 4.11, Ariz. Admin. Ofc. of Courts (1991).

16.3 Selected City Ordinances
The state legislature has preempted municipalities and other political subdivisions from regulating firearms to any extent greater than state law. Thus, firearms carry regulation is uniform throughout the state.

The state has recently enacted a comprehensive knife preemption statute that prohibits local governments and agencies from separately regulating knives to any extent greater than state law. This law is slated to take effect July 29, 2010.

The city ordinances below relate to knife carry. <u>Note:</u> these ordinances remain in effect until the effective date of the new knife preemption law:

Phoenix – Concealed carry of dirks, daggers, bowie knives, or knives other than ordinary pocket knives prohibited. *See,* PHOENIX, ARIZ., CITY CODE § 23-40 (2010).

Tucson – Carry of "weapons of any kind or description" prohibited on any part of Tucson-Pima library grounds posted as prohibiting weapons or firearms. *See,* TUCSON, ARIZ., CODE OF ORD. § 11-160 (2006).

Chandler – Carry of "deadly weapons" in city parks prohibited. Excludes pocket knives with blade lengths no longer than 3½ inches. *See,* CHANDLER, ARIZ., CITY CODE § 31-2.3 (2010).

16.4 State Resources

Arizona Department of Public Safety
2102 W Encanto Blvd
Phoenix, AZ 85009
Phone: (602) 256-6280 or (800) 256-6280
Fax: (602) 223-2928
Website: http://www.azdps.gov/

Arizona Attorney General
1275 West Washington Street
Phoenix, AZ 85007
Phone: (602) 542-5025
Website: http://www.azag.gov/

17 Arkansas – The Natural State

Area: 52,068 sq.mi. (Rank: 27th)   Population: 2,855,390 (Rank: 32rd)
Violent Crime Rate (per 100,000 residents): 503.4 (Rank: 36th Safest)
State Motto: *Regnat Populus (The People Rule)*

Firearms Carry Summary:

Carry considerations	Status
Restaurants and bars	Allowed in restaurants only
Churches / Places of worship	Prohibited
State parks / forests	Concealed handguns allowed with permit (but not in posted buildings)
Vehicle carry	Loaded handguns allowed with permit, otherwise must be unloaded and securely cased; long guns must be unloaded and in plain view or securely cased
LE notification if stopped?	Required. *See*, ARK. CODE § 5-73-315 (2010) and ARK. ADMIN RULES 130.00.08-001, R. 3.2 (2009). See footnote[25]
Retreat requirement for self-defense	Required, except in home. *See*, ARK. CODE § 5-2-607 (2010)
Preemption law	Yes. *See*, ARK. CODE § 14-16-504 (2010)
Open Carry	Generally prohibited
Military-pattern semi-auto restrictions	Not restricted
NFA weapons	NFA-friendly, compliance with federal law only

Reciprocity / Recognition

*Arkansas **recognizes** permits from the following states:*

Alabama	Alaska	Arizona	Colorado

---

[25] State law provides that a permit holder must both carry the permit and valid identification and must "[d]isplay both the license and proper identification upon demand by a law enforcement officer." *See*, ARK CODE § 5-73-315 (2010). An Arkansas State Police administrative rule implements this statutory language, and requires a permit holder in possession of a concealed handgun to produce his or her permit and inform the officer that he or she is carrying a concealed handgun *upon the officer's request for identification*. While the statute does not explicitly require that the permit holder immediately inform the law enforcement officer upon contact that the permit holder is carrying a concealed weapon, as several other states' mandatory notification statutes require, travelers may wish to err on the side of caution and affirmatively inform the officer or deputy if stopped for any official purpose.

Delaware	Florida	Georgia	Idaho
Indiana	Kansas	Kentucky	Louisiana(*)
Michigan	Minnesota	Mississippi	Missouri
Montana	Nebraska	Nevada	North Carolina
North Dakota(*)	Ohio	Oklahoma	Pennsylvania
South Carolina	South Dakota	Tennessee	Texas
Utah	Virginia	Washington	West Virginia
Wyoming			

(*) **Note:** Louisiana: state permits only; North Dakota: Class 1 permits only.

*Arkansas permits **are recognized by** the following states:*

Alabama	Alaska	Arizona	Colorado*
Delaware	Florida*	Georgia	Idaho
Indiana	Kansas	Kentucky	Louisiana
Michigan*	Minnesota	Mississippi	Missouri
Montana	Nebraska	Nevada	North Carolina
North Dakota	Ohio	Oklahoma	Pennsylvania
South Carolina*	South Dakota	Tennessee	Texas
Utah	Vermont	Virginia	Washington
West Virginia	Wyoming		

Note: In the reciprocity / recognition tables above, states with an asterisk (*) require the permit holder to both have a permit from, and be a resident of, the recognized state in order for reciprocity / recognition of the permit.

Knife Carry Summary:

Note: Blade length limits, if any, in parentheses.

Knife Type	Open Carry	Concealed Carry	Notes
Folding	Yes	Yes	
Fixed Blade	Yes	Yes	
Dirks, Daggers, Stilettos	Yes	Yes	
Automatics	Yes	Yes	
Balisongs	Yes	Yes	

17.1 Discussion

Firearms Carry:

Travelers to the Natural State will find a somewhat friendly legal environment for firearms carry. Arkansas requires a permit to carry a handgun concealed on one's person or in a vehicle. Such permits are issued on a "shall issue" basis to qualified residents who are at least twenty-one years old. The state does not issue permits to nonresidents, but does recognize permits from other states that recognize Arkansas permits.

State law prohibits the carry of weapons, whether openly or concealed, on or about the person, in a vehicle, or otherwise readily available for use with the intent to employ the weapon against another person.

Travelers should be aware that open carry of handguns is generally prohibited in most public areas, even with a permit.

In addition, while state law provides a defense to prosecution for those carrying weapons, the definition of which includes firearms and knives, on a bona fide journey, travelers should be aware that this exception nevertheless leaves much room for law enforcement interpretation and discretion. Don't be surprised if you're arrested and have to defend yourself in court to prove that the exception applies to you. Your lawyer will no doubt be happy to take your money to defend you.

A traveler in a vehicle who possesses a recognized permit may carry a loaded handgun concealed on his person. Travelers without recognized permits must transport their handguns in an unloaded and securely cased condition, and should store their weapons in the trunk or cargo compartment of the vehicle. Long guns should be transported unloaded and either in plain view in a gun rack, or securely cased in commercial gun cases.

Visitors to Arkansas should be aware that state law prohibits carry in public of loaded centerfire firearms, other than shotguns, in several specific, statutorily defined parts of the state, to include parts of Baxter, Benton, Carroll, Conway, Garland, in Marion counties.[26] This prohibition does not apply, however, to those with recognized carry permits.

Arkansas's strong preemption statute prohibits local governments from further regulating the carry, transport, or possession of firearms.

Knife Carry:

Travelers to Arkansas will find the state's laws fairly permissive with regards to knife carry. In 2007, the state legislature removed the

---

[26] See, ARK. CODE § 5-73-127 (2010).

long-standing blade length restriction of 3½ inches. Prior to its repeal, Arkansas law provided that any knife with a blade three and a half inches in length or greater was presumptively a weapon, and a corollary statute made carry of any knife with the intent to use as a weapon a crime. In fact, in one case the Arkansas Supreme Court upheld a conviction under the statute for carrying a knife that was *exactly* three and a half inches long. Thankfully, the 3 1/2 inch blade length restriction is now history.

While state law provides an affirmative defense for persons carrying a weapon on a "journey", the exact parameters of what constitutes a journey remain unclear. In addition, once the journey ends, the affirmative defense would no longer be available. Typically, an interstate traveler on a continuous, uninterrupted trip through the state would likely be able to avail him or herself of this defense.

Travelers should note that cities and towns are not preempted from regulating knife carry, unlike the case with firearms, which is exclusively regulated by state and federal law. While state law does not specifically prohibit possession of dirks, daggers, stilettos, balisongs and automatic knives, travelers should be aware that some cities and towns do prohibit such knives, *regardless of blade length*. Under state law, it is illegal to carry a weapon into an establishment that serves alcohol.

17.2 Places Off-Limits While Carrying

Firearms Carry:

Arkansas prohibits the carry of concealed handguns, with or without a permit, into a wide variety of places, including police, sheriff, and state police stations; the buildings and grounds of the Arkansas State Highway and Transportation Department, including that department's highway police division but excluding rest areas and weigh stations; detention facilities, prisons, and jails; courthouses and court rooms; polling places; meeting places of the governing body of any governmental entity; meetings of the legislature or legislative committees; and state offices. *See*, ARK. CODE § 5-73-306 (2010).

Carry of handguns is also prohibited at athletic events not related to firearms, in establishments other than restaurants that serve alcoholic beverages for on premises consumption, and at or in school, college, community college, and university campus buildings or events, except for authorized firearms related activities. *See, id.*

State law prohibits carrying handguns inside the passenger terminal of any airport, with an obvious exception for those possessing unloaded and securely cased firearms to be checked as baggage for lawful transportation on aircraft. *See, id.*

State law further prohibits the carry of handguns into any church or other place of worship, as well as at any location where a parade or demonstration requiring a permit is being held, and the permit holder is a participant in the parade or demonstration. *See, id.*

Private businesses and other private entities may ban the carrying of handguns on their premises by posting clearly visible written notice of such ban at each entrance, or anywhere on the premises if there is no roadway entrance. *See, id.*

State law requires that any permit holder entering a private home must notify the occupant that the permit holder is carrying a concealed handgun. *See*, ARK. CODE § 5-73-306 (2010).

State law prohibits possession or carry of loaded firearms and other deadly weapons in any publicly owned building or facility, or on State Capitol grounds. The definition of the term "facility" includes any municipally owned or maintained park, football, baseball, or soccer field, or other similar recreational structure or property. Exceptions exist for authorized firearms related events. *See*, ARK. CODE § 5-73-122 (2010).

In addition, possession of any firearm, whether loaded or unloaded, is prohibited in the State Capitol building or the Justice building in Little Rock. *See, id.*

Knife Carry:

State law prohibits carrying of weapons in establishments that serve alcohol. *See*, ARK. CODE § 5-73-120 (2010). The definition of weapon specifically includes knives carried with intent to use as a weapon.

State law prohibits possession or carry of deadly weapons in any publicly owned building or facility, or on State Capitol grounds. The definition of the term "facility" includes any municipally owned or maintained park, football, baseball, or soccer field, or other similar recreational structure or property. *See*, ARK. CODE § 5-73-122 (2010).

In addition, towns and cities may pass their own local ordinances prohibiting carry.

17.3 Selected City Ordinances

The state legislature has preempted municipalities and other political subdivisions from regulating most aspects of firearms, including firearms carry, transportation, and possession. Thus, firearms regulation is uniform throughout the state.

The city ordinances below relate to knife carry:

Eureka Springs – Unlawful to carry any knife the blade of which is over three inches in length. Carry of "crabapple switch, dirk, dagger, pick" or similar knives within city limits prohibited. *See*, EUREKA SPRINGS, ARK., MUNICIPAL CODE § 7.32.01 (2007).

17.4 State Resources

Arkansas State Police
One State Police Plaza Drive
Little Rock, AR 72209-2971
Phone: (501) 618-8000
Fax: (501) 618-8647
Website: http://www.asp.state.ar.us/

Office of the Attorney General
200 Catlett-Prien Tower
323 Center Street
Little Rock, AR 72201
Phone: (501) 682-1323 or (800) 448-3014
Website: http://www.ag.state.ar.us/

18 California – The Golden State

Area: 155,959 sq.mi. (Rank: 3rd)   Population: 36,756,666 (Rank: 1st)
Violent Crime Rate (per 100,000 residents): 503.8 (Rank: 37th Safest)
State Motto: *Eureka! (I Have Found It!)*

Firearms Carry Summary:

Carry considerations	Status
Restaurants and bars	Concealed handguns allowed with permit in restaurants (not bars), but cannot consume alcohol and may be subject to additional permit restrictions
Churches / Places of worship	Allowed with permit
State parks / forests	Allowed with permit; otherwise, firearms must be unloaded and securely cased in vehicle
Vehicle carry	Loaded handguns allowed with permit; otherwise, handguns must be unloaded and secured in locked case and/or locked trunk; long guns must be unloaded and should be securely cased
LE notification if stopped?	Not required
Retreat requirement for self-defense	Required
Preemption law	Limited preemption.
Open Carry	Allowed, gun must be unloaded
Military-pattern semi-auto restrictions	Heavily restricted
NFA weapons	Prohibited

Reciprocity / Recognition

*California **does not recognize** permits from any other state. California also does not issue permits to non-residents.*

*California permits **are recognized by** the following states:*

Alaska	Arizona	Idaho	Indiana
Kentucky	Michigan	Missouri	Montana
Nebraska	Oklahoma	South Dakota	Tennessee
Texas	Utah	Vermont	

Note: In the reciprocity / recognition tables above, states with an asterisk (*) require the permit holder to both have a permit from, and be a resident of, the recognized state in order for reciprocity / recognition of the permit.

Knife Carry Summary:

Note: Blade length limits, if any, in parentheses.

Knife Type	Open Carry	Concealed Carry	Notes
Folding	Yes	Yes	Assisted opening ok.
Fixed Blade	Yes	No	
Dirks, Daggers, Stilettos	Yes	No	
Automatics	Yes (< 2")	Yes (< 2")	
Balisongs	Yes (< 2")	Yes (< 2")	
Sword Canes	No	No	

18.1 Discussion

Firearms Carry:

Travelers to the Golden State will find a hostile legal environment for firearms carry. California requires a permit to carry a loaded handgun either concealed, or in a vehicle. Such permits are issued on a highly discretionary "may issue" basis to California residents only. In addition, California does not recognize the carry permits of any other state.

A traveler in a vehicle who does not possess a California-issued permit must transport any handguns in a completely unloaded condition and stored in the locked trunk of a vehicle. If the vehicle does not have a separate trunk compartment, then the handguns must be secured in a *locked* case. Handguns may not be stored in glove compartments or center consoles. Long guns must likewise be transported in an unloaded condition, and should be securely cased and stored in the trunk or cargo compartment of the vehicle. Any ammunition should be separately cased and stored apart from the firearms.

Travelers should be aware that California has enacted its own "assault weapon" ban, and prohibits the importation of such weapons into the state under most circumstances. Note that normal capacity magazines capable of holding more than ten rounds are also prohibited from importation into the state.

Open carry of loaded handguns is prohibited in most urban and suburban areas of the state. A handgun may be openly carried in these areas, however, if carried in a completely unloaded condition.[27] And open carry of a loaded handgun is allowed in rural, unincorporated areas of the state in counties that have not prohibited such carry or the discharge of weapons.[28] In addition, state law allows a person to possess a loaded weapon at his or her place of residence, including a temporary residence or campsite.[29]

Knife Carry:

Visitors to the Golden State will find state law relatively permissive when it comes to knife carry. This relative permissiveness stands in contrast to lawful firearms carry, which is heavily regulated and restricted, especially in the large urban population centers.

Ordinary folding pocket knives, including knives with assisted opening mechanisms, are legal to carry in the closed (folded) position either openly or concealed. Such folding knives must be designed to have a bias towards closure, that is, the design must be such that the mechanism "provides resistance that must be overcome in opening the blade, or that biases the blade back toward its closed position."[30]

Apart from switchblades, no statutorily defined blade length limit exists. Appellate case law has held that blade length refers to the sharpened portion only. Dirks, daggers, stilettos, and other fixed bladed knives must be carried openly, and cannot be carried concealed. Automatic knives ("switchblades") with blades less than two inches long are legal, and may be carried openly or concealed. Balisongs are considered switchblades under California law, and thus are prohibited unless the blade is less than two inches long. Disguised edged weapons, such as sword canes, belt-buckle knives, lipstick case knives, etc. are strictly prohibited.

Carry of most knives on school grounds is prohibited. The statute permits carry of folding knives with *non-locking* blades up to (and including) 2 ½ inches in length. The law does, however, permit carry of folding knives with blades longer than 2 ½ inches, including those with locking blades, on college or university grounds.

---

[27] *See,* CAL. PENAL CODE § 12031 (2009). The statute explicitly authorizes law enforcement to examine and verify the unloaded status of the gun. *See id.* at 12031(e). Failure to allow such examination constitutes probable cause for arrest. *See, id.*

[28] *See id.* at 12031(a).

[29] *See id.* at 12031(l).

[30] *See,* CAL. PENAL CODE § 653k (2009).

California does not preempt its cities and towns from regulating knife carry, unlike the case for firearms, where the state has prohibited cities and towns from enacting their own firearms regulations. As such, carry in towns or cities may be subject to additional restrictions. For example, the city of Los Angeles prohibits open carry of any knife with a blade longer than three inches.[31]

18.2 Places Off-Limits While Carrying

Firearms Carry:

California prohibits the carry of firearms in state or local buildings, or at government meetings open to the public. *See*, CAL. PENAL CODE § 171b (2009).

State law prohibits the possession of firearms in any school zone, the definition of which includes the school buildings and grounds, and any area within 1000 feet of same. Violation of this prohibition may be prosecuted as either a misdemeanor or a felony. Those convicted of a felony under this statute when the firearm is a handgun face the possibility of up to a five-year prison sentence. An exception exists for firearms which are unloaded and secured in a locked case or in the locked trunk of a vehicle. *See*, CAL. PENAL CODE § 626.9 (2009).

Possession of firearms, whether loaded or unloaded, on the premises of any college or university, is prohibited without written permission from the college or university. *See, id.*

Knife Carry:

California prohibits the carry of firearms and other deadly weapons, including knives falling under the switchblade prohibition, or knives or any kind with a blade length over four inches in state or local public buildings, or public meetings. *See*, CAL. PENAL CODE § 171b (2009).

State law prohibits carry of most knives on school grounds. The statute permits carry of folding knives with *non-locking* blades up to (and including) 2 ½ inches in length. The law does, however, permit carry of folding knives with blades longer than 2 ½ inches, including those with locking blades, on college or university grounds.

---

[31] See, LOS ANGELES, CAL., MUNICIPAL CODE § 55.10 (2010)

18.3 Selected City Ordinances

The state legislature has preempted municipalities and other political subdivisions from regulating firearms licensing and registration. Thus, firearms licensing and registration is uniform throughout the state.

The city ordinances below relate to knife carry:

Los Angeles County – Carry in plain view of daggers, ice picks and similar stabbing tools, switchblades, straight-edge razor and knives with blades three inches or longer prohibited. *See*, LOS ANGELES, CAL., COUNTY CODE § 13.62.020 (2010).

Los Angeles – Open carry of knives with blades three inches or more, daggers, dirks, ice picks, and straight edge razors prohibited. *See*, LOS ANGELES, CAL., MUNICIPAL CODE § 55.10 (2010). Exceptions exist for lawful occupational and recreational use. *See, id.*

Oakland – Carry of dirks, daggers, and spring-blade knives with blades of any length prohibited. Carry of knives with blades three inches or longer prohibited. *See*, OAKLAND, CAL., MUNICIPAL CODE § 9.36.020 (2010).

San Francisco – Unlawful to loiter with concealed knife with blade three inches or longer, or with any switchblade knife, ice pick, or straight edge razor. Unlawful to possess switchblade knife of any length. *See*, SAN FRANCISCO, CAL., MUNICIPAL CODE §§ 1291-92 (2010).

18.4 State Resources

California Highway Patrol
P.O. Box 942898
Sacramento, CA 94298-0001
Phone: (916) 657-7261
Website: http://www.chp.ca.gov/

Attorney General of California
4949 Broadway
Sacramento, CA 95820
Phone: (916) 445-9555 or (916) 322-3360
Website: http://caag.state.ca.us/

19 Colorado – The Centennial State

> Area: 103,718 sq.mi. (Rank: 8th)   Population: 4,939,456 (Rank: 22nd)
> Violent Crime Rate (per 100,000 residents): 343.1 (Rank: 25th Safest)
> State Motto: *Nil Sine Numine (Nothing Without Providence)*

Firearms Carry Summary:

Carry considerations	Status
Restaurants and bars	Allowed, but restaurants and bars may prohibit; cannot be intoxicated while carrying. *See,* COLO. REV. STAT. § 18-12-106 (2009)
Churches / Places of worship	Concealed allowed with permit
State parks / forests	Allowed; cannot carry loaded firearm when on snowmobile; must be unloaded and cased. *See,* COLO. REV. STAT. § 33-14-117 (2009)
Vehicle carry	Loaded handguns allowed, long guns must be unloaded (empty chamber), no permit required; *See,* COLO. REV. STAT. § 33-6-125
LE notification if stopped?	Not required
Retreat requirement for self-defense	Required except in home.
Preemption law	Yes. *See,* COLO. REV. STAT. § 29-11.7-101 *et. seq.*
Open Carry	Allowed, but municipalities may prohibit open carry in their buildings and facilities. *See,* COLO. REV. STAT. § 29-11.7-104 (2009)
Military-pattern semi-auto restrictions	Not restricted
NFA weapons	NFA-friendly, compliance with federal law only

Reciprocity / Recognition

Colorado **recognizes** resident permits (only) from the following states (Note: Permit holder must have a permit from, and be a resident of, the recognized state):

Alabama	Alaska	Arizona	Arkansas
Delaware	Florida	Georgia	Idaho
Indiana	Kansas	Kentucky	Louisiana
Michigan	Mississippi	Missouri	Montana
Nebraska	New Hampshire	New Mexico	North Carolina
North Dakota	Oklahoma	Pennsylvania	South Dakota

| Tennessee | Texas | Utah | Wyoming |

Colorado permits **are recognized by** *the following states:*

Alabama	Alaska	Arizona	Arkansas
Delaware	Florida*	Georgia	Idaho
Indiana	Kansas	Kentucky	Louisiana
Michigan*	Mississippi	Missouri	Montana
Nebraska	New Hampshire*	New Mexico	North Carolina
North Dakota	Oklahoma	Pennsylvania	South Dakota
Tennessee	Texas	Utah	Vermont
Wyoming			

Note: In the reciprocity / recognition tables above, states with an asterisk (*) require the permit holder to both have a permit from, and be a resident of, the recognized state in order for reciprocity / recognition of the permit.

Knife Carry Summary:

Note: Blade length limits, if any, in parentheses.

Knife Type	Open Carry	Concealed Carry	Notes
Folding	Yes	Yes (≤ 3.5")	
Fixed Blade	Yes	Yes (≤ 3.5")	
Dirks, Daggers, Stilettos	Yes	Yes (≤ 3.5")	
Automatics	No	No	
Balisongs	No	No	

19.1 Discussion

Firearms Carry:

Visitors to Colorado will find a generally friendly legal environment for firearms carry. Colorado requires a permit to carry a concealed handgun on one's person in public. Such permits are issued on a "shall issue" basis to qualified residents. Colorado does not issue permits to nonresidents, but does recognize the permits of twenty-eight other states. Note that the permit holder must be at least twenty-one years of age, and a resident of the recognized state that issued the permit.

State law does provide an exception to the permit requirement for concealed handguns for those engaged in lawful hunting.

Open carry of a firearm is legal without a permit, although local governments may prohibit open carry in government buildings and specific areas such as city parks under their jurisdiction. Notice of such open carry bans must be conspicuously posted.

A traveler in a vehicle without a recognized permit may nonetheless carry a loaded handgun for self defense. Such handguns may be carried on the person, or in the glove compartment or center console. Long guns may be carried anywhere in the vehicle, provided they are unloaded.

Those on snowmobiles should be aware that state law requires all firearms to be both unloaded and securely cased.

Travelers should also be aware that the city of Denver bans open carry in public areas, and has enacted its own "assault weapons" ban. Unfortunately, both of these restrictions have been upheld by Colorado courts. Included in Denver's "assault weapon" ban is a ban on possession of magazines capable of holding twenty-one or more rounds of ammunition. Denver's latest ordinance includes in its definition of "assault weapon" evil black rifles with any magazine of greater than 20 round capacity, and any shotgun with a folding stock and/or greater than 6 round magazine capacity.[32] *Caveat viator -* traveler beware.

Colorado's preemption law prohibits localities from regulating most aspects of firearms carry, with the exception, noted above, that local governments may prohibit open carry in government buildings and specific areas under their jurisdiction. Denver, due to the nature of their "home rule" status, is able to enact some more restrictive local ordinances that other local governments in the state.

Knife Carry:

Nestled amidst the majestic Rockies, visitors to Colorado will appreciate its scenic grandeur and Western heritage, reflected in the state's firearms-friendly laws. Those carrying knives, however, will find the state somewhat less friendly.

With respect to knives, concealed carry of fixed and folding knives should pose no problem, provided that the blades of such knives do

---

[32] *See,* DENVER, COLO. REV. MUNICIPAL CODE § 38-130 (2009).

not exceed three and a half inches in length. This limit is set by statute. Automatic knives such as ballistic knives, gravity knives, and switchblades are prohibited. Note that concealed carry of any knife, regardless of blade length, with the specific intent to use such knife as a weapon, is a violation of the statutory concealed carry prohibition as well.[33]

Open carry of knives with blades longer than three and a half inches is legal under state law, although travelers should note that some cities and towns restrict such carry. State law permits carry of weapons in private vehicles for lawful hunting or self-defense, and prohibits cities and towns from imposing additional restrictions on private vehicle carry.[34]

Colorado does not preempt its cities and towns from regulating knife carry. As such, cities and towns may impose their own additional restrictions concerning knife carry. In particular, travelers to the state's urban centers will generally find knife carry regulation more restrictive. For example, Denver prohibits both concealed and open carry of knives with blades greater than three and a half inches.[35]

State law prohibits carry of "deadly weapon[s]," whose definition specifically includes knives, on school, college, or university grounds. Violation of this law is a felony. A separate section of the law defines a knife as "any dagger, dirk, knife, or stiletto with a blade over three and one-half inches in length…,"[36] so it would appear that knives with blades three and a half inches or less may be allowable.

19.2 Places Off-Limits While Carrying

Firearms Carry:

Colorado prohibits the carrying of concealed handguns into public schools, although a permit holder may possess a handgun on school grounds in his or her vehicle. If the permit holder leaves the vehicle,

---

[33] See, A.P.E. v. People, 20 P.3d. 1179 (Colo. 2001) (holding state must prove defendant's intent to use as weapon knife with blade less than 3 ½ inches for violation of concealed carry statute to occur).

[34] See, COLO. REV. STAT. ANN. § 18-12-105.6 (2009). While the state's general preemption statute, §§ 29-11.7-101 et. seq., deals exclusively with firearms, the vehicle carry preemption statute appears to apply more broadly. See, id.

[35] See, DENVER REV. MUNICIPAL CODE § 38-117(a) & (b) (2009). Subsection (a) prohibits concealed carry, and subsection (b) prohibits open carry or knives with blades greater than 3 ½ inches. Id.

[36] See, COLO. REV. STAT. ANN. § 18-12-101 (1)(f) (2009)

the handgun must be secured in a compartment within the vehicle (such as a glove compartment) and the vehicle must be locked. A permit holder may also carry a concealed handgun on undeveloped land owned by a school district that is used for hunting or other shooting sports. *See*, COLO. REV. STAT. ANN. § 18-12-214 (2009).

State law prohibits the carrying of concealed handguns into public buildings that electronically screen persons entering the building and require persons carrying weapons to relinquish possession while in the building. *See, id.*

State law prohibits the carry or possession of any loaded firearm in public transportation facilities. Violation of this prohibition is a felony. *See*, COLO. REV. STAT. ANN. § 18-9-118 (2009).

Colorado prohibits the carry or possession of deadly weapons in schools, colleges, universities, and seminaries, whether public or private. Exceptions exist for authorized firearms related activities, and for the storage in a vehicle of unloaded firearms. A person with a recognized carry permit may possess a loaded concealed handgun while in a vehicle on school grounds. *See*, COLO. REV. STAT. ANN. § 18-12-105.5 (2009). A person with a recognized permit may carry on college or university grounds, provided the college or university does not ban firearms carry on their campus.

Possession or carry of firearms in the Colorado General Assembly, or at any legislative hearing or meeting of same, or in any General Assembly office, is prohibited under state law. This prohibition does not apply to a person who carries a concealed handgun and possesses a valid carry permit. *See*, COLO. REV. STAT. ANN. § 18-12-105 (2009).

State law prohibits the carry of loaded firearms while operating or riding on a snowmobile. Such firearms must be transported in an unloaded and securely cased condition. *See*, COLO. REV. STAT. ANN. § 33-14-117 (2009).

Knife Carry:

Colorado prohibits the carry of knives with blades over 3 ½ inches long on school or college grounds. In addition, cities and towns may further limit where such knives are carried on public property, and the manner of carry.

19.3 Selected City Ordinances

The state legislature has preempted municipalities and other political subdivisions from regulating firearms to any extent greater than state law. Thus, firearms carry regulation is uniform throughout the state.

The city ordinances below relate to knife carry:

Denver – Concealed or open carry of switchblades, gravity knives, or knives with blades greater than three and a half inches prohibited. *See*, DENVER, COLO., REV. MUNICIPAL CODE § 38-117 (2010). Exceptions for carry in home, bona fide hunting purpose, etc. exist. *See, id.* at § 38-118 (listing affirmative defenses to prosecution for violations of carry prohibitions).

Steamboat Springs – Concealed carry of knives with blades greater than three and a half inches prohibited. *See*, STEAMBOAT SPRINGS, COLO., REV. MUNICIPAL CODE § 10-169 (2009). Open carry of knives with blades greater than three and a half inches prohibited, with certain exceptions such as on bona fide hunting trip. *See, id.*

Englewood – Concealed carry of knives with blades greater than three and a half inches prohibited. *See*, ENGLEWOOD, COLO., MUNICIPAL CODE § 7-6C-1 (2005).

Boulder – Concealed carry of knives with blades greater than three and a half inches prohibited. *See*, BOULDER, COLO., REV. CODE § 5-8-9. Carry of deadly weapon prohibited in city council chambers while council in session, or in any public building posted as prohibiting carry. *See, id.* at § 5-8-15 (2003).

19.4 State Resources

Colorado State Patrol Headquarters
700 Kipling Street
Lakewood, CO 80215
Phone: (303) 239-4500
Website: http://www.csp.state.co.us/

Attorney General of Colorado
Department of Law
1525 Sherman 5th Floor
Denver, CO 80203

Phone: (303) 866-4500
Fax: (303) 866-5691
Website: http://www.ago.state.co.us/

20 Connecticut – The Constitution State

Area: 4,845 sq.mi. (Rank: 48th)   Population: 3,501,252 (Rank: 29th)
Violent Crime Rate (per 100,000 residents): 297.8 (Rank: 20th Safest)
State Motto: *Qui Transtulit Sustinet (He Who Transplanted Still Sustains)*

Firearms Carry Summary:

Carry considerations	Status
Restaurants and bars	Allowed with permit
Churches / Places of worship	Allowed with permit
State parks / forests	Prohibited; *See,* CONN. DEPT. ENVIR. PROT. R. § 23-4-1 (2007), CONN. GEN. STAT. § 29-28 (2009).
Vehicle carry	Possession prohibited without Connecticut permit
LE notification if stopped?	Not required
Retreat requirement for self-defense	Required, except in home. *See,* CONN. GEN. STAT. § 53a-19 (2009)
Preemption law	None
Open Carry	Allowed with permit, but uncommon
Military-pattern semi-auto restrictions	Heavily restricted
NFA weapons	Heavily restricted

Reciprocity / Recognition

Connecticut **does not recognize** permits from any other state. Connecticut does, however, issue carry permits to non-residents through the Department of Public Safety (see State Resources section for contact information).

Connecticut permits **are recognized by** the following states:

Alaska	Arizona	Idaho	Indiana
Kentucky	Michigan*	Missouri	Montana
Nebraska	Oklahoma	South Dakota	Tennessee
Texas	Utah	Vermont	

Note: In the reciprocity / recognition tables above, states with an asterisk (*) require the permit holder to both have a permit from, and be a resident of, the recognized state in order for reciprocity / recognition of the permit.

Knife Carry Summary:

Note: Blade length limits, if any, in parentheses.

Knife Type	Open Carry	Concealed Carry	Notes
Folding	Yes (< 4")	Yes (< 4")	
Fixed Blade	Yes (< 4")	Yes (< 4")	
Dirks, Daggers, Stilettos	Yes (≤ 1.5")	Yes (≤ 1.5")	Stilettos are banned
Automatics	Yes (≤ 1.5")	Yes (≤ 1.5")	
Balisongs	Yes (≤ 1.5")	Yes (≤ 1.5")	

20.1 Discussion

Firearms Carry:

Travelers to the so-called Constitution State will find their constitutional right to keep and bear arms quite heavily restricted. Possession of *any* firearm in a vehicle, whether handgun or long gun, requires a Connecticut permit. Such permits are issued on a discretionary "may issue" basis to qualified residents and nonresidents. Connecticut does not honor the carry permits of any other state.

Carry of any firearm, whether openly or concealed, requires a Connecticut-issued permit. Open carry, while technically legal with a Connecticut permit, is highly uncommon, and given the quite restrictive tenor of the state's firearms laws, such carry is likely to draw unwanted attention from law enforcement and is not advised, particularly in urban or suburban areas of the state.

Without a Connecticut permit, travelers may not visit the state with firearms, although a limited exception exists for those with permits from their home state who are visiting Connecticut for the purpose of participating in officially recognized firearms competitions or firearms collector exhibitions. Absent such a purpose (and the ability to prove same), travelers may only transit the state with firearms in accordance with the interstate transportation provisions of the federal Firearms Owners Protection Act (also known as the McClure-Volkmer Act), which requires that firearms be transported unloaded and secured, such as in a locked case.

Knife Carry:

Visitors to the Constitution State will find a somewhat restrictive legal environment for knife carry, particularly with regards to blade length.

With respect to knives, travelers to the Constitution State will find that carry of ordinary fixed and folding knives with blades less than the statutorily defined four inches should pose no problem.   Dirks, daggers, and automatic knives, however, are restricted to blade lengths of one and a half inches or less. Carry of stilettos is banned. Knives such as balisongs, while not specifically prohibited, may fall under the switchblade restriction, as balisongs do in some states, and so be limited to blades of one and a half inches or less.

State law prohibits carry of deadly weapons on elementary and secondary school grounds. Violation of this statute is a felony. The definition of "deadly weapon" pertinent to this prohibition includes switchblades and gravity knives of any length.

Connecticut does not preempt its cities and towns from regulating knife carry. As such, cities and towns are free to impose additional restrictions on knife carry, although few municipalities appear to have done so.

20.2 Places Off-Limits While Carrying

Firearms Carry:

Connecticut prohibits the carry of firearms and other deadly weapons on elementary and secondary school grounds, including school-sponsored activities.   Violation of this prohibition is a felony. Exceptions exist for authorized firearms related events and activities, and for those with permission of the school. An exception also exists for those traversing school property for purposes of gaining access to public or private lands for hunting or other lawful activities, provided the firearm is unloaded and the school permits entry onto its property. See, CONN. GEN. STAT. § 53a-217b (2009).

State law prohibits the possession or carry of firearms and other deadly weapons into buildings or offices of the Connecticut General Assembly, or at meetings or legislative hearings of the General Assembly or any of its committees.   Violation of this statute is a felony. See, CONN. GEN. STAT. § 2-1e (2009).

Knife carry:

State law prohibits carry of deadly weapons on elementary and secondary school grounds. Violation of this statute is a felony. See,

CONN. GEN. STAT. § 53a-217b (2009). The definition of "deadly weapon" includes switchblades and gravity knives of any length.

In addition, state law prohibits the possession or carry of switchblades, gravity knives and other deadly weapons into buildings or offices of the Connecticut General Assembly, or at meetings or legislative hearings of the General Assembly or any of its committees. Violation of this statute is a felony. *See*, CONN. GEN. STAT. § 2-1e (2009).

Cities and towns may impose their own restrictions.

20.3 Selected City Ordinances

The state legislature has <u>not</u> preempted municipalities and other political subdivisions from regulating firearms to a greater extent than state law, although few appear to have done so.

Cheshire – Carry of any weapon, including deadly weapon or dangerous instruments prohibited in public parks or recreational facilities, regardless of whether carrier has a permit. *See*, CHESHIRE, CONN., CODE OF ORD. § 11-20 (2010).

20.4 State Resources

Department of Public Safety
Division of State Police
1111 Country Club Road
Middletown, CT 06457-9294
Phone: (860) 685-8000
Fax: (860) 685-8354
Website: http://www.ct.gov/dps/site/default.asp

Attorney General of Connecticut
55 Elm Street
Hartford, CT 06106
Phone: (860) 808-5318
Fax: (860) 808-5387
Website: http://www.ct.gov/ag/site/default.asp

21 Delaware – The First State

Area: 1,954 sq.mi. (Rank: 49th)   Population: 873,092 (Rank: 45th)
Violent Crime Rate (per 100,000 residents): 703.4 (Rank: 47th Safest)
State Motto: *Liberty and Independence*

Firearms Carry Summary:

Carry considerations	Status
Restaurants and bars	Allowed with permit
Churches / Places of worship	Allowed with permit
State parks / forests	Prohibited
Vehicle carry	Open carry (plainly visible) of handgun allowed without permit; long guns must be unloaded
LE notification if stopped?	Not required
Retreat requirement for self-defense	Required, except in home. *See,* DEL CODE tit. 11 § 464 (2009)
Preemption law	Yes, but pre-1985 ordinances grandfathered and still in effect. *See,* DEL CODE tit. 22 § 835 (2009)
Open Carry	Allowed, must by 18 or older, some localities may prohibit
Military-pattern semi-auto restrictions	Not restricted
NFA weapons	Prohibited

Reciprocity / Recognition

Delaware **recognizes** *permits from the following states:*

Alaska	Arizona	Arkansas	Colorado
Florida	Kentucky	Maine	Michigan
Missouri	North Carolina	North Dakota	Ohio
Oklahoma	Tennessee	Texas	Utah
Virginia	West Virginia		

Delaware permits **are recognized by** *the following states:*

Alaska	Arizona	Arkansas	Colorado*
Florida*	Idaho	Indiana	Kentucky
Maine*	Michigan*	Missouri	New Mexico
North Carolina	North Dakota	Ohio	Oklahoma
South Dakota	Tennessee	Texas	Utah
Vermont	Virginia	West Virginia	

Note: In the reciprocity / recognition tables above, states with an asterisk (*) require the permit holder to both have a permit from, and be a resident of, the recognized state in order for reciprocity / recognition of the permit.

Knife Carry Summary:

Note: Blade length limits, if any, in parentheses.

Knife Type	Open Carry	Concealed Carry	Notes
Folding	Yes	Yes (≤ 3")	> 3" concealed with permit
Fixed Blade	Yes	No	Concealed with permit ok
Dirks, Daggers, Stilettos	Yes	No	Concealed with permit ok
Automatics	No	No	See note[37]
Balisongs	No	No	

21.1 Discussion

Firearms Carry:

Visitors to the First State will find this somewhat friendly legal environment for firearms carry. Delaware requires a permit to carry a concealed handgun, whether on the person or in a vehicle. Such permits are issued on a discretionary "may issue" basis to qualified residents. Delaware does not issue permits to nonresidents, but does recognize the carry permits of a number of other states.

Open carry of a loaded handgun is legal without a permit under state law, although travelers should be careful to ensure that the gun remains visible at all times, since carrying a concealed deadly weapon is a felony offense in Delaware. In addition, the state's preemption law allows local ordinances restricting and/or prohibiting open carry that were enacted prior to 1985 to remain in effect.

A traveler without a recognize permits may nonetheless carry a loaded handgun in a vehicle, provided that the gun is openly carried

---

[37] Even though Delaware law provides for the issuance of a concealed weapons permit, which by the statute's wording authorizes the holder to carry deadly weapons concealed, the statute appears to envision, and deals primarily with, firearms. *See*, DEL. CODE tit. 11 § 1441 (2009). Furthermore, Title 11, § 1446 appears to completely ban even mere possession of switchblades, the definition of which includes gravity knives. See, DEL CODE tit. 11 § 1446 (2009). The cautious traveler would thus be well advised to avoid carry or possession of switchblades or gravity knives in the state.

in plain view. Handguns may not be stored in glove compartments or center consoles without a recognized permit. For those without a recognized permit, handguns must be transported in an unloaded condition, securely cased and stored in the trunk or cargo area of the vehicle.

A traveler with long guns must transport them in an unloaded condition, regardless of whether the traveler possesses a recognized permit or not. Such guns may be stored in a visible gun rack, or in commercial gun cases. These long gun transport requirements apply to both motorized vehicles and to watercraft.

Knife Carry:

Visitors to Delaware, the first state to sign the Declaration of Independence, will find the state typical of its Eastern brethren when it comes to laws governing knife carry.

State law allows ordinary fixed and folding knives to be carried openly, although carry of large fixed bladed knives should be avoided in urban areas, due to the likelihood of unwanted law enforcement attention. Ordinary folding pocket knives with blades three inches or less may be carried concealed without a permit. Note that the Delaware Supreme Court has held that blade length measurement includes the *entire* length of the blade from the tip to the handle, and includes any unsharpened portion.[38]

Concealed carry of knives with longer blades requires a concealed weapon permit issued or otherwise recognized by the state. Delaware provides for reciprocity for other states' permits that meet certain statutory requirements. Travelers wishing to determine whether Delaware recognizes a particular state's permit may contact the Delaware Attorney General (See State Resources section for contact information).

State law bans automatic knives, the definition of which includes gravity knives. Knives such as balisongs, while not specifically prohibited, may fall under the switchblade ban (as balisongs do in some states), so the careful traveler would do well to avoid carry of such knives in the state.

---

[38] *See*, State v. Harmon, No. 606-2001 (Del. Supr. 2002) (reinstating conviction for weapons offense for possession of knife with blade greater than three inches long).

State law also bans possession of so-called "undetectable knives", defined as knives which are undetectable by a metal detector or magnetometer. Possession of such knives is a felony.[39]

State law prohibits carry on educational institution property and school or municipal recreational facilities, such as sports stadiums, athletic fields, etc. An exception exists, however, for legitimate educational instruction, sporting or recreational use.

21.2 Places Off-Limits While Carrying

Firearms Carry:

Delaware prohibits the carry of firearms and other deadly weapons in schools and on school grounds, or within 1000 feet of same, and on school buses for school-supplied transportation. The term "school" includes kindergartens, elementary and secondary schools, vocational technical schools, as well as colleges and universities. See, DEL. CODE tit. 11 § 1457 (2009).

Carry of such weapons is also prohibited in or on any municipal or county owned or operated building or structure used as a recreation center, athletic field or sports stadium. See, id.

Knife Carry:

Delaware prohibits the carry of deadly weapons, the definition of which includes knives other than ordinary pocket knives with blades three inches or less in length, on school grounds or school or municipal recreational facilities. See, DEL CODE tit. 11 § 1457 (2009).

21.3 Selected City Ordinances

The state legislature has preempted municipalities and other political subdivisions from regulating firearms to any extent greater than state law. The legislature, unfortunately, grandfathered existing firearms ordinances and regulations enacted prior to 1985, and thus those ordinances are not preempted and are still in effect. See, DEL. CODE tit. 22 § 835 (2009).

---

[39] See, DEL CODE tit. 11 § 1446A (2009).

The city ordinances below relate to knife carry:

Dover – Carry of knives of any type or length without permit prohibited. *See,* DOVER , DEL., CODE OF ORDINANCES § 70-2 (2009). Carry of knife with blade more than three inches long prohibited in parks or other recreational facilities owned, operated or maintained by the city. See, id. at § 74-24 (2009).

21.4 State Resources

Delaware State Police
P.O. Box 430
Dover, DE 9903-0430
Phone: (302) 739-5901
Website: http://dsp.delaware.gov/

Attorney General of Delaware
Carvel State Office Building
820 N. French Street
Wilmington, DE 19801
Phone: (302) 577-8400
Website: http://attorneygeneral.delaware.gov/

22 District of Columbia – D.C.

Area: 68.25 sq.mi. (Rank: N/A)   Population: 591,833 (Rank: N/A)
Violent Crime Rate (per 100,000 residents): 1,437.7 (Rank: N/A)
State Motto: *Justia Omnibus (Justice for All)*

Firearms Carry Summary:

Carry considerations	Status
Restaurants and bars	Allowed with DC permit
Churches / Places of worship	Allowed with DC permit
State parks / forests	N/A
Vehicle carry	Allowed with DC permit; otherwise, must be unloaded, secured in locked case and stored in trunk or cargo area. Without DC permit, can only travel through the city without stopping
LE notification if stopped?	Not required
Retreat requirement for self-defense	Required
Preemption law	N/A
Open Carry	Prohibited
Military-pattern semi-auto restrictions	Prohibited
NFA weapons	Prohibited

Reciprocity / Recognition

The District of Columbia **does _not_ recognize** permits from any other state.

District of Columbia permits **are recognized by** the following states:

Alaska	Idaho	Indiana	Kentucky
Missouri	Nebraska	South Dakota	Utah
Vermont			

Note: In the reciprocity / recognition tables above, states with an asterisk (*) require the permit holder to both have a permit from, and be a resident of, the recognized state in order for reciprocity / recognition of the permit.

Knife Carry Summary:

Note: Blade length limits, if any, in parentheses.

Knife Type	Open Carry	Concealed Carry	Notes
Folding	Yes (≤ 3")	Yes (≤ 3")	
Fixed Blade	No	No	
Dirks, Daggers, Stilettos	No	No	
Automatics	No	No	
Balisongs	No	No	

22.1 Discussion

Firearms Carry:

Visitors to our nation's capital will find a hostile legal environment for firearms carry. Ironically, the city which houses our nation's founding documents has done everything in its power to suppress the constitutionally guaranteed right to keep and bear arms of its residents and anyone who visits.

Indeed, it was only in June 2008 that Washington DC's draconian 30+ year handgun ban and ban on the possession of any operable firearm, even in your own home, was struck down by the United States Supreme Court in the landmark case of District of Columbia v. Heller. In the wake of Heller, the city's politicians have grudgingly modified their laws to permit the registration of some handguns. Perhaps not surprisingly, those virulently anti-gun politicians have made the registration process a time-consuming and arduous one. It seems clear that Washington DC's leaders will continue to do their best to suppress the Second Amendment rights of its residents, and any visitors to that city.

Washington DC forbids the possession or carrying of any firearms, whether openly or concealed, in public.[40] Possession of ammunition is also prohibited.

A traveler in a vehicle may not possess any firearms or ammunition in the city. A limited exception exists for those travelers who are merely transiting the city; those travelers with firearms may legally travel through the city without stopping if their firearms are unloaded, secured in a commercial gun case, and stored in a locked vehicle trunk. If the vehicle has no trunk, then the firearms should be

---

[40] In 2009, the city apparently repealed its carry permit statute, D.C. CODE ANN. § 22-4506, thus eliminating even the theoretical possibility of obtaining a carry permit.

secured in a locked case, and stored in the vehicle's cargo area.[41] Any ammunition should be separately cased and stored apart from the firearms.

Knife Carry:

Visitors to our nation's capital will encounter a decidedly hostile legal environment for knife carry. The District of Columbia, which has the dubious distinction of being one of the most violent cities in the country (if D.C. was a state, it would be the most violent state by a wide margin), has enacted a fairly draconian series of laws ostensibly designed to curb violent crime. For example, D.C. law prohibits carry on or about the person, whether open or concealed, of any deadly or dangerous weapon.[42] Period. Even in your own home.[43] Carry in public of any such weapon is a felony, punishable by up to five years in prison.[44]

Another statute prohibits possession, with intent to use unlawfully against another, of any dagger, dirk, stiletto, razor, or knife with a blade greater than three inches long, or other dangerous weapon.[45] While technically the Code permits possession (but not carry) of such knives so long as the possessor has no intent to use them unlawfully against another, as a practical matter, and as is the case in some states with similar statutes, unlawful intent will often be presumed, especially for larger or aggressive looking knives.

Switchblades are prohibited. Balisongs, while not specifically listed as a prohibited knife, may fall under the switchblade prohibition, as balisongs do in some states. In addition, balisongs are often associated with, and perceived as, martial arts weapons. As such, visitors should avoid carry of balisongs in the District.

In addition to the broad carry prohibitions already codified in the D.C. Code, many buildings in the District are home to government agencies and institutions, many of which prohibit weapons under their own regulatory authority, or which are federal buildings and thus

---

[41] *See*, D.C. CODE ANN. § 22-4504.02 (2009).

[42] *See*, D.C. CODE ANN. § 22-4504 (2009).

[43] *See, id.* The current statute, strictly interpreted, reads that carry in your home is a misdemeanor (less than one year in prison), while carry outside your home (or fixed place of business, etc.) is a felony punishable by up to five years in prison. *See, id.* Interestingly, a predecessor statute did have an exception for carry at home, fixed place of business, etc. *See, e.g.*, Monroe v. U.S., 598 A.2d 439, note 1 (D.C. 1991) (citing predecessor statute).

[44] *See*, D.C. CODE ANN. § 22-4504 (2009).

[45] *See, id.* at § 22-4514.

are subject to the weapon-related statutes pertaining to such buildings and facilities.[46] Weapons are also prohibited in such places as, e.g., Capitol grounds. D.C. law incorporates enhanced penalties for firearms possession on school property, although apparently not for other dangerous weapons such as knives. Of course, such possession is prohibited, and is already subject to harsh penalties.

22.2 Places Off-Limits While Carrying

Our nation's capital prohibits the carry of firearms in disarmed victims zones, euphemistically referred to as "gun free zones" in the politically correct vernacular. The district defines such zones as encompassing all areas within 1,000 feet of appropriately identified public or private day care centers, elementary schools, vocational schools, secondary schools, colleges, junior colleges, universities, public swimming pools, playgrounds, video arcades, youth centers, public libraries, and in or around public housing locations. Such "gun free zones" are supposed to be identified by a sign to that effect. See, D.C. CODE ANN. § 22-4502.01 (2009).

In addition to the broad carry prohibitions already codified in the D.C. Code, many buildings in the District are home to government agencies and institutions, many of which prohibit weapons under their own regulatory authority, or which are federal buildings and thus are subject to the weapon-related statutes pertaining to such buildings and facilities. Weapons are also prohibited in such places as, e.g., Capitol grounds. D.C. law incorporates enhanced penalties for firearms possession on school property, although apparently not for other dangerous weapons such as knives. Of course, such possession is prohibited, and is already subject to harsh penalties.

22.3 Selected City Ordinances

Not applicable.

22.4 State Resources

Metropolitan Police Department
300 Indiana Avenue, NW

---

[46] See supra Section 7.4 for a discussion of federal knife-related law.

Washington, DC 20001
Phone: (202) 727-4218
Fax: (202) 727-9524
Website: http://mpdc.dc.gov/mpdc/site/default.asp

Office of Corporation Counsel
441 4th Street, NW, Suite 1060N
Washington, DC 20001
Phone: (202) 727-3400
Website: http://occ.dc.gov/occ/site/default.asp

23 Florida – The Sunshine State

Area: 53,927 sq.mi. (Rank: 26th)   Population: 18,328,340 (Rank: 4th)
Violent Crime Rate (per 100,000 residents): 688.9 (Rank: 46th Safest)
State Motto: *In God We Trust*

Firearms Carry Summary:

Carry considerations	Status
Restaurants and bars	Concealed allowed with permit in restaurant dining areas
Churches / Places of worship	Concealed allowed with permit
State parks / forests	Concealed carry only allowed with recognized permit
Vehicle carry	Concealed with permit ok, otherwise must be "securely encased" or "not readily accessible for immediate use"[47]
LE notification if stopped?	Not required
Retreat requirement for self-defense	Not required, *See*, FLA. STAT. CH. 776.013 (2009)
Preemption law	Yes, *See*, FLA. STAT. CH. 790.33 (2009)
Open Carry	Prohibited even with permit. *See*, FLA. STAT. CH. 790.053 (2009)
Military-pattern semi-auto restrictions	Not restricted
NFA weapons	NFA-friendly, compliance with federal law only

Reciprocity / Recognition

*Florida **recognizes** resident permits (only) from the following states (Note: Permit holder must have a permit from, and be a resident of, the recognized state):*

Alabama	Alaska	Arizona	Arkansas
Colorado	Delaware	Georgia	Idaho
Indiana	Kansas	Kentucky	Louisiana
Michigan	Mississippi	Missouri	Montana
New Hampshire	Nebraska	New Mexico	North Carolina
North Dakota	Ohio	Oklahoma	Pennsylvania
South Carolina	South Dakota	Tennessee	Texas
Utah	Virginia	Washington	West Virginia

---

[47] *See*, FLA. STAT. CH. 790.25(5) (2009). The term "securely encased" is defined as meaning "in a glove compartment, whether or not locked; snapped in a holster; in a gun case, whether or not locked; in a zippered gun case; or in a closed box or container which requires a lid or cover to be opened for access." FLA. STAT. CH. 790.001(17).

Wyoming

Note: Florida does not recognize any nonresident permits except Florida-issued nonresident permits.

*Florida permits **are recognized by** the following states:*

Alabama	Alaska	Arizona	Arkansas
Colorado*	Delaware	Georgia	Idaho
Indiana	Kansas	Kentucky	Louisiana
Michigan*	Mississippi	Missouri	Montana
Nebraska	New Hampshire*	New Mexico	North Carolina
North Dakota	Ohio	Oklahoma	Pennsylvania
South Carolina*	South Dakota	Tennessee	Texas
Utah	Vermont	Virginia	Washington
West Virginia	Wyoming		

Note: In the reciprocity / recognition tables above, states with an asterisk (*) require the permit holder to both have a permit from, and be a resident of, the recognized state in order for reciprocity / recognition of the permit.

Knife Carry Summary:

Note: Blade length limits, if any, in parentheses.

Knife Type	Open Carry	Concealed Carry	Notes
Folding	Yes	Yes	See note[48]
Fixed Blade	Yes	No	Concealed with permit ok.
Dirks, Daggers, Stilettos	Yes	No	Concealed with permit ok.
Automatics	Yes	No	Concealed with permit ok.
Balisongs	Yes	No	Concealed with permit ok.

23.1 Discussion

Firearms Carry:

Visitors to the Sunshine State will find a generally a hospitable legal environment for firearms carry so long as the visitor possesses a recognized permit and carries concealed. Florida issues a true

---

[48] Concealed carry of a "common pocketknife" is legal, although case law relating to what exactly that term means is not definitive, and in some cases, conflicting. Concealed carry of folding knives that do not meet the definition of "common pocketknife" is, however, legal with a concealed weapon permit.

concealed weapons permit to both residents and a non-residents, which covers not just firearms, but also such weapons as collapsible batons and knives. State law requires that the holder of the permit be at least 21 years old, and have the permit readily available in their possession when carrying. Florida requires that the permit holder be a resident of the state that issued the permit, unless of course the permit is a Florida-issued non-resident permit.

State law prohibits open carry in public, and requires a permit to carry concealed on foot on in a vehicle.

Holders of a recognized permit may carry concealed while in a vehicle. Carry in a vehicle without benefit of a recognized permit, however, requires that the weapon be "securely encased" or otherwise "not readily accessible for immediate use". Florida law defines "securely encased" as meaning "in a glove compartment, whether or not locked; snapped in a holster; in a gun case, whether or not locked; in a zippered gun case; or in a closed box or container which requires a lid or cover to be opened for access."[49]

A recent state law prohibits most businesses from banning firearms possession by customers (and employees) in their locked vehicles in company-owned parking lots.[50]

Florida allows carry within state parks with a recognized permit. Thus, carry in National Forests and National Parks located within the state is also permitted, except for federal facilities and buildings within those federal lands.

Knife Carry:

Visitors to the Sunshine State will find a generally hospitable legal environment for knife carry so long as the visitor possesses a recognized permit. The law provides an exception for "common pocketknives" to the prohibition against concealed carry of weapons without a permit. Unfortunately, Florida courts have struggled to define what exactly constitutes a "common pocketknife," and so the cautious traveler would be wise to avoid overly "large" or "aggressive" looking folders.

Folding pocket knives that do not meet the definition of "common pocketknife" may still be carried concealed if the carrier possesses a valid concealed weapon permit. Fortunately, Florida recognizes a

---

[49] See, FLA. STAT. CH. 790.001(17) (2009)
[50] See, FLA. STAT. CH. 790.251 (2009)

large number of out-of-state permits. Concealed carry of fixed blades, dirks, daggers, stilettos, and automatic knives is prohibited without a permit, although open carry is legal. Florida law prohibits possession (and thus carry) of ballistic knives.[51]

State law bans carry on school property. Florida does not preempt its cities and towns from regulating knife carry, unlike the case for firearms, where the state has prohibited cities and towns from enacting their own firearms carry restrictions, ensuring uniform state-wide firearms laws. As such, municipalities may pass their own additional knife carry restrictions, although not many appear to have done so.

23.2 Places Off-Limits While Carrying

Florida law prohibits carry of a concealed weapon or firearm into "any police, sheriff, or highway patrol station; any detention facility, prison, or jail; any courthouse; any courtroom, …; any polling place; any meeting of the governing body of a county, public school district, municipality, or special district; any meeting of the Legislature or a committee thereof; any school, college, or professional athletic event not related to firearms; any school administration building; any portion of an establishment licensed to dispense alcoholic beverages for consumption on the premises, *which portion of the establishment is primarily devoted to such purpose*; [emphasis added] any elementary or secondary school facility; any career center; any college or university facility unless the licensee is a registered student, employee, or faculty member of such college or university and the weapon is a stun gun or nonlethal electric weapon or device designed solely for defensive purposes and the weapon does not fire a dart or projectile; inside the passenger terminal and sterile area of any airport, provided that no person shall be prohibited from carrying any legal firearm into the terminal, which firearm is encased for shipment for purposes of checking such firearm as baggage to be lawfully transported on any aircraft; or any place where the carrying of firearms is prohibited by federal law. …." See, FLA. STAT. CH. 790.06(12) (2009). In addition, the law prohibits carry into locations declared as "places of nuisance", typically those involving criminal gang activity, illegal gambling, and the like. *See, id.*

Florida law prohibits firearm and knife carry on school grounds. *See,* FLA. STAT. CH. 790.115 (2009). In addition, towns and cities may

---

[51] *See,* FLA. STAT. CH. 790.225 (2009)

pass their own local ordinances prohibiting or otherwise restricting knife carry in other areas within their jurisdictions.

23.3 Selected City Ordinances

The state legislature has preempted municipalities and other political subdivisions from regulating firearms to any extent greater than state law. Thus, firearms regulation pertaining to possession and carry is uniform throughout the state. See, FLA. STAT. CH. 790.33 (2009)

The city ordinances below relate to knife carry:

Metropolitan Miami-Dade County – Concealed carry of dirks, daggers, bowie knives, switchblades, or other "dangerous or deadly weapon[s]" prohibited. Carry, whether open or concealed, of switchblades prohibited. See, METRO. MIAMI-DADE COUNTY, FLA., CODE § 21-14 (2010).

23.4 State Resources

Florida Department of Law Enforcement
P.O. Box 1489
Tallahassee, FL 32302-1489
Phone: (850) 410-7000
E-Mail: info@fdle.state.fl.us
Website: http://www.fdle.state.fl.us/Content/home.aspx

Attorney General of Florida
Office of Attorney General
Tallahasse, FL 32399-1050
Phone: (850) 487-1963
Fax: (850) 487-2564
Website: http://myfloridalegal.com/

Florida Dept. of Agriculture and Consumer Services
Division of Licensing (CCW permits)
Post Office Box 6687
Tallahassee, Florida 32314-6687
Phone: (850) 245-5491
Website: http://licgweb.doacs.state.fl.us/index.html

24 Georgia – The Peach State

Area: 57,906 sq.mi. (Rank: 21st)   Population: 9,685,744 (Rank: 9th)
Violent Crime Rate (per 100,000 residents): 478.9 (Rank: 34nd Safest)
State Motto: *Wisdom, Justice, and Moderation*

Firearms Carry Summary:

Carry considerations	Status
Restaurants and bars	Allowed with permit in restaurants provided no alcohol consumed. Prohibited in bars. *See,* GA. CODE § 16-11-127(b), (f)
Churches / Places of worship	Prohibited. *See,* GA. CODE § 16-11-127(b)
State parks / forests	Allowed with permit, excluding public buildings.
Vehicle carry	Open or concealed carry in motor vehicle allowed, no permit required. *See,* GA. CODE § 16-11-126(c)
LE notification if stopped?	Not required
Retreat requirement for self-defense	Not required. *See,* GA. CODE § 16-3-23.1
Preemption law	Yes. *See,* GA. CODE § 16-11-173
Open Carry	Allowed with permit
Military-pattern semi-auto restrictions	Not restricted
NFA weapons	NFA-friendly, compliance with federal law only

Reciprocity / Recognition

Georgia **recognizes** *permits from the following states:*

Alabama	Alaska	Arizona	Arkansas
Colorado	Florida	Idaho	Indiana
Kentucky	Louisiana	Michigan	Mississippi
Missouri	Montana	New Hampshire	North Carolina
North Dakota	Oklahoma	Pennsylvania	South Dakota
Tennessee	Texas	Utah	Wyoming

Georgia permits **are recognized by** *the following states:*

Alabama	Alaska	Arizona	Arkansas
Colorado*	Florida*	Idaho	Indiana
Kentucky	Louisiana	Michigan*	Mississippi
Missouri	Montana	New Hampshire*	North Carolina

North Dakota	Oklahoma	Pennsylvania	South Dakota
Tennessee	Texas	Utah	Vermont
Wyoming			

Note: In the reciprocity / recognition tables above, states with an asterisk (*) require the permit holder to both have a permit from, and be a resident of, the recognized state in order for reciprocity / recognition of the permit.

Knife Carry Summary:

Note: Blade length limits, if any, in parentheses.

Knife Type	Open Carry	Concealed Carry	Notes
Folding	Yes	Yes	See note[52]
Fixed Blade	Yes	No	Local restrictions may apply
Dirks, Daggers, Stilettos	Yes	No	Local restrictions may apply
Automatics	Yes	No	Local restrictions may apply
Balisongs	Yes	No	Local restrictions may apply

24.1 Discussion

Firearms Carry:

Travelers to Georgia will find a generally hospitable legal environment for firearms carry, with a few minor quirks. State law requires a recognized permit to carry either openly or concealed. Georgia does not issue permits to nonresidents but will recognize permits issued by states that also recognize Georgia's permits, so long as the holder of the permit is not a Georgia resident.

Those carrying concealed handguns must do so only "in a shoulder holster, waist belt holster, any other holster, hipgrip, or any other similar device, in which event the weapon may be concealed by the person's clothing, or a handbag, purse, attache case, briefcase, or other closed container."[53]

---

[52] State law prohibits concealed carry of any knife "designed for the purpose of offense and defense." *See*, GA. CODE § 16-11-126 (2009). Travelers should thus exercise caution when describing the reasons for concealed carry of a particular knife, and should avoid concealed carry of "tactical" type folders.
[53] *See*, GA. CODE § 16-11-126(c).

A traveler without a recognized permit may still carry a loaded handgun or long gun anywhere in her motor vehicle, so long as the traveler is not a prohibited possessor, i.e., can legally own a firearm.

Hunters and sportsmen engaged in "legal hunting, fishing, or sport shooting when the persons have the permission of the owner of the land on which the activities are being conducted" may carry loaded handguns without a permit, provided that they do so "only in an open and fully exposed manner."[54]

Travelers should be aware that Georgia prohibits firearms carry of any kind at so-called "public gatherings". This prohibition applies even to those with recognized permits. The law defines "public gathering" as including, but not limited to, "athletic or sporting events, churches or church functions, political rallies or functions, publicly owned or operated buildings, or establishments at which alcoholic beverages are sold for consumption on the premises and which derive less than 50 percent of their total annual gross food and beverage sales from the sale of prepared meals or food."[55] Note that "publicly owned or operated buildings" would also typically encompass those buildings at roadside rest areas, and thus carry would be prohibited even for those with recognized permits.

Those wishing to visit Georgia's state and local parks, historical sites, recreational areas, and wildlife management areas may carry handguns in those areas provided they have a recognized permit. Note, however, that public buildings in those parks, historical sites, etc., are off-limits for firearms carry.[56]

Knife Carry:

Visitors to the Peach State will find that state law prohibits concealed carry of knives "designed for the purpose of offense and defense." Thus, cautious travelers would be well advised to avoid concealed carry of so-called "tactical" knives that appear overly aggressive or weapon-like. Open carry, however, is legal. Note, however, that Georgia does not preempt its cities and towns from regulating knife carry, and so municipalities may impose additional, more restrictive requirements on knife carry within their jurisdictions. For example,

---

[54] *See*, GA. CODE § 16-11-128 (2009).

[55] *See*, GA. CODE § 16-11-127(b).

[56] There appears to exist some ambiguity in the wording of the law in this regard. On the one hand, GA. CODE § 16-11-127(e) would appear to allow carry in public buildings in parks, etc. However, section (b) of that law prohibits carry in all "publicly owned or operated buildings". *See, id.* Thus, a cautious traveler would be wise to avoid carry in public buildings in parks, historical sites, etc.

Atlanta prohibits carry of automatic knives with blades more than two inches, or any other knife with a blade more than three inches.

State law prohibits carry of dirks, bowie knives, switchblades, ballistic knives, straight razors, and razor blades of any blade length, or any other knife with a blade of two or more inches on school grounds.

24.2 Places Off-Limits While Carrying

In addition to the "public gathering" prohibition discussed above, state law also specifically prohibits carry of firearms and knives in the "state capitol building or any building housing committee offices, committee rooms, or offices of members, officials, or employees of the General Assembly or either house[.]"[57]

State law also prohibits carry of firearms within 150 feet of a polling place.[58]

Firearms carry is prohibited within 1,000 feet of schools and colleges and other educational institutions.[59] Violation of this law is a felony. An exception exists for holders of a Georgia permit.

Georgia prohibits carry of dirks, bowie knives, switchblades, ballistic knives, straight razors, and razor blades of any blade length, or any other knife with a blade of two or more inches on school or college grounds. Violation of this law is a felony, with a two year mandatory minimum sentence. *See*, GA. CODE § 16-11-127.1 (2009). In addition, towns and cities may pass their own more restrictive local ordinances prohibiting knife carry.

24.3 Selected City Ordinances

The state legislature has preempted municipalities and other political subdivisions from regulating firearms to any extent greater than state law. Thus, laws and regulations pertaining to firearms carry are uniform throughout the state.

---

[57] *See*, GA. CODE § 16-11-34.1(b) (2009).
[58] *See*, GA. CODE § 21-2-413.
[59] *See*, GA. CODE § 16-11-127.1.

The city ordinances below relate to knife carry:

Atlanta – Sale of dirks, bowie knives, and switchblades prohibited. *See*, ATLANTA, GA., CODE OF ORDINANCES § 106-305 (2008). Carry, whether open or concealed, of automatic knives with blades more than two inches, or any other knife with a blade more than three inches, or any razor or ice pick prohibited. *See, id.* at § 106-306. Carry of any knife, regardless of blade length, prohibited at parades or public assemblies. *See, id.* at § 142-88.

Macon – Carry of automatic knives with blade over two inches, any other knife with a blade more than three inches, or razors and ice picks prohibited. *See*, MACON, GA., CODE OF ORDINANCES § 13-26 (2010). Carry of any knife "designed for the purpose of offense or defense" prohibited in terminal building of airport. Exception exists for weapons packaged for shipment and for checking as baggage. *See, id.* at § 3-22 (2010).

24.4 State Resources

Georgia Bureau of Investigation
3121 Panthersville Road
Decatur, GA 30037-0808
Phone: (404) 244-2639
Website: http://gbi.georgia.gov/

Georgia Attorney General
40 Capitol Square, SW
Atlanta, GA 30334-1300
Phone: (404) 656-3300
Fax: (404) 657-8733
Website: http://law.ga.gov/
Website: http://www.ganet.org/ago/

25 Hawaii – The Aloha State

Area: 6,423 sq.mi. (Rank: 47th)   Population: 1,288,198 (Rank: 42nd)
Violent Crime Rate (per 100,000 residents): 272.6 (Rank: 14th Safest)
State Motto: *Ua mau ke ea o ka aina I ka pono (The life of the Land is Perpetuated in Righteousness)*

Firearms Carry Summary:

Carry considerations	Status
Restaurants and bars	Allowed with permit, unless permit restricts
Churches / Places of worship	Allowed with permit, unless permit restricts
State parks / forests	Prohibited. Unloaded, securely cased, and stowed in vehicle allowed
Vehicle carry	Prohibited without permit
LE notification if stopped?	Not required
Retreat requirement for self-defense	Required for deadly force. *See*, HAW. REV. STAT. § 703-304 (5) (2009)
Preemption law	None, cities and towns can regulate separately. *See*, HAW. REV. STAT. § 46-1.5 (2009)
Open Carry	Prohibited without permit (and good luck getting a permit)
Military-pattern semi-auto restrictions	Registration required
NFA weapons	Possession prohibited

Reciprocity / Recognition

*Hawaii **does not recognize** permits from any other state.*

*Hawaii permits **are recognized by** the following states:*

Alaska	Arizona	Idaho	Indiana
Kansas	Kentucky	Michigan	Missouri
Nebraska	Oklahoma	South Dakota	Tennessee
Texas	Utah	Vermont	

Note: In the reciprocity / recognition tables above, states with an asterisk (*) require the permit holder to both have a permit from, and be a resident of, the recognized state in order for reciprocity / recognition of the permit.

Knife Carry Summary:

Note: Blade length limits, if any, in parentheses.

Knife Type	Open Carry	Concealed Carry	Notes
Folding	Yes	Yes	See note[60]
Fixed Blade	Yes	Yes	See note[60]
Dirks, Daggers, Stilettos	No	No	
Automatics	No	No	
Balisongs	No	No	

25.1 Discussion

Firearms Carry:

Visitors to the Aloha State will find a decidedly inhospitable and unwelcoming legal climate for firearms in general, and firearms carry in particular. In fact, unless you are a current or retired law enforcement officer and fall under the provisions of LEOSA, you can pretty much forget about being able to defend your life or the lives of your loved ones with a firearm. The state of Hawaii simply will not tolerate such a radical exercise of fundamental human rights by mere citizens, even its own. Heck, even out of state law enforcement officers visiting Hawaii and not on official duty are subject to the mandatory firearm registration requirement, as well as magazine capacity limits (ten rounds max) and ammo restrictions.[61]

While Hawaii is in theory a "may issue" state, it's "no issue" in practice. Fortunately, state law is much more amenable to knife carry (see below). You carry a knife, don't you?

State law requires mandatory registration within three days of *any* firearm brought into the state. Mere possession (not carry) of handguns requires a possession permit, although possession of long

---

[60] State law prohibits carry of dirks, daggers, or deadly or dangerous weapons. *See*, HAW. REV. STAT. § 134-51 (2009). The statute prohibits concealed carry on the person, in a vehicle, or being otherwise "armed with" such weapons, which may be interpreted to include open carry. *See, id.* The cautious traveler should avoid carry of knives that appear overly "tactical", aggressive, or weapon like.

[61] *See*, Guidelines for Carrying a Concealed Firearm in the State of Hawaii by a "Qualified Law Enforcement Officer" pursuant to 18 USC § 926B, Hawaii Dept. of Attorney General, available at http://hawaii.gov/ag/LEO.

guns does not. State law prohibits possession of normal capacity pistol magazines capable of holding more than 10 rounds.

Even transporting any firearm in a vehicle requires a permit, with a limited exception for transporting a firearm from the place of purchase to the owner's residence or to and from a firing range, provided that the gun is transported unloaded and securely cased and stowed in the vehicle.

Knife Carry:

America's 50th state, Hawaii beckons travelers with its beautiful beaches and tropical climate. Visitors to the Aloha State will find that with respect to knives, ordinary fixed and folding knives should pose no problem, and may be carried openly or concealed. As in many states, the open carry of large fixed blades may result in unwanted law enforcement attention, especially in urban areas. There is no statutorily defined blade length limit. State law prohibits carry of dirks, daggers, and stilettos. In addition, state law prohibits mere possession of automatic knives such as switchblades and gravity knives, as well as balisongs (butterfly knives).

No state-wide statutory prohibitions on off-limit locations for legal knife carry appear to exist. Cities and towns, however, may pass their own ordinances restricting knife carry, although few appear to have done so.

25.2 Places Off-Limits While Carrying

No state law limitations. Each permit issuing authority may place whatever permit restrictions they choose.

Towns and cities, however, may pass their own local ordinances restricting carry, although not many appear to have done so.

25.3 Selected City Ordinances

No relevant ordinances. An examination of ordinances for a number of municipalities shows no knife-related ordinances with restrictions greater than those embodied in state law.

25.4 State Resources

Honolulu Police Department
801 S. Beretania
Honolulu, HI 96818
Phone: (808) 529-3371
Fax: (808) 529-3525
Website: http://www.honolulupd.org/

Attorney General of Hawaii
Department of the Attorney General
425 Queen Street
Honolulu, HI 96813
Phone: (808) 586-1500
Website: http://hawaii.gov/ag

26 Idaho – The Gem State

Area: 82,747 sq.mi. (Rank: 11th)   Population: 1,523,816 (Rank: 39th)
Violent Crime Rate (per 100,000 residents): 228.6 (Rank: 7th Safest)
State Motto: *Esto Perpetua (May It Endure Forever)*

Firearms Carry Summary:

Carry considerations	Status
Restaurants and bars	Allowed
Churches / Places of worship	Allowed
State parks / forests	Allowed
Vehicle carry	Open carry allowed, concealed with permit
LE notification if stopped?	Not required
Retreat requirement for self-defense	(unknown)
Preemption law	Yes. *See*, IDAHO CODE §§ 18-3302J, 31-872, 50-343 (2009)
Open Carry	Allowed, no permit required
Military-pattern semi-auto restrictions	No restrictions
NFA weapons	NFA-friendly, compliance with federal law only

Reciprocity / Recognition

*Idaho **recognizes** permits from **all other states**.*

*Idaho permits **are recognized by** the following states:*

Alabama	Alaska	Arizona	Arkansas
Colorado*	Florida*	Georgia	Indiana
Kentucky	Louisiana	Michigan*	Missouri
Montana	Nebraska	New Hampshire*	North Carolina
North Dakota	Ohio	Oklahoma	Pennsylvania
South Dakota	Tennessee	Texas	Utah
Vermont	Wyoming		

Note: In the reciprocity / recognition tables above, states with an asterisk (*) require the permit holder to both have a permit from, and be a resident of, the recognized state in order for reciprocity / recognition of the permit.

Knife Carry Summary:

Note: Blade length limits, if any, in parentheses.

Knife Type	Open Carry	Concealed Carry	Notes
Folding	Yes	Yes	
Fixed Blade	Yes	No	Concealed with permit ok.
Dirks, Daggers, Stilettos	No	No	
Automatics	Yes	No	Concealed with permit ok.
Balisongs	Yes	No	Concealed with permit ok.

26.1 Discussion

Firearms Carry:

Idaho's scenic beauty, from the mountains, rivers and lakes of the Idaho Panhandle to the plains of Southern Idaho, embrace a frontier heritage that persists to this day outside the major population centers, and the few trendier vacation spots such as Sun Valley. Not surprisingly, the state has firearms-friendly laws and a low violent crime rate, which make for pleasant family vacationing for the outdoors-inclined.

Idaho honors carry permits from any state. Open carry is legal without a permit and is increasingly common, particularly in more rural areas. Travelers without permits may carry loaded handguns in their vehicles so long as the firearms are in plain view. Unloaded handguns may be carried anywhere in the vehicle.

Loaded long guns may be carried anywhere in a vehicle either openly visible or secured in gun cases.

In addition, state law allows the permitless concealed carry of handguns in the unincorporated areas of the state, except in a vehicle or on a public highway.

Knife Carry:

With respect to knives, ordinary fixed and folding knives carried openly should pose no problem. There is no statutorily defined blade length limit. Dirks, daggers, and stilettos, however, are prohibited.

State law prohibits carry, open or otherwise, of firearms or other deadly or dangerous weapons, in courthouses, jails, juvenile detention facilities, and schools, regardless of whether the person possesses a concealed weapon permit or not.[62] Pocket knives with blades less than 2½ inches in length are exempted from the definition of "deadly or dangerous weapon."[63]

Idaho does not preempt its cities and towns from regulating knife carry, unlike the case for firearms, where the state has prohibited cities and towns from enacting their own firearms carry restrictions, ensuring uniform state-wide firearms laws. As such, towns and cities may enact their own restrictions on knife carry, although few appear to have done so.

26.2 Places Off-Limits While Carrying

State law prohibits the carry of firearms and other deadly weapons, the definition of which includes knives, in courthouses, jails or juvenile detention facilities, or public or private schools. *See*, IDAHO CODE § 18-3302C (2009).

26.3 Selected City Ordinances

The state legislature has preempted municipalities and other political subdivisions from regulating firearms to any extent greater than state law. Thus, firearms carry regulation is uniform throughout the state.

The city ordinances below relate to knife carry:

Boise – Concealed carry of knives, dirks, daggers, and other deadly or dangerous weapons prohibited. *See*, BOISE, IDAHO, CITY CODE § 6-04-02 (2006). This prohibition may not apply to holders of concealed weapon permits.

26.4 State Resources

Idaho State Police
700 S. Stratford Drive

---

[62] *See*, IDAHO CODE § 18-3302D (2009). The statute refers to the definition of "deadly or dangerous weapon" used in 18 U.S.C. 930. *Id.*
[63] *See*, 18 U.S.C. 930 (2009).

Meridian, ID 83642
Phone: (208) 884-7000
Fax: (208) 884-7090
Website: http://www.isp.idaho.gov/

Idaho Attorney General
700 W. Jefferson Street
Boise, ID 83720-0010
Phone: (208) 334-2400
Fax: (208) 334-2530
Website: http://www.state.id.us/ag/

27 Illinois – Land of Lincoln

Area: 55,584 sq.mi. (Rank: 24th)   Population: 12,901,563 (Rank: 5th)
Violent Crime Rate (per 100,000 residents): 525.4 (Rank: 40th Safest)
State Motto: *State Sovereignty, National Union*

Firearms Carry Summary:

Carry considerations	Status
Restaurants and bars	Prohibited
Churches / Places of worship	Prohibited
State parks / forests	Prohibited
Vehicle carry	Must be unloaded and securely cased. *See*, 720 ILL. COMP. STAT. § 5/24.1(a)(4)
LE notification if stopped?	N/A
Retreat requirement for self-defense	Unknown; statutory law is silent on the retreat requirement. Cf. 720 ILL. COMP. STAT. § 5/7 *et. seq.*
Preemption law	No preemption law. *See*, 430 ILL. COMP. STAT. § 65/13.1
Open Carry	Prohibited
Military-pattern semi-auto restrictions	Towns and cities may restrict
NFA weapons	Possession prohibited

Reciprocity / Recognition

*Illinois **does not recognize** permits from any other state.*

*Illinois **does not issue** carry permits, and thus there is no permit for another state to recognize. Illinois residents who can lawfully possess firearms, however, may carry concealed handguns in Alaska and Vermont, because those states do not require a permit to carry concealed handguns. After July 29, 2010, such residents may also carry concealed handguns without a permit in Arizona.*

Knife Carry Summary:

Note: Blade length limits, if any, in parentheses.

Knife Type	Open Carry	Concealed Carry	Notes
Folding	Yes	Yes	See note[64]

---

[64] State law considers daggers, dirks, switchblades, stilettos, axes, hatchets and any knife with a blade at least three inches or longer to be *per se* dangerous weapons.

Knife Type	Open Carry	Concealed Carry	Notes
Fixed Blade	Yes	Yes	See note[64]
Dirks, Daggers, Stilettos	Yes	Yes	See note[64]
Automatics	No	No	
Balisongs	Yes	Yes	Some localities prohibit carry

27.1 Discussion

Firearms Carry:

Travelers to Illinois will find the state generally inhospitable to firearms in general, and firearms carry in particular. State law prohibits concealed carry of loaded firearms by "mere citizens", and the law has no provision for issuance of carry permits. Illinois is only one of two states (Wisconsin, its neighbor to the North, is the other one) that prohibit concealed carry loaded firearms and have no provision in state law for the issuance of permits to do so. So unless you are a current or retired law enforcement officer who falls within the provisions of LEOSA, you're out of luck in the Land of Lincoln when it comes to carrying a firearm for self-defense.

State law requires possession of a firearm identification card in order to purchase or possess a handgun, long gun, or ammunition.

Furthermore, the state legislature has not seen fit to preempt municipal governments from enacting their own regulations concerning firearms ownership and possession. The result, not surprisingly, is a patchwork of laws further regulating firearms ownership, possession, transport and the like, depending on where in the state you are. Some cities and towns, notably in the Chicago area, have enacted ordinances completely banning the possession of firearms, even in residents' own homes, although a relatively recent state law provides an affirmative defense against such ordinances for those using a firearm in self-defense. Note that in light of the historic Supreme Court ruling in *District of Columbia v. Heller*, a number (but not all) of those towns have caved and repealed their gun bans.

Chicago, of course, has long banned handgun possession for its law-abiding residents. Naturally, the Windy City's violent criminals suffer

---

See, 720 ILL. COMP. STAT. § 5/33A-1 (2009). Carry as weapon with intent to use unlawfully against another is prohibited. *See, id.* at § 5/24-1.

no such infirmity. Technically, only handguns that were possessed in the city and properly registered prior to the 1982 ban are allowed, provided that their registration has not lapsed. The United States Supreme Court is poised to address this constitutional outrage in a case called *McDonald v. Chicago*. Hopefully, the Court will consign Chicago's notorious handgun ban to the dustbin of history.

Visitors traveling through Illinois may possess firearms and ammunition without the requisite firearms identification card if the weapons are unloaded and securely cased in the trunk or storage compartment of the vehicle. Any ammunition must be stored separately and not with the weapons. Note that even residents with valid firearms identification cards must comply with these transport requirements (unloaded, securely cased, ammo stored separately).

Travelers should be aware that due to the lack of preemption and the resulting patchwork of laws, some municipalities may impose additional or different transport requirements for those traveling through their jurisdictions. Some jurisdictions may even ban firearms transport completely. Welcome to Illinois.

Nonresidents may possess firearms on licensed firing ranges, modified gun shows, or when hunting, provided the hunter has a valid hunting license.

Knife Carry:

As it the case with firearms, travelers to Illinois will find state law generally unfriendly to knife carry. While folding knives, fixed bladed knives, daggers, dirks, stilettos, and balisongs may technically be legal to carry under state law absent an intent to use such knife unlawfully against another, as a practical matter carry of anything but a small folder is likely asking for trouble should you be stopped, especially in any of the larger cities. Indeed, Chicago prohibits concealed carry of a bewildering variety of knives, including dirks, daggers, stilettos, bowie knives, "commando knives", switchblades, and any other knife with a blade longer than two and a half inches.[65] Oh, did I forget razors and "other dangerous weapons"? Chicago didn't, and bans concealed carry of those too.[66]

State law considers daggers, dirks, stilettos, and any knife with a blade three inches or longer to be *per se* dangerous weapons.

---

[65] *See*, CHICAGO, ILL., MUNICIPAL CODE § 8-24-020 (2010).
[66] *See, id.*

Switchblades and ballistic knives are completely banned and are illegal to even possess. Balisongs, while not specifically prohibited, may fall under the switchblade prohibition, as balisongs do in some states. Note that some cities, such as Aurora, specifically prohibit carry of balisongs. The cautious traveler would be well advised to avoid larger knives, daggers, dirks, stilettos, and the like on your visit to the land of Lincoln, especially in the larger cities.

State law prohibits carry of deadly weapons in establishments that serve alcohol, or at "public gatherings" such as concerts. In addition, carry of knives with intent to use unlawfully is a felony if carried in or on school property, public housing, public parks, courthouses, or on a public way within 1,000 feet of such locations.

27.2 Places Off-Limits While Carrying

Carry of deadly weapons prohibited in any place "licensed to sell intoxicating beverages, or at any public gathering held pursuant to a license issued by any governmental body or any public gathering at which an admission is charged." See, 720 ILL. COMP. STAT. § 5/24-1 (2009). Carry of a knife with intent to use unlawfully prohibited on school property, public housing, public parks, courthouses, or on any public way within 1,000 feet of same. Violation of this prohibition is a felony. See, id. In addition, towns and cities may pass their own local ordinances prohibiting or restricting knife carry.

27.3 Selected City Ordinances

The city ordinances below relate to knife carry:

Aurora – Carry of switchblades and ballistic knives prohibited. Carry or possession of switchblades, ballistic knives, and butterfly knives (balisongs) prohibited on school, college, or university premises, and in public parks, playground forest preserve or public housing property, or on any public way within 1,000 feet of any school or public park or residential property owned, operated, or managed by a public housing agency. See, AURORA, ILL., CODE OF ORDINANCES § 29-43 (2009).

Chicago – Unlawful to possess switchblades. See, CHICAGO, ILL., MUNICIPAL CODE § 8-24-020 (2010). Concealed carry of dirks, daggers, stilettos, bowie knives, "commando knives", any knife with blade greater than two and a half inches, ordinary razors, and "other dangerous weapon[s]" prohibited. *See, id.* Unlawful for person under 18 years of age to carry or possess knife with blade two inches in length or longer. *See, id.* Carry on person or in vehicle passenger compartment of "utility knife" (e.g., box cutter) by person under 18 years of age prohibited. Certain exceptions apply. *See, id.* at § 8-24-021.

27.4 State Resources

Illinois state Police
P.O. Box 19461
Springfield, IL 62794-9461
Phone: (217) 782-7263
Fax: (217) 785-2821
Website: http://www.isp.state.il.us/

Attorney General of Illinois
500 South Second St.
Springfield, IL 62706
Phone: (217) 782-1090
Website: http://www.ag.state.il.us/

28 Indiana – The Hoosier State

Area: 35,867 sq.mi. (Rank: 38th)   Population: 6,376,792 (Rank: 16th)
Violent Crime Rate (per 100,000 residents): 333.8 (Rank: 24nd Safest)
State Motto: *The Crossroads of America*

Firearms Carry Summary:

Carry considerations	Status
Restaurants and bars	Allowed with permit
Churches / Places of worship	Concealed with permit allowed
State parks / forests	Concealed with permit allowed
Vehicle carry	Loaded handguns with permit ok, loaded long guns allowed in plain view or securely cased
LE notification if stopped?	Not required
Retreat requirement for self-defense	Not required. *See*, IND. CODE § 35-41-3-2 (2010)
Preemption law	Yes, *see*, IND. CODE § 35-47-11 (2010); ordinances in effect prior to January 1, 1994 grandfathered
Open Carry	Allowed with permit
Military-pattern semi-auto restrictions	Not restricted
NFA weapons	NFA-friendly, compliance with federal law only

Reciprocity / Recognition

Indiana **recognizes** permits from **all other states**.

Indiana permits **are recognized by** the following states:

Alabama	Alaska	Arizona	Arkansas
Colorado*	Florida*	Georgia	Idaho
Kentucky	Louisiana	Michigan*	Mississippi
Missouri	Montana	New Hampshire*	North Carolina
North Dakota	Oklahoma	Pennsylvania	South Dakota
Tennessee	Texas	Utah	Vermont
Wyoming			

Note: In the reciprocity / recognition tables above, states with an asterisk (*) require the permit holder to both have a permit from, and be a resident of, the recognized state in order for reciprocity / recognition of the permit.

Knife Carry Summary:

Note: Blade length limits, if any, in parentheses.

Knife Type	Open Carry	Concealed Carry	Notes
Folding	Yes	Yes	
Fixed Blade	Yes	Yes	Municipalities may regulate
Dirks, Daggers, Stilettos	Yes	Yes	Municipalities may regulate
Automatics	No	No	
Balisongs	Yes	Yes	

28.1 Discussion

Firearms Carry:

Visitors to Indiana will find a generally favorable legal environment for firearms and firearms carry. Indiana recognizes all other states' carry permits. If you've got a carry permit from your home state, it's valid in Indiana. Open carry of firearms is legal, provided you have a recognized permit.

Carry of loaded handguns in the vehicle requires a recognized permit. For those without permits, the handgun must be unloaded and securely cased such that the gun is not readily accessible for immediate use.

Loaded long guns may be carried in a vehicle. Such firearms should be in plain view or securely cased. Appellate case law has resulted in pistol grip shotguns without shoulder stocks being deemed handguns under Indiana law.[67] As such, loaded carry of such shotguns requires a recognized permit.

Knife Carry:

Visitors to the Hoosier State will find a generally favorable environment for lawful knife carry, in addition to excellent reciprocity and/or recognition of other states' concealed carry handgun permits. With respect to knives, ordinary fixed and folding knives should pose no problem, and may be carried openly or concealed. There is no

---

[67] *See*, Estep v. Indiana, 716 N.E.2d 986 (Ind. Ct. App. 1999) (holding pistol grip shotgun without shoulder stock meets statutory definition of handgun).

statutorily defined blade length limit. Automatic knives, such as switchblades and ballistic knives, however, are prohibited. Note that balisongs may fall under the switchblade prohibition, as balisongs do in some states.

No specific state-wide statutory prohibitions on off-limits areas for knife carry exist, although cities and towns may pass their own ordinances restricting knife carry. Indiana does not preempt its cities and towns from regulating knife carry, unlike the case for firearms, where the state has prohibited cities and towns from enacting their own firearms carry restrictions, ensuring uniform state-wide firearms laws. As such, towns and cities may regulate knife carry within their jurisdictions, such as in schools or public parks.

28.2 Places Off-Limits While Carrying

Firearms Carry:

State law prohibits firearms carry in public and private schools (certain exceptions exist), the secure areas of airports, and commercial or charter aircraft. *See,* IND. CODE §§ 35-47-9 (2010) *et. seq.* (schools); 35-47-6 *et. seq.* (airports and aircraft).

In addition, the state administrative code prohibits firearms carry on riverboat casinos, at the annual State Fair (permit holders must secure their firearms in their vehicle and out of sight), and on shipping port property. *See,* 68 IND. ADMIN. CODE § 1-7-1 (riverboat casinos); 80 IND. ADMIN. CODE § 4-4-4 (state fair); 130 IND. ADMIN. CODE § 4-1-7 (shipping ports).

Knife Carry:

State law prohibits the possession of knives, the definition of which includes daggers, dirks, poniards, stilettos, switchblades and gravity knives, on school property and school buses. Exceptions exist for school-provided or authorized knives and uses, or if the knives are secured in a private motor vehicle. *See,* IND. CODE § 35-47-5-2.5 (2010). The state administrative code prohibits knife carry at the annual state fair. *See,* 80 IND. ADMIN. CODE § 4-4-4.

In addition, towns and cities may pass their own local ordinances prohibiting knife carry.

28.3 Selected City Ordinances

The state legislature has preempted municipalities and other political subdivisions from regulating firearms to any extent greater than state law. Thus, firearms carry regulation is uniform throughout the state, although a few ordinances that were in effect prior to January 1st, 1994 have been grandfathered and are still in effect.

The city ordinances below relate to knife carry:

Indianapolis – Marion County – Carry of ice picks and similar instruments prohibited. *See*, INDIANAPOLIS – MARION COUNTY, IND., CODE OF ORDINANCES § 451-1 (2009). Selling, or otherwise supplying dagger, dirk, bowie knife, stiletto or other dangerous weapon of similar character to suspected criminal or person with criminal purpose prohibited. *See, id.* at § 451-5.

South Bend – Carry of switchblades, daggers, and hunting knives prohibited in city parks. *See*, SOUTH BEND, IND., CODE OF ORDINANCES § 19-44 (2009).

28.4 State Resources

Indiana State Police
100 North Senate Avenue
Indiana Government Center North, 3rd Floor
Indianapolis, IN 46204-2259
Phone: (317) 232-8200
Website: http://www.state.in.us/isp/

Indiana Attorney General
State House, Room 219
Indianapolis, IN 46204
Phone: (317) 232-6201
Website: http://www.in.gov/attorneygeneral/

29 Iowa – The Hawkeye State

Area: 55,869 sq.mi. (Rank: 23rd)   Population: 3,002,555 (Rank: 30th)
Violent Crime Rate (per 100,000 residents): 283.8 (Rank: 17th Safest)
State Motto: *Our Liberties We Prize and Our Rights We Will Maintain*

Firearms Carry Summary:

Carry considerations	Status
Restaurants and bars	Allowed with permit
Churches / Places of worship	Allowed with permit
State parks / forests	Prohibited. *See*, IOWA CODE § 724.4A (2009) (public parks); § 461A.42 (state parks and preserves)
Vehicle carry	Handguns: allowed with permit; long guns: unloaded and cased
LE notification if stopped?	Not required
Retreat requirement for self-defense	Retreat from home or place of business or employment not required. *See*, IOWA CODE § 704.1 (2009)
Preemption law	Yes. *See*, IOWA CODE § 724.28 (2009).
Open Carry	Prohibited without permit in vehicles and within city or town limits
Military-pattern semi-auto restrictions	Not restricted
NFA weapons	Ownership and possession prohibited

Reciprocity / Recognition

*Iowa **does not recognize** permits from any other state.*

*Iowa permits **are recognized by** the following states:*

Alaska	Arizona	Idaho	Indiana
Kentucky	Michigan*	Missouri	Montana
Nebraska	Oklahoma	South Dakota	Tennessee
Texas	Utah	Vermont	

Note: In the reciprocity / recognition tables above, states with an asterisk (*) require the permit holder to both have a permit from, and be a resident of, the recognized state in order for reciprocity / recognition of the permit.

Knife Carry Summary:

Note: Blade length limits, if any, in parentheses.

Knife Type	Open Carry	Concealed Carry	Notes
Folding	Yes	Yes (≤ 5")	
Fixed Blade	Yes	Yes (≤ 5")	Some municipalities regulate
Dirks, Daggers, Stilettos	Yes	No	
Automatics	Yes	No	Ballistic knives are prohibited
Balisongs	Yes	No	

29.1 Discussion

Firearms Carry:

Travelers to the Hawkeye State will find a fairly restrictive legal environment for defensive handgun carry. State law prohibits concealed carry of a loaded handgun without an Iowa-issued carry permit. Iowa does not recognize carry permits from any other state. State law provides for issuance of "professional" (employment-related, such as security guards) and "nonprofessional" classes of license. Iowa residents apply for a license through the Sheriff of the county in which they reside, while nonresidents will apply through the Department of Public Safety.

Unfortunately, nonprofessional licenses are issued on a "may issue" discretionary basis, and thus the issuing authority has broad discretion to deny such permits. Indeed, reports are that some sheriffs rarely issue nonprofessional licenses, and that nonresident nonprofessional licenses are especially hard to obtain. Thus, the average traveler will likely find it difficult to be able to legally carry a concealed defensive firearm. (Note: Iowa has recently adopted a "shall issue" permit licensing law, but that law will not take effect until January, 2011).

Travelers in a vehicle who do not possess the requisite Iowa-issued permit must transport their handguns unloaded and securely cased and/or in the trunk or cargo area of the vehicle in order to comply with state law. Similarly, long guns must be transported unloaded and securely cased.

State law permits open carry a loaded handgun without a permit outside municipal (city or town) limits and when not in a vehicle.

Open carry is technically legal within city or town limits with an Iowa carry permit. Given the "may issue" discretionary nature of Iowa nonprofessional carry permits, however, prudence would advise against doing so, particularly as some sheriffs have reportedly indicated that they will revoke the permits of those who open carry.

Knife Carry:

Located in the heart of the Midwest, travelers to Iowa will find only moderate restrictions on knife carry outside of the state's cities. As is perhaps typical of most states, larger cities such as Des Moines impose their own, more restrictive regulations on what legal to carry, and where.

In general, ordinary fixed and folding knives with blades no longer than five inches should pose no problem, and may be carried openly or concealed. Larger folders or fixed blades must be carried openly, although an exception exists for hunting or fishing knives carried concealed while actually engaged in lawful hunting or fishing.[68] State law prohibits concealed carry of dangerous weapons, the definition of which includes daggers, razors, stilettos, switchblades (of any blade length) or any knife with a blade exceeding five inches in length.[69] Note that case law indicates that balisongs, of any blade length, are considered dangerous weapons, and thus may not be carried concealed.[70] The Iowa Supreme Court has ruled that sword canes fall under the prohibition on carrying concealed weapons.[71] Thus, you may not carry a sword cane.

While no specific state-wide statutory prohibitions on off-limits areas for knife carry exist, cities and towns may pass their own ordinances, as the state does not preempt its cities and towns from regulating knife carry, unlike the case for firearms. As such, some municipalities, such as Des Moines, have enacted their own carry restrictions.

29.2 *Places Off-Limits While Carrying*

Firearms Carry:
State law provides for enhanced penalties for carry in so-called "weapons free zones", defined as being on or within 1000 feet of

---

[68] *See*, IOWA CODE § 724.4(4)(h) (2009).
[69] *See*, IOWA CODE §§ 702.7, 724.4 (2009).
[70] *See*, In the Interest of F.A.B., No. 4-086/03-1638 (Iowa Ct. App. 2004).
[71] *See*, State v. McCoy, 618 N.W.2d 324 (Iowa 2000).

elementary or secondary schools, or parts of public parks not designated for hunting. *See*, IOWA CODE § 724.4A (2009). A person who " goes armed with, carries, or transports a firearm of any kind, whether concealed or not" on school grounds commits a felony under state law. *See*, IOWA CODE § 724.4B (2009).

Knife Carry:

No specific state law prohibition on carry. State law provides for enhanced penalties, however, for public offenses in so-called "weapons-free zones", defined as the area in, on, or within one thousand feet of a school or in a public park. *See*, IOWA CODE § 724.4A (2009).

29.3 Selected City Ordinances

The state legislature has preempted municipalities and other political subdivisions from regulating firearms to any extent greater than state law. Thus, firearms carry regulation is uniform throughout the state.

The city ordinances below relate to knife carry:

Des Moines – Carry of knives of any type, openly or concealed, on school property prohibited. *See*, DES MOINES, IOWA, MUNICIPAL CODE § 70-78 (2010). Concealed carry within the city of daggers, bowie knives, butterfly knives, stilettos, or switchblades prohibited. *See, id.* at § 70-85.

29.4 State Resources

Iowa Department of Public Safety
Wallace State Office Building
Des Moines, IA 50319
Phone: (515) 281-3211
Website: http://www.dps.state.ia.us/index.shtml

Attorney General of Iowa
Department Of Justice
1305 E. Walnut Street
Des Moines, IA 50319
Phone: (515) 281-5164
Fax: (515) 281-4209
Website: http://www.state.ia.us/government/ag/index.html

30 Kansas – The Sunflower State

Area: 81,815 sq.mi. (Rank: 13th)   Population: 2,802,134 (Rank: 33rd)
Violent Crime Rate (per 100,000 residents): 410.6 (Rank: 29th Safest)
State Motto: *Ad Astra Per Aspera (To the Stars Through Difficulties)*

Firearms Carry Summary:

Carry considerations	Status
Restaurants and bars	Allowed with permit in restaurants only, unless posted otherwise. *See*, KAN. STAT. ANN. § 75-7c10 (2009)
Churches / Places of worship	Allowed with permit unless posted otherwise. *See*, KAN. STAT. ANN. § 75-7c10 (2009)
State parks / forests	Allowed with permit unless posted otherwise
Vehicle carry	Loaded handgun carry allowed in plain view, or in glove or storage compartment, or concealed with permit. Note: Some cities and towns may prohibit loaded carry without permit.
LE notification if stopped?	Not required
Retreat requirement for self-defense	Not required. *See*, KAN. STAT. ANN. §§ 21-3211, 21-3212 (2009)
Preemption law	Limited preemption only, cities and towns can regulate open carry. *See*, KAN. STAT. ANN. § 12-16,124 (2009)
Open Carry	Generally legal, although some cities and towns prohibit open carry in vehicle without permit
Military-pattern semi-auto restrictions	Not restricted
NFA weapons	NFA-friendly, compliance with federal law only

Reciprocity / Recognition

*Kansas **recognizes** permits from the following states:*

Alaska	Arizona	Arkansas	Colorado
Florida	Hawaii	Kentucky	Louisiana
Michigan	Minnesota	Missouri	Nebraska
Nevada	New Jersey	New Mexico	North Carolina
Ohio	Oklahoma	South Carolina	Tennessee
Texas	West Virginia		

Kansas permits **are recognized by** *the following states:*

Alaska	Arizona	Arkansas	Colorado*
Florida*	Idaho	Indiana	Kentucky
Louisiana	Michigan*	Minnesota	Missouri
Montana	Nebraska	Nevada	North Carolina
Oklahoma	South Carolina*	South Dakota	Tennessee
Texas	Utah	Vermont	

Note: In the reciprocity / recognition tables above, states with an asterisk (*) require the permit holder to both have a permit from, and be a resident of, the recognized state in order for reciprocity / recognition of the permit.

Knife Carry Summary:

Note: Blade length limits, if any, in parentheses.

Knife Type	Open Carry	Concealed Carry	Notes
Folding	Yes	Yes (≤ 4")	
Fixed Blade	Yes	No	See note[72]
Dirks, Daggers, Stilettos	Yes	No	
Automatics	No	No	
Balisongs	No	No	See note[72]

30.1 Discussion

Firearms Carry:

In 2006, Kansas passed its first "shall issue" concealed carry law. That law also provides for recognition of other states' carry permits whose issuance standards are at least as strict as those of Kansas. To date, the state recognizes the permits of over 20 states. State law for bids concealed carry of a firearm without a recognized permit.

Open carry a loaded firearm is legal without a permit, although travelers should be aware that the state allows cities and towns to regulate (read: prohibit) this mode of carry. Carry of a loaded firearm in a vehicle without a recognized permit is allowed if the firearm is in plain view and visible to casual observation. Firearms may also be kept in the glove compartment, console storage area, trunk or vehicle cargo area.

Kansas' limited preemption law prevents local governments from regulating firearms carry or transport in a vehicle, provided that the guns are unloaded and securely cased. As noted above, some cities and towns to regulate open carry of loaded firearms while on foot or traveling in a vehicle.

Knife Carry:

Visitors to Kansas, with its vast expanses of rolling plains, will find state law regarding knife carry to be somewhat restrictive as to concealed carry. Ordinary folding pocket knives with blades four inches or less may be carried concealed. Automatic knives, such as switchblades, gravity knives, and ballistic knives, are strictly prohibited.

State law prohibits concealed carry of dirks, daggers, and stilettos. In addition, state law also prohibits possession or carry of any kind with "intent to use ... unlawfully against another."[72] As is the case with many such vaguely worded carry statutes, law enforcement will have broad discretion in interpreting "intent." You may very well prevail in the end, but you'll have an arrest record to show for it. The cautious traveler would do well to avoid dirks, daggers, stilettos, or any knife with an overly aggressive or weapon-like "tactical" appearance.

Note that knives such as balisongs, while not specifically prohibited, may fall under the switchblade prohibition, as balisongs do in some states.

While no specific state-wide statutory prohibitions on off-limits areas for knife carry exist, cities and towns may pass their own ordinances, as the state does not preempt its cities and towns from regulating knife carry.

30.2 Places Off-Limits While Carrying

Firearms Carry:

Unfortunately, state law defines a wide-ranging panoply of places where concealed firearms (which carry necessarily requires a permit) may be prohibited, if posted to that effect.[73] The list of such places includes police, sheriff or highway patrol stations, prisons and jails, courthouses and courtrooms, polling places on election day,

---

[72] *See*, KAN. STAT. § 21-4201 (2005).
[73] *See*, KAN. STAT. ANN. § 75-7c10 (2009).

municipal government meetings, the state fairgrounds, state office buildings, athletic sporting events not related to firearms held by any elementary, secondary, or post-secondary (i.e., college or university) educational institution, professional athletic sporting events not related to firearms, and drinking establishments other than restaurants.[74]

Also included in the list of off-limits locations if posted are elementary or secondary schools, attendance centers, administrative offices, services centers or other facilities, community colleges and college or university facilities, child exchange and visitation centers, community mental health centers, mental health clinics, and psychiatric hospitals.

Not to mention city halls, public libraries, day care or group day care homes, preschool or childcare centers, and churches or temples. Got all that?

Travelers should be aware that "state office buildings" includes places like the State Capitol building, so those wishing to visit such places should be on the lookout for signs prohibiting carry. The state Attorney General's office has promulgated regulations requiring that such "gun free zones" must conspicuously display a sign of at least eight inches by eight inches and bearing a "no firearms" graphic.[75]

Knife Carry:

No state law limitation. Towns and cities, however, may pass their own local ordinances regulating or restricting carry.

---

[74] State law defines "restaurant" thusly:
(1)   In the case of a club, a licensed food service establishment which, as determined by the director, derives from sales of food for consumption on the licensed club premises not less than 50% of its gross receipts from all sales of food and beverages on such premises in a 12-month period;
(2)   in the case of a drinking establishment subject to a food sales requirement under K.S.A. 41-2642 and amendments thereto, a licensed food service establishment which, as determined by the director, derives from sales of food for consumption on the licensed drinking establishment premises not less than 30% of its gross receipts from all sales of food and beverages on such premises in a 12-month period; and
(3)   in the case of a drinking establishment subject to no food sales requirement under K.S.A. 41-2642 and amendments thereto, a licensed food service establishment.
See, KAN. STAT. ANN. § 41-2601(o) (2009).
[75] The required signage can be found on the Kansas Attorney General's website at http://www.ksag.org/files/shared/concealcarrysignage.pdf

30.3 Selected City Ordinances

The state legislature has preempted municipalities and other political subdivisions from regulating firearms to any extent greater than state law. Thus, firearms regulation is uniform throughout the state.

The city ordinances below relate to knife carry:

Atchison – Carry in public park of dangerous or deadly weapons prohibited. *See*, ATCHISON, KAN., CODE OF ORDINANCES § 22-5 (2010).

Manhattan – Concealed carry of bowie knives, switchblades, dirks and other deadly weapons prohibited. *See*, MANHATTAN, KAN., CODE OF ORDINANCES § 22-66 (2010).

Sedgwick County – Carry, concealed or otherwise, of dirks, straight-edge razors, stilettos, switchblades, gravity knives, or other dangerous knives in clubs or establishments licensed to serve alcohol prohibited. Ordinary pocket knives with blades of four inches or less are excluded from the definition of "dangerous knife" for purposes of these ordinances. *See*, SEDGWICK COUNTY, KAN., CODE OF ORDINANCES §§ 4-36, 4-81 (2009).

30.4 State Resources

Kansas Highway Patrol
General Headquarters
122 SW 7th
Topeka, KS 66603
Phone: (785) 296-6800
Fax: (785) 296-3049
Website: http://www.kansashighwaypatrol.org/

Attorney General of Kansas
120 SW 10th Street
Topeka, KS 66612
Phone: (888) 428-8436 or (785) 296-2215
Fax: (785) 296-6296
Website: http://www.ksag.org/home/

31 Kentucky – The Bluegrass State

Area: 39,728 sq.mi. (Rank: 36th)   Population: 4,269,245 (Rank: 26th)
Violent Crime Rate (per 100,000 residents): 296.2 (Rank: 19th Safest)
State Motto: *United We Stand, Divided We Fall*

Firearms Carry Summary:

Carry considerations	Status
Restaurants and bars	Allowed with permit in restaurants only, carry in bars prohibited. *See*, KY. REV. STAT. § 237.110 (2009)
Churches / Places of worship	Allowed
State parks / forests	Concealed with permit allowed
Vehicle carry	Loaded firearms allowed if in plain view, loaded handguns allowed in glove compartment (note: <u>cannot</u> be in center console storage area)
LE notification if stopped?	Not required
Retreat requirement for self-defense	Not required. *See*, KY. REV. STAT. § 503.050 (2009)
Preemption law	Yes. *See*, KY. REV. STAT. § 65.870 (2009)
Open Carry	Allowed, no permit needed
Military-pattern semi-auto restrictions	Not restricted
NFA weapons	NFA-friendly, compliance with federal law only

Reciprocity / Recognition

Kentucky **recognizes** permits from **all other states**.

Kentucky permits **are recognized by** the following states:

Alabama	Alaska	Arizona	Arkansas
Colorado*	Delaware	Florida*	Georgia
Idaho	Indiana	Kansas	Louisiana
Michigan*	Minnesota	Mississippi	Missouri
Montana	Nebraska	New Hampshire*	New Mexico
North Carolina	North Dakota	Ohio	Oklahoma
Pennsylvania	South Carolina*	South Dakota	Tennessee
Texas	Utah	Vermont	Virginia
West Virginia	Wyoming		

Note: In the reciprocity / recognition tables above, states with an asterisk (*) require the permit holder to both have a permit from, and be a resident of, the recognized state in order for reciprocity / recognition of the permit.

Knife Carry Summary:

Note: Blade length limits, if any, in parentheses.

Knife Type	Open Carry	Concealed Carry	Notes
Folding	Yes	Yes	See note[76]
Fixed Blade	Yes	Yes	See note[76]
Dirks, Daggers, Stilettos	Yes	No	Concealed with permit ok
Automatics	Yes	No	Concealed with permit ok
Balisongs	Yes	No	Concealed with permit ok

31.1 Discussion

Firearms Carry:

Travelers to the Bluegrass State will find a generally firearms-friendly legal environment. Open carry of loaded firearms is legal without a permit and generally accepted, particularly in the rural areas of the state. Concealed carry of loaded firearms, however, is prohibited without a recognized permit. Fortunately, Kentucky recognizes permits from all other states.

Travelers without permits may carry loaded firearms in their vehicle so long as the firearms are in plain view and visible to casual observation. Loaded handguns may also be stored in the passenger-side glove compartment of the vehicle. Note that storage of loaded handguns in other storage areas of the passenger compartment, such as the center console, requires the traveler to possess a recognized permit. Loaded long guns may be carried anywhere in a vehicle provided they are in plain view.

Knife Carry:

Visitors to Kentucky will find generally favorable state laws concerning knife carry, in addition to favorable firearms carry laws.

---

[76] State law excludes "ordinary pocket knife or hunting knife" from the statutory definition of "deadly weapon", and so the statutory prohibition on carrying concealed deadly weapons does not apply, because such knives are not *per se* deadly weapons under the statute. Of course, ordinary pocket knives and hunting knives may indeed be considered deadly weapons if used as such. *See*, KY. REV. STAT. § 500.080 (2009).

Knives may be carried openly, and no statutorily defined blade length limit exists. Ordinary hunting knives and pocket knives are excluded from the statutory definition of deadly weapon, and may thus be carried concealed. As is the case with most states, caution is advised when carrying any large fixed blade, especially in urban areas. This is particularly true given that an older decision from the state's highest court has upheld a deadly weapon concealed carry conviction for carrying a fixed bladed knife with a six inch blade.[77]

Dirks, daggers, and stilettos are considered deadly weapons and may not be carried concealed without a recognized permit. While not specifically prohibited, automatic knives and balisongs may fall outside the "ordinary pocket knife" exception to the concealed carry prohibition. Thus, cautious travelers would be wise to avoid carrying such knives concealed without a valid permit. Fortunately, Kentucky will recognize any valid concealed weapons permit, so out-of-state travelers with such permits may legally carry concealed weapons, subject to Kentucky law, while visiting the state.

Note, however, that municipalities may pass their own ordinances regarding knife carry in their jurisdictions. The state has prohibited municipalities from regulating firearms carry, however.

With respect to knives, no state-wide statutory prohibitions on off-limits areas for otherwise legal knife carry exist, although as mentioned before, cities and towns may pass their own ordinances restricting knife carry. Fortunately, few cities or towns appear to have done so. Note that state law does restrict firearms carry in a number of places, including police stations, courthouses, and schools, even with a valid concealed weapons permit.

31.2 Places Off-Limits While Carrying

Firearms Carry:

State law prohibits concealed firearms in a variety of places, including
police stations, sheriff's offices, detention facilities such as prisons and jails, courthouses solely occupied by Court of Justice courtrooms, and at court proceedings, meetings of state or local

---

[77] *See*, Asher v. Commonwealth, 473 S.W.2d 145 (Ky. 1971).

government, and the secured areas of airports or any place prohibited by federal law.

In addition, concealed carry even with a permit is prohibited in bars, defined as "[a]ny portion of an establishment licensed to dispense beer or alcoholic beverages for consumption on the premises, which portion of the establishment is primarily devoted to that purpose." *See*, KY. REV. STAT. § 237.110 (2009). Restaurants that serve alcoholic beverages would likely be excluded from this definition, although any bar area in such restaurant would be off limits to those carrying concealed firearms.

Finally, state law prohibits concealed firearms in elementary or secondary school facilities without the consent of school authorities, and child-caring facilities and day-care centers.

Knife Carry:

State law prohibits carry of concealed firearms, but not specifically other deadly weapons such as knives, in a variety of places, such as police stations, jails, courthouses, schools, and bars. *See*, KY. REV. STAT. § 237.110 (2009). Note that such locations may prohibit knife carry by ordinance or other regulatory authority provided under state law.

31.3 Selected City Ordinances

The state legislature has preempted municipalities and other political subdivisions from regulating firearms to any extent greater than state law. Thus, firearms carry regulation is uniform throughout the state.

The city ordinances below relate to knife carry:

Owensboro – Knife throwing in city parks prohibited. *See*, OWENSBORO, KY. MUNICIPAL CODE § 19-6 (2005).

31.4 State Resources

Kentucky State Police
919 Versailles Road
Frankfort, KY 40601
Phone: (270) 856-3721
Website: http://www.kentuckystatepolice.org/

Office of the Attorney General
The Capitol, Suite 118
Frankfort, KY 40601-3449
Phone: (502) 696-5300
Fax: (502) 564-2894.
Website: http://ag.ky.gov/

32 Louisiana – The Pelican State

Area: 43,562 sq.mi. (Rank: 33rd)   Population: 4,410,796 (Rank: 25th)
Violent Crime Rate (per 100,000 residents): 656.2 (Rank: 45th Safest)
State Motto: *Union, Justice, and Confidence*

Firearms Carry Summary:

Carry considerations	Status
Restaurants and bars	Prohibited even with permit
Churches / Places of worship	Prohibited
State parks / forests	Prohibited, firearms must be unloaded and cased in vehicle
Vehicle carry	Loaded firearms allowed if carried in plain view (openly), or in glove compartment, console, trunk or vehicle storage area.
LE notification if stopped?	Required. *See*, LA. REV. STAT. § 40:1379.3 (2009)
Retreat requirement for self-defense	Not required. *See*, LA. REV. STAT. §§ 14:19, 14:20 (2009)
Preemption law	Yes, but ordinances in effect prior to July 16, 1985 grandfathered. *See*, LA. REV. STAT. § 40:1796 (2009)
Open Carry	Allowed, no license required, but certain grandfathered ordinances restricting carry exist
Military-pattern semi-auto restrictions	Not restricted
NFA weapons	Ownership and possession restricted to machine guns that are "war relics". *See*, LA. REV. STAT. § 40:1752 (2009)

Reciprocity / Recognition

*Louisiana **recognizes** permits from the following states:*

Alabama	Alaska	Arizona	Arkansas
Colorado	Florida	Georgia	Idaho
Indiana	Kansas	Kentucky	Maine
Michigan	Minnesota	Mississippi	Missouri
Montana	Nevada	New Hampshire	North Carolina
North Dakota	Oklahoma	Pennsylvania	South Carolina
South Dakota	Tennessee	Texas	Utah
Virginia	Washington	West Virginia	Wyoming

*Louisiana permits **are recognized by** the following states:*

Alabama	Alaska	Arizona	Arkansas
Colorado*	Florida*	Georgia	Idaho
Indiana	Kansas	Kentucky	Maine*
Michigan*	Minnesota	Mississippi	Missouri
Montana	Nebraska	Nevada	New Hampshire*
North Carolina	North Dakota	Oklahoma	Pennsylvania
South Carolina*	South Dakota	Tennessee	Texas
Utah	Vermont	Virginia	Washington
West Virginia	Wyoming		

Note: In the reciprocity / recognition tables above, states with an asterisk (*) require the permit holder to both have a permit from, and be a resident of, the recognized state in order for reciprocity / recognition of the permit.

Knife Carry Summary:

Note: Blade length limits, if any, in parentheses.

Knife Type	Open Carry	Concealed Carry	Notes
Folding	Yes	Yes	See notes[78,79]
Fixed Blade	Yes	No	
Dirks, Daggers, Stilettos	Yes	No	
Automatics	No	No	
Balisongs	No	No	See note[79]

32.1 Discussion

Firearms Carry:

Travelers to the Pelican State will find state law generally friendly to those wishing to carry firearms for self protection. Louisiana requires

---

[78] State law criminalizes concealed carry of any "instrumentality customarily used or intended for probable use as a dangerous weapon." *See*, LA. REV. STAT. § 14:95 (2009). Knives marketed for "tactical" use as weapons will likely fall under this prohibition. The cautious traveler would do well to avoid concealed carry of such knives.

[79] The state law switchblade definition, which includes any "knife or similar instrument having a blade which may be automatically unfolded or extended from a handle by the manipulation of a button, switch, latch or similar contrivance", may be read to encompass balisongs and assisted opening knives. See, LA. REV. STAT. § 14:95 (2009).

a recognized carry permit for carry of handguns concealed on one's person. Travelers should be aware that state law requires those carrying concealed firearms with a recognized permit who are approached by a law enforcement officer in an official capacity to notify such officer that they are carrying a concealed firearm(s), submit to a pat down search, and to allow the officer to temporarily disarm them.[80]

Travelers without a recognized permit may carry loaded handguns in their vehicle if the gun is in plain view, or stored in the glove compartment or center console. Loaded long guns may be transported in commercial storage cases anywhere in the vehicle.

Open carry of firearms is legal without a permit.

The state's preemption law prohibits municipalities from regulating firearms ownership, possession, transport or licensing to any extent greater than state law. Note, however, that the state has grandfathered ordinances in effect prior to July 16, 1985.

Knife Carry:

Travelers to Louisiana will find a legal environment that strongly favors open carry, versus concealed carry of knives. State law prohibits concealed carry of any item customarily used or intended for use as a dangerous weapon. Thus, travelers should be wary of carrying even pocket knives with aggressive, weapon-like features or appearance, as such features or appearance simply increase the likelihood that such a knife will be judged a dangerous weapon.

There is no statutorily defined blade length limit. Dirks, daggers, and stilettos, may be carried openly, but not concealed. Automatic knives, however, are prohibited. Note that folding knives with assisted opening devices and balisongs may run afoul of the prohibition on switchblade knives, based on the wording of the statute.

State law prohibits carry of dangerous weapons, concealed or otherwise, on school grounds or school buses. Towns and cities may enact their own additional restrictions or regulations affecting knife carry in their jurisdictions.

---

[80] *See,* LA. REV. STAT. § 40:1379.3(I)(2) (2009).

32.2 Places Off-Limits While Carrying

Firearms Carry:

State law prohibits carry of a concealed firearm in law enforcement offices, stations, or buildings, detention facilities such as prisons or jails, courthouses or courtrooms, polling places, meeting places of the governing authority of a political subdivision, the state capitol building, the secure areas of airports, as well as churches, synagogues, mosques, or other places of worship, and parades or demonstrations for which permits have been issued by a governmental entity.[81]

In addition, carry is prohibited in any restaurant or bar or other establishment that serves alcoholic beverages for on-premises consumption.[82]

Carry is also prohibited, regardless of whether one has a recognized permit or not, in any so-called "firearm-free zone", defined as "area inclusive of any school campus and within one thousand feet of any such school campus, and within a school bus." *See,* LA. REV. STAT. § 14:95.6 (2009)

Knife Carry:

State law prohibits carry of dangerous weapons on school grounds or school buses. Towns and cities may pass their own local ordinances prohibiting or restricting carry.

32.3 Selected City Ordinances

The state legislature has preempted municipalities and other political subdivisions from regulating firearms to any extent greater than state law, although municipal ordinances in effect prior to July 16, 1985 are grandfathered. Thus, for the most part, most firearms carry regulation is uniform throughout the state.

The city ordinances below relate to knife carry:

New Orleans – Unlawful to carry any weapon while participating in or attending a demonstration held in a public place. The definition of

---

[81] *See,* LA. REV. STAT. § 40:1379.3 (2009)
[82] *See, id.*

"weapon" specifically includes knives. *See*, NEW ORLEANS, LA., CODE OF ORDINANCES § 54-342 (2006). Carry of knives in Louisiana Nature and Science Center prohibited. *See*, *id.* at § 106-296. Possession of knives prohibited in public buildings with posted signs prohibiting weapons, "regardless of whether person may otherwise be in lawful possession of such weapon." *See*, *id.* at § 54-410.

Baton Rouge, and East Baton Rouge Parish – Carry of dangerous weapons prohibited in places that serve alcohol. *See*, BATON ROUGE, AND EAST BATON ROUGE PARISH, LA., CODE OF ORDINANCES § 13:95.3 (2005).

Shreveport – Carry of dangerous weapons in courthouses, city hall or other public city buildings and facilities prohibited. *See*, SHREVEPORT, LA., CODE OF ORDINANCES § 50-135.2 (2010). Possession of switchblades prohibited. *See*, *id.* at § 50-135.1 (2010).

32.4 State Resources

Louisiana State Police
P.O. Box 66614
Baton Rouge, LA 70896-6614
Phone: (225) 925-4239
Fax: (225) 925-3717
Website: http://www.lsp.org/

Louisiana Attorney General
State Capitol, 24th Floor
Baton Rouge, LA 70802
Phone: (225) 342-7876
Fax: (225) 342-3790
Website: http://www.ag.state.la.us/

33 Maine – The Pine Tree State

Area: 30,862 sq.mi. (Rank: 39th)   Population: 1,316,456 (Rank: 40th)
Violent Crime Rate (per 100,000 residents): 117.5 (Rank: Safest State!)
State Motto: *Dirigo (I Direct)*

Firearms Carry Summary:

Carry considerations	Status
Restaurants and bars	Allowed
Churches / Places of worship	Allowed
State parks / forests	Allowed in most areas; prohibited in Baxter State Park
Vehicle carry	Open or concealed handguns allowed with permit, otherwise unloaded and in plain view or securely cased and stored; long guns must be unloaded
LE notification if stopped?	Not required
Retreat requirement for self-defense	Retreat required except in home. *See,* ME. REV. STAT. tit. 17-A, § 108 (2009)
Preemption law	Yes. *See,* ME. REV. STAT. tit. 25, § 2011 (2009)
Open Carry	Allowed, no permit needed. Carry in vehicle requires permit.
Military-pattern semi-auto restrictions	Not restricted
NFA weapons	NFA-friendly, compliance with federal law only

Reciprocity / Recognition

Maine **recognizes** resident permits (only) from the following states *(Note: Permit holder must have a permit from, and be a resident of, the recognized state):*

Delaware   Louisiana   South Dakota

Maine permits **are recognized by** the following states:

Alaska	Arizona	Delaware	Idaho
Indiana	Kentucky	Louisiana	Michigan*
Missouri	Nebraska	Oklahoma	South Dakota
Tennessee	Utah	Vermont	

Note: In the reciprocity / recognition tables above, states with an asterisk (*) require the permit holder to both have a permit from, and be a resident of, the recognized state in order for reciprocity / recognition of the permit.

Knife Carry Summary:

Note: Blade length limits, if any, in parentheses.

Knife Type	Open Carry	Concealed Carry	Notes
Folding	Yes	Yes	See note[83]
Fixed Blade	Yes	No	See note[84]
Dirks, Daggers, Stilettos	Yes	No	See note[84]
Automatics	No	No	
Balisongs	No	No	See note[86]

33.1 Discussion

Firearms Carry:

Visitors to Maine looking to enjoy its rustic New England charm will also find a fairly favorable environment for legal firearms carry. State law requires a recognized permit for concealed carry or loaded carry (whether openly visible or concealed) in a vehicle. Unfortunately, Maine recognizes only a few other states permits, although Maine does issue permits to nonresidents. Nonresidents may apply for a permit through the state police.

Open carry of firearms is legal and does not require a permit, except if carrying in a vehicle. Licensed hunters and trappers may carry a concealed firearm when on foot and engaged in those activities with the appropriate hunting or trapping license.

Travelers in a vehicle and without a recognized permit must carry their firearms unloaded and either in plain view, or securely cased. Loaded carry of a firearm in a vehicle is prohibited without a recognized permit.

---

[83] State law prohibits concealed carry of dangerous weapons (other than firearms with a valid permit). *See*, ME. REV. STAT. tit. 25, § 2001-A (2009). Travelers should exercise caution when carrying any concealed folding pocket knife with an aggressive weapon-like appearance.
[84] Concealed carry of knives such as bowies, dirks, and stilettos is specifically prohibited. The statute also bans any other dangerous weapon "usually employed in the attack on or defense of a person." *See, id.* Travelers would be wise to avoid concealed carry of any fixed bladed knife, except for a typical hunting or fishing knife carried while actually pursuing such activities.

With regard to the use of defensive force, state law requires that the defender retreat from an unlawful attack before resorting to deadly force, if the defender can retreat "with complete safety" from the encounter, except that the defender is not required to retreat if the defender is in his or her dwelling place and was not the initial aggressor.[85]

Knife Carry:

Visitors to Maine will also find a fairly favorable environment for legal knife carry, unlike the case with Massachusetts, its neighbor to the South. Ordinary pocket knives may be carried openly or concealed. Ordinary fixed knives should pose no problem, and may be carried openly. Dirks, daggers, and stilettos may similarly be carried openly. No statutorily defined blade length limit exists. Automatic knives, however, are prohibited. In addition, recent case law from the state's highest court has held that butterfly knives (balisongs) fall under the statutory switchblade definition, and are thus prohibited.[86]

Knives used for hunting or fishing may be carried concealed, although prudence suggests that such knives should only be so carried when actually engaged in hunting or fishing. State law prohibits concealed carry of bowie knives, dirks, stilettos and other dangerous or deadly weapons commonly used as weapons for either offense or personal defense.

State courts prohibit carry of weapons in court facilities. In addition, state law prohibits persons involved in a labor dispute or strike to carry weapons at the site of such dispute or strike. Towns and cities may enact their own prohibitions or restrictions affecting knife (but not firearm) carry, although few appear to have done so.

33.2 Places Off-Limits While Carrying

Firearms Carry:

State law prohibits possession or carry of firearms in courthouses, or in an establishment that serves alcoholic beverages if the establishment is "posted to prohibit or restrict the possession of firearms in a manner reasonably likely to come to the attention of

---

[85] See, ME. REV. STAT. tit. 17-A, § 108 (2009).
[86] See, State v. Michael M., 772 A.2d 1179, 1179 (Me. 2001) (describing butterfly knife as falling under switchblade prohibition and thus illegal).

patrons[.]"[87]   State law also prohibits carry of dangerous weapons, the definition of which includes firearms, at the site of a labor dispute or strike, regardless of whether the person has a concealed firearms permit.[88]

The Department of Public Safety has adopted an administrative rule that prohibits persons, except on duty police officers, from carrying firearms in the state Capitol Area and other state-controlled locations within Augusta (the state capital). Includes in the "Capitol Area" definition are the District Court Building on State Street, State Police Barracks and Garage on Hospital Street, Blaine House Complex, Blaine Memorial, and Augusta Mental Health Institute Complex.[89]

Knife Carry:

State courts, through administrative rule, prohibit the carry of firearms, other dangerous weapons, and disabling chemicals, into courthouses. *See*, ME. SUPR. JUDICIAL CT. ADMIN. ORD. JB05-9 (2005). State law prohibits carry of firearms and other dangerous weapons by any person involved in a labor dispute or strike at the site of such dispute or strike. The statute specifically states that "[a] person who possesses a valid permit to carry a concealed firearm is *not* exempt" from this prohibition. (emphasis added) *See*, ME. REV. STAT. tit. 32, § 9412(5) (2009). State law also prohibits carry of firearms in establishments licensed to serve alcohol that have posted signs to that effect. *See, id.* at tit. 17-A, § 1057.

33.3 Selected City Ordinances

The state legislature has preempted municipalities and other political subdivisions from regulating firearms to any extent greater than state law. Thus, firearms carry regulation is uniform throughout the state.

The city ordinances below relate to knife carry:

No relevant ordinances. An examination of ordinances for a number of municipalities shows no knife-related ordinances with restrictions greater than those embodied in state law.

---

[87] *See*, ME. REV. STAT. tit. 17-A, §§ 1058 (courthouses), 1057 (bars and restaurants).
[88] *See*, ME. REV. STAT. tit. 32, § 9412. The term "dangerous weapon" is defined in ME. REV. STAT. tit. 17-A, § 2, and includes firearms.
[89] *See*, CODE ME. R. § 16-219, ch. 41 (2009).

33.4 State Resources

Maine Department of Public Safety
45 Commerce Drive
Augusta, ME 04333-0104
Phone: (207) 626-3800
TTY: (207) 287-3659
Fax: (207) 287-3042
Website: http://www.state.me.us/dps/index.html

Attorney General of Maine
6 State House Station
Augusta, ME 04333
Phone: (207) 626-8800
TTY: (207) 626-8865
Website: http://www.state.me.us/ag/

34 Maryland – The Old Line State

Area: 9,774 sq.mi. (Rank: 42nd)   Population: 5,633,597 (Rank: 19th)
Violent Crime Rate (per 100,000 residents): 628.2 (Rank: 42th Safest)
State Motto: *Fatti Maschii, Parole Femine (Manly Deeds, Womanly Words)*

Firearms Carry Summary:

Carry considerations	Status
Restaurants and bars	Allowed with permit
Churches / Places of worship	Allowed with permit, localities may prohibit
State parks / forests	Allowed with permit, otherwise unloaded, securely cased and stored in vehicle
Vehicle carry	Allowed with permit, otherwise firearms must be unloaded, securely cased, and inaccessible
LE notification if stopped?	Not required
Retreat requirement for self-defense	Required
Preemption law	Limited preemption. *See*, MD. CODE. ANN., CRIM. LAW § 4-209 (2009)
Open Carry	Allowed only with permit
Military-pattern semi-auto restrictions	Restricted, magazine capacity limits, certain types prohibited
NFA weapons	State registration, in addition to compliance with federal law

Reciprocity / Recognition

Maryland **does not recognize** permits from any other state.

Maryland permits **are recognized by** the following states:

Alaska	Arizona	Idaho	Indiana
Kentucky	Michigan*	Missouri	Montana
Oklahoma	South Dakota	Tennessee	Texas
Utah	Vermont		

Note: In the reciprocity / recognition tables above, states with an asterisk (*) require the permit holder to both have a permit from, and be a resident of, the recognized state in order for reciprocity / recognition of the permit.

Knife Carry Summary:

Note: Blade length limits, if any, in parentheses.

Knife Type	Open Carry	Concealed Carry	Notes
Folding	Yes	Yes	
Fixed Blade	Yes	No	See note[90]
Dirks, Daggers, Stilettos	Yes	No	See note[90]
Automatics	Yes	No	See note[90]
Balisongs	Yes	No	See note[90]

34.1 Discussion

Firearms Carry:

Travelers to Maryland will find restrictive laws pertaining to firearms. State law prohibits the open or concealed carry of handguns without a Maryland-issued permit. Maryland does not recognize permits from any other state. While Maryland theoretically issues permits to nonresidents, as a practical matter the state is "no issue" for nonresidents.

Indeed, even those living in Maryland who are not famous, wealthy, or very well-connected politically (or some combination thereof) will likely find it difficult to obtain a carry permit, as such permits are issued on a highly discretionary basis. Maryland does issue permits to residents; I have met and trained individuals with Maryland carry permits, so they do exist.

Travelers in a vehicle traveling without benefit of a Maryland-issued permit must transport their firearms in an unloaded condition, securely cased, and stored in the trunk. If the vehicle has no trunk, such as is the case with SUVs, then the gun case should be secured with a lock and stowed in the vehicle's cargo area. This applies to both handguns and long guns.

---

[90] State law prohibits concealed carry of dirks, bowie knives, and switchblades. *See*, MD. CODE § 4-101 (2009). Travelers should exercise care in the concealed carry of any fixed bladed knife, lest such knife be judged a bowie knife, dagger or dirk. In addition, state law prohibits open carry of any dangerous weapon with the "intent or purpose of injuring an individual in an unlawful manner." *Id.*

Note that the state legislature has passed a limited preemption law that prohibits municipalities from regulating firearms, except within 100 yards of parks, churches, schools, public buildings, and other places of public assembly. That's a pretty broad exception, particularly as applied to urban areas.

Knife Carry:

As is the case with firearms, travelers to Maryland will find, as a practical matter, some fairly restrictive carry laws pertaining to knives.

With respect to knives, concealed or open carry of ordinary folding pocket knives, referred to as "penknives" by statute and in case law, should pose no problem. There is no statutorily defined blade length limit. Bowie knives, dirks, daggers, stilettos, and automatic knives may not be carried concealed. Visitors should note that knives such as balisongs, while not specifically prohibited, may fall under the switchblade restriction, as balisongs do in some states.

While state law technically allows open (but not concealed) carry of a wide variety of knives such as bowie knives, dirks, daggers, stilettos, automatics, and balisongs, so long as the knife is not carried "with the intent or purpose of injuring an individual in an unlawful manner", travelers should be aware that this somewhat nebulous standard will often provide slim protection from arrest, especially in the more urban areas of the state. Regardless of whether such charge actually results in conviction, and bearing in mind that the statute provides for up to three years incarceration under certain circumstances, such an arrest will, at the very least, likely ruin your visit to, and impression of, the state.

State law prohibits the carry of any knife on school grounds. In addition, towns and cities may enact their own prohibitions or restrictions on knife carry.

34.2 Places Off-Limits While Carrying

Firearms Carry:

Maryland prohibits carry or possession of firearms on public school property. *See*, MD. CODE. ANN., CRIM. LAW § 4-102. In addition, state law prohibits possession of firearms within 1,000 feet of a demonstration in a public place. *See*, MD. CODE. ANN., CRIM. LAW § 4-102.

Knife Carry:

Maryland prohibits the carry of firearms, knives and other deadly weapons on public school property. *See*, MD. CODE § 4-102 (2009).

34.3 Selected City Ordinances

The state legislature has preempted municipalities and other political subdivisions from regulating firearms to any extent greater than state law. Thus, firearms regulation is uniform throughout the state.

The city ordinances below relate to knife carry:

Gaithersburg – Unlawful to carry razors or other dangerous weapons. *See*, GAITHERSBURG, MD., CODE OF ORDINANCES § 15-16 (2009).

Cumberland – Concealed carry of sword canes and dirks prohibited. *See*, CUMBERLAND, MD., CODE OF ORDINANCES § 11-91 (2009). Possession of switchblades prohibited. *See, id.* § 11-95.

34.4 State Resources

Maryland State Police
1201 Reisterstown Road
Pikesville, MD 21208
Phone: (410) 268-6101
Website: http://www.mdsp.org/

Attorney General of Maryland
200 St. Paul Place
Baltimore, MD 21202
Phone: (410) 576-6300
TDD: (410) 576-6372
Website: http://www.oag.state.md.us/

35 Massachusetts – The Bay State

Area: 8,257 sq.mi. (Rank: 45th)   Population: 6,497,967 (Rank: 15th)
Violent Crime Rate (per 100,000 residents): 449.0 (Rank: 31st Safest)
State Motto: *Ense Petit Placidam Sub Libertate Quietem (By the Sword We Seek Peace, But Peace Only Under Liberty)*

Firearms Carry Summary:

Carry considerations	Status
Restaurants and bars	Allowed with permit
Churches / Places of worship	Allowed with permit
State parks / forests	Allowed with permit
Vehicle carry	Allowed with permit, otherwise must be unloaded and securely cased
LE notification if stopped?	Not required
Retreat requirement for self-defense	Required, except in home / dwelling
Preemption law	Yes
Open Carry	Technically allowed with permit, but will likely result in permit revocation if done in urban areas
Military-pattern semi-auto restrictions	Restricted, post-Sept. 1994 "assault weapons" prohibited
NFA weapons	Restricted, permit required for possession; possession of silencers (sound suppressors) prohibited

Reciprocity / Recognition

*Massachusetts **does not recognize** permits from any other state.*

*Massachusetts permits **are recognized by** the following states:*

Alaska	Arizona	Idaho	Indiana
Kentucky	Michigan*	Missouri	Montana
Oklahoma	South Dakota	Tennessee	Texas
Utah	Vermont		

Note: In the reciprocity / recognition tables above, states with an asterisk (*) require the permit holder to both have a permit from, and be a resident of, the recognized state in order for reciprocity / recognition of the permit.

Knife Carry Summary:

Note: Blade length limits, if any, in parentheses.

Knife Type	Open Carry	Concealed Carry	Notes
Folding	Yes	Yes	See note[91]
Fixed Blade	Yes	Yes	See note[91]
Dirks, Daggers, Stilettos	No	No	
Automatics	No	No	See note[92]
Balisongs	Yes	Yes	See note[93]
Sword Canes	No	No	

35.1 Discussion

Firearms Carry:

Being one of the original thirteen colonies, and the site of several key battles of the Revolutionary War that gave birth to this great Nation, one might be inclined to think that Massachusetts law would favor citizens' right to carry defensive tools. Indeed, the state motto, *Ense Petit Placidam Sub Libertate Quietem*, meaning "by the sword we seek peace, but peace only under liberty," harkens to a freedom-loving revolutionary spirit that embraces arms as the means to achieve and secure both peace and liberty. Such notions, however, would be greatly at odds with current Massachusetts law, as the state strictly regulates both firearms and a wide variety of weapons, including knives.

The Commonwealth of Massachusetts requires a permit to carry loaded firearms either openly or concealed. Massachusetts does not recognize permits from any other state. Permits are issued to both residents and nonresidents on a discretionary basis to those who can convince the issuing authority of their need for a carry permit.

---

[91] Note that some cities regulate carry and blade length. In addition, certain assisted-opening mechanisms are prohibited, to wit, any mechanism "which enables a knife with a locking blade to be drawn at a locked position[.]" *See*, MASS. GEN. LAWS ch. 269, § 10 (2009).

[92] The law appears to allow automatic knives whose blades do not exceed 1.5 inches in length. The statute wording is somewhat ambiguous, however, and appears to ban "switch knives", typically a synonym for automatic knives.

[93] Note that balisongs may fall under the switchblade prohibition, as balisongs do in some states, and thus be subject to the same restrictions or prohibitions as switchblades.

Basically, you must be able to convince them that you have "good reason to fear injury" to your "person or property".[94] Massachusetts issues two classes of so-called "License to Carry" (LTC); only the Class A LTC allows a person to carry loaded firearms. The issuing authority – the local police chief for residents, or the State Police for nonresidents – has broad discretion to grant or deny your permit.

Nonresidents thinking of applying for a nonresident permit should note that, as of August 2009 the nonresident permit application process now requires an in-person interview at the licensing bureau's office in Chelsea, MA. Non-resident permits cost $100 and are valid only for one year.

Naturally, this broad discretion for permit issuance has resulted in widely divergent, often arbitrary, probabilities for permit applications being approved, with some cities and towns (e.g., Boston) being essentially "no issue" to "ordinary" residents, i.e., those who aren't famous, wealthy, or well-connected. Welcome to Massachusetts.

With regards to open carry, while possession of a Class A LTC technically allows both open and concealed carry, permit holders should be advised that such carry is extremely rare, and will likely result in permit revocation (you may be deemed "no longer a suitable person" for licensure) and possible arrest, particularly if done in an urban or suburban area.

Massachusetts prohibits possession of handguns by non-citizens. Non-citizens may possess long guns with the appropriate permit.

State law prohibits possession of ammunition without a permit. Even the purchase and possession of pepper spray in Massachusetts requires a license, as the state regulates the purchase, possession and carry of chemical sprays such as mace and pepper spray. In addition, state law prohibits possession of stun guns and tasers to non-law enforcement personnel.

State law prohibits the carry of handguns in a vehicle, loaded or unloaded, without a permit. A limited exception exists for those traveling to participate in organized pistol or revolver competition, or attending any meeting or exhibition of any organized group of firearm collectors, or for the purpose of hunting. To fall within this exception, the traveler must be a resident of the United States and must possess a firearms carry permit from another state. Hunters must possess a valid hunting license. Note that in all cases the handgun

---

[94] *See*, MASS. GEN. LAWS ch. 140 § 131(d) (2009).

must be unloaded, unless the traveler possesses a Massachusetts-issued Class A license to carry.[95]

Travelers who do not fall within this limited exception would have to rely on the provisions of McClure-Volkmer, which would apply only if the traveler was transiting the state on a continuous and uninterrupted journey, and where possession of the firearms being transported is legal at both his starting point and destination.

Transport of long guns is allowed, provided that they are unloaded, securely cased, and stored in the vehicle's trunk. If the vehicle does not have a separate trunk compartment, then the gun case should be secured with a lock. Note, however, that transport of pre-1994 so-called "assault weapons" requires a Massachusetts-issued permit, and post-1994 "assault weapons" are prohibited in the state (and thus may not be possessed and transported unless transiting through the state in accordance with the McClure-Volkmer interstate transportation provisions of federal law).

Knife Carry:

There is no statutorily defined blade length limit for ordinary fixed or folding knives. Massachusetts prohibits folding knives equipped with certain types of assisted opening mechanisms that enable the blade to be drawn at a locked position. In addition, dirks, daggers, stilettos, and "switch knives" are likewise prohibited. State law would appear to allow automatic knives with blades of one and a half inches or less, although the statute also appears to ban switch knives, typically a synonym for an automatic-type knife, completely. The cautious traveler visiting the Bay State would do well to consider any automatic knife, of any length blade, off limits in the Commonwealth. Note that balisongs, while not specifically prohibited, may fall within the switchblade prohibition, as balisongs do in some states.

Carry of ordinary fixed and folding knives, while permissible under state law, may be independently regulated by towns and cities, and a number of municipalities have done so. Some cities and towns variously prohibit the sale, possession, and carry of knives of certain types and/or certain blade lengths. For example, travelers to Boston should be aware that the Boston Municipal Code prohibits carry of any knife, fixed or folding, with a blade length over two and a half inches in length. Other Massachusetts cities and towns have similar ordinances prohibiting carry within town or city limits. Travelers

---

[95] *See*, MASS. GEN. LAWS ch. 140 § 131G (2009).

visiting particular cities may wish to contact the local authorities in those cities to verify that the knife they plan on carrying will be acceptable.

State law prohibits carry of dangerous weapons in the buildings or upon the grounds of any elementary or secondary school, or college or university without written authorization from that educational institution.

35.2 Places Off-Limits While Carrying

Firearms Carry:

State law prohibits carry in courthouses. Firearms carry is also prohibited on school, college, or university property without written authorization from the school, college, or university. *See*, MASS. GEN. LAWS ch. 269, § 10(j) (2009).

Knife Carry:

Carry of "dangerous weapons" on school, college, or university property is prohibited without written authorization from the school, college, or university. *See*, MASS. GEN. LAWS ch. 269, § 10(j) (2009).

35.3 Selected City Ordinances

The state legislature has preempted municipalities and other political subdivisions from regulating firearms to any extent greater than state law. Thus, firearms regulation is uniform throughout the state.

The city ordinances below relate to knife carry:

Boston – Carry on person or under person's control in vehicle of any knife with a blade over 2½ inches in length prohibited. *See*, BOSTON, MASS., MUNICIPAL CODE, § 16-45 *et. seq.* (2005).

Revere – Carry on person or under person's control in vehicle of any saber, sword, or similar weapon prohibited. Carry on person or under person's control in vehicle of any knife with a blade over 2½ inches in length prohibited, unless actually engaged in hunting or fishing or in going directly to and/or returning directly from such activities, or in any employment which requires the use of any type of knife. *See*, REVERE, MASS., REV. ORD. § 9.20.020 (2007).

35.4 State Resources

Massachusetts State Police
470 Worcester Road
Framingham, MA 01702
Phone: (508) 820-2300
Website: http://www.mass.gov (Search for "State Police")

Attorney General of Massachusetts
1350 Main Street, 4th Floor
Springfield, MA 01103
Phone: (413) 784-1240
Fax: (413) 784-1244
Website: http://www.ago.state.ma.us/

36 Michigan – The Wolverine State

Area: 56,804 sq.mi. (Rank: 22nd)   Population: 10,003,422 (Rank: 8th)
Violent Crime Rate (per 100,000 residents): 501.5 (Rank: 35th Safest)
State Motto: *Si Quaeris Peninsulam Amoenam, Circum Spice (If You are Seeking an Amenable (Pleasant) Peninsula, Look Around You)*

Firearms Carry Summary:

Carry considerations	Status
Restaurants and bars	Allowed in restaurants, prohibited in bars and taverns. *See*, MICH. COMP. LAWS § 28.425o (2009)
Churches / Places of worship	Allowed with permission of church
State parks / forests	Allowed with permit. *See*, MICH. COMP. LAWS § 324.504 (2009)
Vehicle carry	Handguns allowed with permit; long guns must be unloaded and securely cased and/or stored in trunk. *See*, MICH. COMP. LAWS §§ 750.227c, 750.227d (2009)
LE notification if stopped?	Required
Retreat requirement for self-defense	Not required. *See*, MICH. COMP. LAWS § 780.972 (2009)
Preemption law	Yes. *See*, MICH. COMP. LAWS § 123.1102 (2009)
Open Carry	Allowed, no permit required.
Military-pattern semi-auto restrictions	Some restrictions for certain folding stock weapons
NFA weapons	NFA-friendly, compliance with federal law only

Reciprocity / Recognition

Michigan **recognizes** permits from **all other states**, provided the permit holder is a resident of the state that issued his or her permit.

Michigan permits **are recognized by** the following states:

Alabama	Alaska	Arizona	Arkansas
Colorado*	Delaware	Florida*	Georgia
Idaho	Indiana	Kansas	Kentucky
Louisiana	Montana	Minnesota	Mississippi
Missouri	Nebraska	Nevada	New Hampshire*
New Mexico	North Carolina	North Dakota	Ohio
Oklahoma	Pennsylvania	South Carolina*	South Dakota
Tennessee	Texas	Utah	Vermont
Virginia	Washington	West Virginia	Wyoming

Note: In the reciprocity / recognition tables above, states with an asterisk (*) require the permit holder to both have a permit from, and be a resident of, the recognized state in order for reciprocity / recognition of the permit.

Knife Carry Summary:

Note: Blade length limits, if any, in parentheses.

Knife Type	Open Carry	Concealed Carry	Notes
Folding	Yes	Yes (≤ 3")	See notes[96,97]
Fixed Blade	Yes	Yes	See note[98]
Dirks, Daggers, Stilettos	Yes	No	See note[98]
Automatics	No	No	
Balisongs	No	No	See note[97]

36.1 Discussion

Firearms Carry:

Visitors to Michigan will find a perhaps somewhat surprisingly restrictive legal environment for firearms carry and transport. State law requires a permit to carry a loaded handgun either concealed on your person or in a vehicle. Michigan honors carry permits from all other states, provided that the holder of the permit is a resident of the state that issued it.

Open carry of firearms is legal without a permit, except in a vehicle. As is the case in most states, open carry is uncommon in urban areas of the state.

---

[96] The state's "unlawful intent" statute includes in its definition of "dangerous weapon" any knife with a blade longer than three inches. *See*, MICH. COMP. LAWS § 750.226 (2009). A separate statute prohibits concealed carry of weapons, including dirks, daggers, stilettos, and "other dangerous weapon[s]". *See, id.* at § 750.227. Thus, folding pocket knives with blades greater than three inches likely fall under this prohibition.

[97] State law prohibits automatic knives, the definition of which includes any knife having "the appearance of a pocket knife, the blade or blades of which can be opened by the flick of a button, pressure on a handle or other mechanical contrivance[.]" *See*, MICH. COMP. LAWS § 750.226a (2009). Note that this definition may include balisongs and assisted opening folding knives.

[98] State law prohibits carry, whether concealed or open, in a vehicle. *See*, MICH. COMP. LAWS § 750.227 (2009).

State law prohibits carrying or transporting long guns in a loaded condition; to be legally transported, all long guns must be unloaded and meet one or more of the following conditions: (a) taken down (disassembled); (b) enclosed in the case; (c) carried in the trunk of the vehicle; or (d) inaccessible from the interior of the vehicle.

As noted above, loaded handguns in vehicles requires a permit. Note that nonresidents may not transport handguns without a permit from their home state, because while state law allows Michigan residents without permits to transport handguns for a "lawful purpose", the definition of "lawful purpose" requires that the handgun owner must have obtained a purchase permit when he acquired the handgun.

Although not related to firearms, visitors to Michigan should be aware that the state prohibits possession of electric stun guns.[99] In addition, state law has very specific restrictions on the type and quantity of chemical defense sprays that may be possessed or use for self-defense. For non-law enforcement, possession and use is limited to pepper spray (oleoresin capsicum) with a maximum concentration of 2% (law enforcement officers have a 10% limit).[100]

Knife Carry:

As is the case with firearms, visitors to the Wolverine State will find a perhaps somewhat surprisingly restrictive legal environment for knife carry. With respect to knives, ordinary folding pocket knives should pose no problem, carried either openly or concealed. Note, however, that the statutory definition of "dangerous weapon" under the state's "unlawful intent" statute includes knives with blades over three inches

---

[99] See, MICH. COMP. LAWS § 750.224a (2009).
[100] See, MICH. COMP. LAWS § 750.224d (2009). Subsection (2) provides: "Except as otherwise provided in this section, a person who uses a self-defense spray or foam device to eject, release, or emit orthochlorobenzalmalononitrile or oleoresin capsicum at another person is guilty of a misdemeanor, punishable by imprisonment for not more than 2 years, or a fine of not more than $2,000.00, or both.", and Subsection (5) allows the use of 10% OC for law enforcement, 2% for non-law enforcement persons: Subsection (2) does not prohibit either of the following: (a) The reasonable use of a self-defense spray or foam device containing not more than 10% oleoresin capsicum by a person who is employed by a county sheriff or a chief of police and who is authorized in writing by the county sheriff or chief of police to carry and use a self-defense spray or foam device and has been trained in the use, effects, and risks of the device, while in performance of his or her official duties. (b) The reasonable use of a self-defense spray or foam device containing not more than 2% oleoresin capsicum by a person in the protection of a person or property under circumstances which would justify the person's use of physical force.

in length, and a corollary statute prohibits concealed carry of *per se* weapons. Thus, prudent travelers would be wise to avoid concealed carry of folding knives with blades over three inches long.

State law provides that dirks, daggers, stilettos, and knives with blades over three inches in length may be carried openly so long as the wearer does not intend to use such knife unlawfully against another. The careful traveler should realize that such "unlawful intent" statutes provide considerable discretion to law enforcement for arrest of persons carrying such knives. In addition, such knives may not be carried either openly or concealed in a vehicle. As such, it is recommended that travelers seriously consider alternatives to dirk, dagger, stiletto, and large fixed bladed knife carry. Fixed bladed knives such as hunting or fishing knives, however, may be carried concealed if legitimately engaged in those activities, subject to the vehicle carry prohibition.

State law prohibits automatic knives. Knives such as balisongs, while not specifically prohibited, may fall under the switchblade prohibition, as balisongs do in some states. In addition, based on the broad statutory wording of the automatic knife prohibition, some assisted opening knives may also fall under the switchblade prohibition, and thus may be illegal to carry.

Other that a state law prohibition on any knife carry in the sterile (secure) area of commercial airports[101] (already prohibited under federal law), no general state-wide off-limits locations on legal knife carry exist. Note that state law does prohibit possession of dangerous weapons, including knives with blades over three inches, by students in schools or at school activities. In addition, cities and towns may pass their own ordinances restricting knife carry within their jurisdictions.

36.2 *Places Off-Limits While Carrying*

Firearms Carry:

Michigan prohibits concealed carry of handguns in schools or school property, with a limited exception for parents or legal guardians picking up or dropping off students, provided that the firearm remains in the vehicle. Concealed carry is also prohibited in public or private child care centers, sports arenas and stadiums, bars and taverns

---

[101] *See*, MICH. COMP. LAWS § 259.80f (2009).

serving alcoholic beverages, places of worship such as churches, synagogues, mosques and temples without permission from the presiding official of the place of worship, entertainment facilities with seating capacities of 2,500 or more, hospitals, and dormitories or classrooms of community colleges, colleges, and universities. *See*, MICH. COMP. LAWS § 28.425o (2009).

Concealed carry of firearms is also prohibited in casinos. *See*, MICH. ADMIN. CODE r. 432.1212 (2009).

Knife Carry:

State law prohibits carry of knives, razors, box cutters and similar bladed items in the sterile (secure) areas of commercial airports. *See*, MICH. COMP. LAWS § 259.80f (2009).

State law prohibits possession of dangerous weapons by students on school grounds or at school activities. The definition of "dangerous weapon" includes dirks, daggers, stilettos, knives with blades over three inches long, or a "pocket knife opened by a mechanical device[.] " *See*, MICH. COMP. LAWS § 380.1313 (2009).

Note that towns and cities may pass their own additional restrictions of prohibitions on knife carry by non-students on school grounds.

36.3 Selected City Ordinances

The state legislature has preempted municipalities and other political subdivisions from regulating firearms to any extent greater than state law. Thus, firearms carry regulation is uniform throughout the state.

The city ordinances below relate to knife carry:

Detroit – Possession of cane swords, umbrella swords, switchblades and other self-opening knives prohibited, with exception for possession of switchblade by one-armed person. *See*, DETROIT, MICH., CITY CODE § 38-10-40 (2009). Carry in public, openly or concealed, of knife with blade three inches or longer prohibited. Exceptions exist for work, sporting, and recreational uses. *See, id.* at § 38-10-42. Possession of knives in public city buildings with blades over three inches in length prohibited. *See, id.* at § 38-4-11.

Lansing – Carry, concealed or otherwise, of any knife with blade over three inches in length prohibited. *See*, LANSING, MICH., CODIFIED

ORDINANCES § 696.04 (2005). Possession of knives on college campus property prohibited. *See, id.* at § 696.05.

36.4 State Resources

Michigan Department of State Police
714 S. Harrison Road
East Lansing, MI 48823
Phone: (517) 332-2521
Website: http://www.michigan.gov/msp

Michigan Attorney General
525 W. Ottawa St.
Lansing, MI 48909
Phone: (517) 373-1110
Fax: (517) 373-3042
Website: http://www.michigan.gov/ag

37 Minnesota – The North Star State

Area: 79,610 sq.mi. (Rank: 14th)   Population: 5,220,393 (Rank: 21st)
Violent Crime Rate (per 100,000 residents): 262.8 (Rank: 13th Safest)
State Motto: *L'Etoile du Nord (The Star of the North)*

Firearms Carry Summary:

Carry considerations	Status
Restaurants and bars	Allowed in restaurants with permit
Churches / Places of worship	Allowed with permit
State parks / forests	Concealed with permit allowed
Vehicle carry	Loaded handguns allowed with permit; long guns must be unloaded and securely cased
LE notification if stopped?	Not required
Retreat requirement for self-defense	Required
Preemption law	Yes. *See,* MINN. STAT. § 471.633 (2009)
Open Carry	Allowed with permit
Military-pattern semi-auto restrictions	Possession not restricted, but waiting period for purchase. *See,* MINN. STAT. § 624.7132 (2009)
NFA weapons	Restricted, possession limited to certain curio and relic machine guns and short-barreled shotguns. *See,* MINN. STAT. § 609.67 (2009)

Reciprocity / Recognition

Minnesota **recognizes** *permits from the following states:*

Alaska	Arkansas	Kansas	Kentucky
Louisiana	Michigan	Missouri	New Mexico
Nevada	Ohio	Oklahoma	Tennessee
Texas	Utah	Wyoming	

Minnesota permits **are recognized by** *the following states:*

Alaska	Arizona	Arkansas	Idaho
Indiana	Kansas	Kentucky	Louisiana
Michigan*	Mississippi	Missouri	Montana
Nebraska	New Mexico	Oklahoma	South Dakota
Tennessee	Utah	Vermont	Virginia
Wyoming			

Note: In the reciprocity / recognition tables above, states with an asterisk (*) require the permit holder to both have a permit from, and be a resident of, the recognized state in order for reciprocity / recognition of the permit.

Knife Carry Summary:

Note: Blade length limits, if any, in parentheses.

Knife Type	Open Carry	Concealed Carry	Notes
Folding	Yes	Yes	See note[102]
Fixed Blade	Yes	Yes	See note[102]
Dirks, Daggers, Stilettos	No	No	
Automatics	No	No	
Balisongs	No	No	

37.1 Discussion

Firearms Carry:

Travelers to Minnesota will find it somewhat restrictive legal environment for firearms carry. Minnesota requires a recognized permit for either open or concealed carry of handguns. Currently, Minnesota will honor the carry permits from fifteen other states. Nonresidents without a recognized out-of-state permit may obtain a Minnesota-issued carry permit by applying to any sheriff in the state. Such permits are granted on a "shall issue" basis.

State law requires a recognized permit in order to lawfully carry a loaded handgun in a vehicle. Those without such permits must transport their handguns in an unloaded condition, securely encased in a commercial gun case. Lawful transport of long guns requires that they be unloaded and securely cased, regardless of whether the traveler possesses a recognized permit or not.

---

[102] State law prohibits the carry of dangerous weapons for use as such unlawfully against another. *See,* MINN. STAT. § 609.66 (1)(a) (2009). The cautious traveler should avoid carry of "tactical" knives with weapon-like appearances or overly large knives. Knives such as hunting and fishing knives should only be carried while engaged in those activities, and certainly not within urban areas.

Open carry of loaded handguns requires a recognized permit. Open carry of loaded long guns is limited to those lawfully engaged in hunting or target shooting on shooting ranges. Transporting long guns to and from those activities requires that they be unloaded and securely cased.[103]

Knife Carry:

Travelers to Minnesota will find a fairly restrictive legal environment for knife carry, especially within the urban population areas.

With respect to knives, ordinary folding pocket knives should pose no problem. There is no statutorily defined blade length limit under state law, although at least one major city imposes a blade length limit for knives considered *per se* weapons. Automatic knives are prohibited under state law. Dirks, daggers and stilettos are prohibited under some city ordinances, and likely would be considered *per se* dangerous weapons under state law as well. Balisongs, while not specifically prohibited, may fall under the statutory switchblade prohibition, as balisongs do in some states.

State law prohibits carry of dangerous weapons in courthouses and on school property. Minnesota does not preempt its cities and towns from regulating knife carry, unlike the case for firearms, and so towns and cities may impose their own restrictions on knife carry.

37.2 *Places Off-Limits While Carrying*

Firearms Carry:

State law prohibits carry of loaded firearms in schools or on school property. A limited exception exists for those with permits while in a vehicle, or outside the vehicle leasing or retrieving a firearm from the trunk or rear storage area of the vehicle. *See*, MINN. STAT. § 609.66. State law also prohibits carry on school buses and in buildings or facilities under the temporary and exclusive control of a school, provided that the location is prominently and conspicuously posted at each entrance to give actual notice of the school related use. *See, id.*

---

[103] Note that state law provides a limited exception for unloaded but uncased transport for hunting and target shooting, but this exception is itself subject to numerous exceptions that are county and/or location specific. *See*, MINN. STAT. § 97B.045 (2009). The prudent traveler would be well advised to *always* transport their long guns in an unloaded and securely cased condition when in Minnesota.

Carry is also prohibited in child care centers. *See, id.*

Minnesota prohibits firearms possession within courthouses, and state buildings within the Capitol Area (except the National Guard Armory). Certain exceptions exist, including an exception for those with recognized permits who notify the sheriff or the commissioner of public safety, as appropriate. *See, id.* at Subd. 1G.

Knife Carry:

Minnesota state law prohibits the carry of dangerous weapons on school grounds, courthouses, and state buildings in the Capitol Area, subject to certain limited exceptions.

In addition, towns and cities may pass their own local ordinances restricting or prohibiting carry. Minneapolis, for example, explicitly prohibits carry of knives of any kind on school property, with certain exceptions not normally applicable to the average traveler.

37.3 *Selected City Ordinances*

The state legislature has preempted municipalities and other political subdivisions from regulating firearms to any extent greater than state law. Thus, firearms regulation is uniform throughout the state.

The city ordinances below relate to knife carry:

Minneapolis – Carry of weapons on or about the person within the city prohibited. *See*, MINNEAPOLIS, MINN., CODE OF ORDINANCES § 393.90 (2010). The definition of "weapon" normally excludes folding knives with blades four inches or less, unless such knife is actually used as a weapon. *See, id.* at § 393.10. Carry of weapons while intoxicated also prohibited. *See, id.* at § 393.50. Possession of knives on school property prohibited (limited exceptions exist). *See, id.* at § 393.60.

Duluth – Possession of daggers, stilettos, and switchblades prohibited. *See*, DULUTH, MINN., LEGISLATIVE CODE § 49-10 (2010).

37.4 *State Resources*

Minnesota Department of Public Safety

444 Cedar Street
Saint Paul, MN 55101
Phone: (651) 201-7000
Website: http://www.dps.state.mn.us/

Minnesota Attorney General's Office
1400 Bremer Tower
445 Minnesota Street
St. Paul, MN 55101
Phone: (651) 296-3353
Phone: (800) 657-3787
TTY: (651) 297-7206
TTY: (800) 366-4812
Website: http://www.ag.state.mn.us/

38 Mississippi – The Magnolia State

Area: 46,907 sq.mi. (Rank: 31st)   Population: 2,938,618 (Rank: 31st)
Violent Crime Rate (per 100,000 residents): 284.9 (Rank: 18th Safest)
State Motto: *Virtute et Armis (By Valor and Arms)*

Firearms Carry Summary:

Carry considerations	Status
Restaurants and bars	Allowed in dining area of restaurants with permit
Churches / Places of worship	Prohibited. *See*, MISS. CODE ANN. § 45-9-101(13) (2009)
State parks / forests	Prohibited. *See*, MISS. CODE ANN. § 45-9-101(13) (2009)
Vehicle carry	Loaded handguns allowed, long guns should be unloaded and cased during hunting season
LE notification if stopped?	Not required
Retreat requirement for self-defense	Not required. *See*, MISS. CODE ANN. § 97-3-15 (2009)
Preemption law	Yes, some limited exceptions exist. *See*, MISS. CODE ANN. § 45-9-51 *et. seq.*
Open Carry	Allowed with permit
Military-pattern semi-auto restrictions	Not restricted
NFA weapons	NFA-friendly, compliance with federal law only

Reciprocity / Recognition

Mississippi **recognizes** *permits from the following states:*

Alabama	Alaska	Arizona	Arkansas
Colorado	Florida	Georgia	Indiana
Kentucky	Louisiana	Michigan	Minnesota
Missouri	Montana	New Hampshire	North Carolina
Oklahoma	South Dakota	Tennessee	Texas
Utah	Virginia	Washington	West Virginia
Wyoming			

Mississippi permits **are recognized by** *the following states:*

Alabama	Alaska	Arizona	Arkansas
Colorado*	Georgia	Florida*	Idaho
Indiana	Kentucky	Louisiana	Michigan*
Missouri	Montana	New Hampshire*	North Carolina

Oklahoma	South Dakota	Tennessee	Texas
Utah	Vermont	Virginia	Washington
West Virginia	Wyoming		

Note: In the reciprocity / recognition tables above, states with an asterisk (*) require the permit holder to both have a permit from, and be a resident of, the recognized state in order for reciprocity / recognition of the permit.

Knife Carry Summary:

Note: Blade length limits, if any, in parentheses.

Knife Type	Open Carry	Concealed Carry	Notes
Folding	Yes	Yes	
Fixed Blade	Yes	No	
Dirks, Daggers, Stilettos	Yes	No	
Automatics	Yes	No	
Balisongs	Yes	No	

38.1 Discussion

Firearms Carry:

Visitors to the Magnolia State will find a relatively friendly legal environment for firearms carry, provided that the visitor possesses a recognized permit. Mississippi does not issue permits to nonresidents, but currently recognizes the carry permits of twenty-five other states.

Mississippi requires a recognized permit to carry a concealed handgun in public outside of a vehicle. No permit is required to carry a loaded handgun, concealed or unconcealed, in a vehicle. A loaded handgun may be kept in the glove compartment or console or other storage area without a permit. Long guns may be carried loaded in the vehicle, except during deer or turkey hunting season, during which they must be transported in an unloaded condition.

State law prohibits carry in public (outside of a vehicle) of handguns, short barreled rifles, short barreled shotguns, machine guns (any with or without silencers) and a variety of knives (see discussion in the knife carry section below) in any manner that renders them "concealed in whole or in part", unless the carrier is engaged in a "legitimate weapon-related sports activity" such as hunting, fishing, target shooting or firearms competition, or is going to or returning from such activity.[104] Standard length rifles and shotguns do not fall under this prohibition. Handguns, of course, may be carried concealed with a recognized permit.

Travelers should be aware that Mississippi courts have ruled that a handgun carried in a visible holster, i.e., in what would be considered open carry in most other states, is considered "concealed in whole or in part" in Mississippi, and thus falls under the prohibition of such carry.[105] Thus, open carry of handguns in visible holsters requires a recognized concealed carry permit.

Those travelers who have the misfortune of running afoul of the concealed deadly weapon statute should note that the law provides for several affirmative defenses against such a charge or indictment. The two that would typically apply to travelers allow the person charged to demonstrate that he "was threatened, and had good and sufficient reason to apprehend a serious attack from any enemy, and that he did so apprehend", or that he is an upstanding citizen ("not a tramp", as the statute so indelicately states) and was on a bona fide journey, at the time of the charged offense.[106] Assuming the person charged can convince the court that one or more of these conditions apply to his case, this would operate as a successful defense against the charge.

Knife Carry:

Visitors to the Magnolia State will find a fairly permissive legal environment for open knife carry, with a more restrictive environment for concealed carry. Open or concealed carry of ordinary pocket knives should pose no problem. Fixed bladed knives may be carried openly, but travelers should exercise care when carrying such knives concealed. Mississippi state law prohibits concealed carry of bowie knives, dirks, butcher knives and switchblades, although state law does not define these types of knives. The statute prohibits concealment "in whole or in part."[107] As such, travelers should exercise considerable caution carrying any fixed bladed knife, lest they inadvertently run afoul of the statutory language and be accused of carrying one of the prohibited knife types.

---

[104] See, MISS. CODE § 97-37-1 (2009).
[105] See, L.M., Jr. v. State, 600 So.2d 967, 971 (Miss., 1992) (Lee, C.J., concurring) (discussing concealed weapons statute).
[106] See, MISS. CODE § 97-37-9 (2009).
[107] See, MISS. CODE § 97-37-1 (2009).

Note that balisongs, while not specifically prohibited, may fall under the switchblade prohibition, as balisongs do in some states.

Unlike with firearms, no state-wide statutory prohibitions on off-limits locations for otherwise legal knife carry appear to exist, although travelers should be aware that cities and towns may pass their own ordinances restricting knife carry. Tupelo, for example, prohibits carry of knives with blades greater than three and a half inches in length in a wide variety of places within that city, such as in government buildings, in establishments that serve alcohol for on-premises consumption, and at political rallies or meetings, among others.

38.2 *Places Off-Limits While Carrying*

Firearms Carry:

Mississippi prohibits the carry, with or without a permit, of stun guns and concealed handguns in police, sheriff, and highway patrol stations, detention facilities such as prisons and jails, courthouses and court rooms, polling places, meeting places of local governments, meetings of the Legislature of legislative committees, public parks (except for the purpose of participating in authorized firearms-related activities), and at school, college or professional athletic events not related to firearms. *See*, MISS. CODE ANN. § 45-9-101(13) (2009).

State law also prohibits carry in "any portion of an establishment, licensed to dispense alcoholic beverages for consumption on the premises, that is primarily devoted to dispensing alcoholic beverages" and in "any portion of an establishment in which beer or light wine is consumed on the premises, that is primarily devoted to such purpose[.]" *See, id.*

Carry is prohibited in elementary or secondary school facilities, junior colleges, community colleges, colleges and university facilities unless for the purpose of participating in any authorized firearms-related activities. *See, id.*

State law prohibits carry inside the passenger terminal of any airport (not just the secure areas of the airport), with the obvious exception for those with unloaded and securely cased firearms for purposes of checking such firearms as baggage for lawful transport on aircraft. *See, id.*

MISSISSIPPI – THE MAGNOLIA STATE | 171

Mississippi prohibits carry in churches or other place of worship, and while participating in the parade or demonstration for which a permit is required. *See, id.*

Note that private businesses can then carry on their premises by conspicuously posting a sign to that effect. *See*, MISS. CODE ANN. § 45-9-101(13) (2009).

Knife Carry:

No state law limitation. Towns and cities, however, may pass their own local ordinances prohibiting or restricting carry.

38.3 Selected City Ordinances

The state legislature has preempted municipalities and other political subdivisions from regulating firearms to any extent greater than state law. Thus, firearms regulation is uniform throughout the state.

The city ordinances below relate to knife carry:

Jackson – Carry of firearms or deadly weapons as defined in state law prohibited at city council meetings, parades, political rallies, or other political meetings held in or on public buildings. *See*, JACKSON, MISS., CODE OF ORDINANCES § 86-12 (2009).

Tupelo – Carry of "dangerous weapons," the definition of which includes automatic knives and knives with blades greater than three and a half inches, prohibited in, on, or at public parks, public meetings, political rallies, parades, at school, college, or professional events, including concerts and lectures, financial institution premises, commercial retail establishments, including shopping malls and centers, on government owned buildings or property, and in establishments serving alcohol for on-premises consumption. *See*, TUPELO, MISS., CODE OF ORDINANCES § 19-4 (2009).

38.4 State Resources

Mississippi Department of Public Safety
1900 East Woodrow Wilson Drive
Jackson, MS 39216
Phone: (601) 987-1212

Fax: (601) 987-1498
Website: http://www.dps.state.ms.us/

Attorney General of Mississippi
P.O. Box 220
Jackson, MS 39205-0220
Phone: (601) 359-3680
Fax: (601) 987-1547
Website: http://www.ago.state.ms.us/

39 Missouri – The Show Me State

Area: 66,886 sq.mi. (Rank: 18th)   Population: 5,911,605 (Rank: 18th)
Violent Crime Rate (per 100,000 residents): 504.4 (Rank: 38th Safest)
State Motto: *Salus Populi Suprema Lex Esto (The Welfare of the People Shall Be the Supreme Law)*

Firearms Carry Summary:

Carry considerations	Status
Restaurants and bars	Allowed in restaurants with permit; prohibited in bars without permission of bar owner or manager. *See,* Mo. Rev. Stat. § 571.107 (2009)
Churches / Places of worship	Prohibited without permission of church or place or worship. *See,* Mo. Rev. Stat. § 571.107 (2009)
State parks / forests	Concealed with permit allowed
Vehicle carry	Concealed carry of loaded handguns allowed; loaded long guns must be in plain view
LE notification if stopped?	Not required
Retreat requirement for self-defense	Required, except if in your own dwelling, residence, or vehicle. *See,* Mo. Rev. Stat. § 563.031 (2009)
Preemption law	Yes, but local governments can regulate open carry. *See,* Mo. Rev. Stat. § 21.750 (2009)
Open Carry	Allowed, but municipalities can prohibit.
Military-pattern semi-auto restrictions	Not restricted
NFA weapons	Possession prohibited, except for items classified as curio and relics. *See,* Mo. Rev. Stat. § 571.020 (2009)

Reciprocity / Recognition

Missouri **recognizes** permits from **all other states**.

Missouri permits **are recognized by** the following states:

Alabama	Alaska	Arkansas	Arizona
Colorado*	Delaware	Georgia	Florida*
Idaho	Indiana	Kansas	Kentucky
Louisiana	Michigan*	Minnesota	Mississippi
Montana	Nebraska	Nevada	New Hampshire*
New Mexico	North Carolina	North Dakota	Ohio
Oklahoma	Pennsylvania	South Carolina*	South Dakota

| Tennessee | Texas | Utah | Vermont |
| Virginia | Washington | West Virginia | Wyoming |

Note: In the reciprocity / recognition tables above, states with an asterisk (*) require the permit holder to both have a permit from, and be a resident of, the recognized state in order for reciprocity / recognition of the permit.

Knife Carry Summary:

Note: Blade length limits, if any, in parentheses.

Knife Type	Open Carry	Concealed Carry	Notes
Folding	Yes (≤ 4")	Yes (≤ 4")	
Fixed Blade	Yes	No	
Dirks, Daggers, Stilettos	Yes	No	
Automatics	No	No	
Balisongs	No	No	

39.1 Discussion

Firearms Carry:

Travelers to Missouri will find that the Show Me State has a friendly legal environment for firearms carry. Missouri issues conceal carry permits on a "shall issue" basis to its residents, and recognizes the carry permits of all other states. Thus, if you have a carry permit from any state, you can legally carry concealed in Missouri. Subject, of course, to the same laws that apply to Missouri permit holders.

State law allows anyone twenty-one years or older to carry a loaded, concealed handgun in a vehicle without a permit. The loaded handgun may be stored in the glove compartment or console or any other storage area in the vehicle. Persons under twenty-one who do not possess a valid permit must transport handguns unloaded and securely cased, with any ammunition cased or stored separately from the gun.

Long guns may be carried loaded in a vehicle, provided that they are in plain view. If not, they must be transported unloaded and securely cased, with any ammunition cased or stored separately from the gun.

State law requires a permit to carry a concealed handgun in public. While open carry is generally legal in Missouri, travelers should be aware that the state allows municipal governments to regulate and/or prohibit open carry in their jurisdictions. This regulatory "loophole" concerning open carry is the only glaring omission in the state's otherwise comprehensive preemption law. Thus, visitors to the state who possess a valid permit would be well advised to keep their firearms concealed, lest they run afoul of an open carry prohibition in their travels in the Show Me State.

Knife Carry:

Visitors to the Show Me State will find that the legal environment for knife carry, in keeping with the state's nickname, strongly favors open, versus concealed, knife carry. (Firearms-carrying travelers with recognized permits should note that while open carry is permitted under state law, many municipalities restrict or prohibit such carry.)

With respect to knives, ordinary folding pocket knives with blades no longer than four inches may be carried openly or concealed. Under state law, fixed bladed knives, including dirks, daggers, and stilettos, may be carried openly, although travelers would be well advised to exercise caution whenever carrying such knives, especially in urban areas. Automatic knives are prohibited. Knives such as balisongs, while not specifically prohibited, may fall under the switchblade prohibition, as balisongs do in some states, and thus the careful traveler would do well to avoid carry of such knives.

State law prohibits carry of weapons in schools, school buses, and at school sponsored or sanctioned events. As is the case in many states, travelers should be aware that cities and towns may pass their own ordinances prohibiting or otherwise restricting knife carry within their jurisdictions.

39.2 Places Off-Limits While Carrying

Firearms Carry:

Missouri prohibits carry of concealed firearms in a wide variety of places, including police stations, sheriff's offices, and Highway Patrol offices without the consent of the chief law enforcement officer in charge of the office or station; within 25 feet of polling places on election day; in detention or correctional institutions; courthouses and court rooms; and meetings of local government or of the state's General Assembly or legislative committees. *See*, MO. REV. STAT. § 571-107 (2009).

Carry of firearms is also prohibited in bars, to wit, "[a]ny establishment licensed to dispense intoxicating liquor for consumption on the premises, which portion is primarily devoted to that purpose," without the permission of the owner or manager. This restriction does not apply to restaurants with a seating capacity of fifty or more and which receive at least 51% of their gross annual income from the dining facilities by the sale of food. *See, id.*

Carry of firearms is prohibited in the secure areas of airports.

Carry of firearms is also prohibited in schools, colleges and universities without permission of the educational institution, childcare facilities without permission of the manager, and riverboat gambling operations without permission of the owner or manager, as well as the gated area of an amusement park. *See, id.*

Carry in churches or other places of religious worship requires permission of the church or place of worship. *See, id.*

Private property owners and private businesses and organizations may prohibit concealed firearms by posting signs to that effect in a conspicuous place. Possession of a firearm in a vehicle on the premises shall not be a criminal offense so long as the firearm is not removed from the vehicle or brandished while the vehicle is on the premises. *See*, MO. REV. STAT. § 571-107 (2009).

State law forbids concealed carry in sports arenas and stadiums with a seating capacity of 5,000 or more, as well as hospitals accessible by the public. *See, id.*

Note that while this is a daunting list of off-limits locations, in general state law provides that firearms kept in the vehicle at those locations do not constitute a criminal offense so long as the firearm is not removed from the vehicle or brandished while the vehicle is on the premises of the prohibited location. Additionally, carrying a concealed firearm with a recognized permit in a prohibited location will generally subject the person to denial to the premises or removal from the premises, and will generally not result in criminal sanctions, unless the person refuses to leave the prohibited premises. *See*, MO. REV. STAT. § 571-107 (2009).

Knife Carry:

State law prohibits carry of weapons "readily capable of lethal use" in schools, school buses, and at school sponsored or sanctioned events. *See*, MO. REV. STAT. § 571.030 (2009). Municipal governments may also pass their own local ordinances prohibiting or otherwise restricting carry within their respective jurisdictions.

39.3 Selected City Ordinances

The state legislature has preempted municipalities and other political subdivisions from regulating firearms to any extent greater than state law. Thus, firearms regulation is uniform throughout the state.

The city ordinances below relate to knife carry:

Independence – Possession of deadly weapons prohibited on school grounds, playgrounds, parks, and city buildings or facilities. The definition of "deadly weapon" includes knives with blades greater than four inches in length. *See*, INDEPENDENCE, MO., CODE OF ORDINANCES § 12.03.001 (2009). Possession of switchblades prohibited. *See, id.* at § 12.03.002. Concealed carry of firearms and knives prohibited, unless one has a valid concealed carry permit. Carry of firearms and other weapons "readily capable of lethal use" into any church or other place of worship, election precinct on election day, or government building prohibited, unless one has a valid permit. *See, id.* at § 12.03.003. The definition of "knife" excludes "any ordinary pocket knife with no blade more than four inches in length." *See, id.* at § 12.03.008.

Jackson – Carry of firearm and any weapon readily capable of lethal use prohibited in churches, schools, polling places on election day, or any government building, unless one has valid carry permit. *See*, JACKSON, MO., CODE OF ORDINANCES § 45-502 (2009). The definition of "knife" excludes "any ordinary pocket knife with no blade more than four (4) inches in length." *See, id.* at § 45-500.

39.4 State Resources

Missouri Department of Public Safety
Truman State Office Building, Rm. 870
Jefferson City, MO 65102-0749
Phone: (888) FYI-MDPS

Fax: (573) 751-5399
Website: http://www.dps.mo.gov/

Attorney General of Missouri
Supreme Court Building
207 W. High Street
Jefferson City, MO 65102
Phone: (573) 751-3321
Fax: (573) 751-0774
Website: http://ago.mo.gov/

40 Montana – The Treasure State

Area: 145,552 sq.mi. (Rank: 4th)   Population: 967,440 (Rank: 44th)
Violent Crime Rate (per 100,000 residents): 258.1 (Rank: 12th Safest)
State Motto: *Oro y Plata (Gold and Silver)*

Firearms Carry Summary:

Carry considerations	Status
Restaurants and bars	Allowed, open carry required
Churches / Places of worship	Allowed
State parks / forests	Allowed
Vehicle carry	Loaded allowed if in plain view, of in glove compartment or center console; weapons cannot be concealed *on one's person* without a permit
LE notification if stopped?	Not required
Retreat requirement for self-defense	Not required. *See*, MONT. CODE ANN. § 45-3-110 (2009).
Preemption law	Yes, but local governments can regulate carry in certain areas. *See*, MONT. CODE ANN. § 45-8-351 (2009).
Open Carry	Allowed without permit, and generally accepted. Local governments can prohibit in certain areas
Military-pattern semi-auto restrictions	Not restricted
NFA weapons	NFA-friendly, compliance with federal law only

Reciprocity / Recognition

*Montana **recognizes** permits from the following states:*

Alaska	Arizona	Arkansas	California
Colorado	Connecticut	Florida	Georgia
Idaho	Indiana	Iowa	Kansas
Kentucky	Louisiana	Maryland	Massachusetts
Michigan	Minnesota	Mississippi	Missouri
Nebraska	Nevada	New Jersey	New Mexico
New York	North Carolina	North Dakota	Ohio
Oklahoma	Oregon	Pennsylvania	South Carolina
South Dakota	Tennessee	Texas	Utah
Virginia	Washington	West Virginia	Wyoming

*Montana permits **are recognized by** the following states:*

Alaska	Arizona	Arkansas	Colorado*
Florida*	Georgia	Idaho	Indiana
Kentucky	Louisiana	Michigan*	Mississippi
Missouri	Nebraska	New Mexico	North Carolina
North Dakota	Oklahoma	Pennsylvania	South Dakota
Tennessee	Texas	Utah	Vermont
Virginia	Wyoming		

Note: In the reciprocity / recognition tables above, states with an asterisk (*) require the permit holder to both have a permit from, and be a resident of, the recognized state in order for reciprocity / recognition of the permit.

Knife Carry Summary:

Note: Blade length limits, if any, in parentheses.

Knife Type	Open Carry	Concealed Carry	Notes
Folding	Yes	Yes (< 4")	
Fixed Blade	Yes	Yes (< 4")	
Dirks, Daggers, Stilettos	Yes	No	
Automatics	No	No	
Balisongs	Yes	Yes (< 4")	

40.1 Discussion

Firearms Carry:

First-time visitors to Montana will no doubt wonder at the state's natural beauty, from the rolling plains in the Eastern half of the state, to the state's Western snow-capped mountains. As the license plates proclaim, this *is* Big Sky Country. Perhaps not surprisingly, with few urban population centers of any appreciable size, the state's firearm and knife carry laws tend to be fairly unburdened with restrictions on law-abiding citizens.

State law requires a permit to carry a concealed firearm only within city and town limits, and logging camps. Montana issues concealed carry permits to residents on a "shall issue" basis. Unfortunately, the state does not issue permits to nonresidents, although Montana currently recognizes the permits of forty states.

No permit is required to carry a loaded firearm either openly or concealed in the approximately 99% of the state that is not within the boundaries of a city, town, or logging camp. Thus, visitors who wish to hunt, fish, hike, and camp in Montana's beautiful outdoors may carry defensive firearms concealed without a permit, so long as they do so outside the property limits of cities, towns, and logging camps. Note that no permit is required for open carry, even within cities and towns.

Travelers in vehicles may carry loaded firearms without a permit in plain view. Note that, with respect to firearms carry, Montana defines "concealed weapon" as a weapon that is "wholly or partially covered by the clothing or wearing apparel of the person carrying or bearing the weapon."[108] Thus, loaded firearms may be carried in glove compartments or center consoles of vehicles, because even though not in plain view, they do not meet the definition of concealed weapon under Montana law.

Montana prohibits the concealed carry of weapons in places that serve alcoholic beverages for consumption on the premises. Thus, those wishing to patronize such establishments while armed must carry their weapons openly.

Visitors to Montana should be aware that the state's preemption law nevertheless allows local governments to prohibit carry of weapons, whether openly or concealed, at public assemblies, in publicly owned buildings, parks or schools.[109]

Knife Carry:

With respect to knives, state law has a bias towards open carry. Knives with blades four inches or greater in length must be carried openly. Ordinary pocket knives with blades less than four inches long may be carried concealed. Fixed bladed knives, other than dirks, daggers, and stilettos, with blades less than four inches may also be carried concealed. Possession of automatic knives of any kind, however, is prohibited. Travelers should note that balisongs, while not specifically prohibited, may also fall under the switchblade prohibition, as balisongs do in some states.

---

[108] *See*, MONT. CODE ANN. § 45-8-315 (2009).
[109] *See*, MONT. CODE ANN. § 45-8-351 (2009).

State law specifically prohibits carry of concealed weapons while intoxicated. In addition, state law prohibits carry of concealed weapons in government buildings, financial institutions, and places serving alcohol. Note that, unlike the case for firearms, municipalities may pass and enforce their own restrictions on knife carry within their jurisdictions.

40.2 Places Off-Limits While Carrying

Firearms Carry:

Montana prohibits the carrying of concealed weapons, with or without a permit, in state or local government offices, inside banks, credit unions, savings and loan and similar institutions (drive-up teller windows and ATMs are not included in this prohibition), and any location in which alcoholic beverages are sold, dispensed, and consumed on the premises. *See*, MONT. CODE ANN. § 45-8-328 (2009).

In addition, state law prohibits the carry or transport of firearms on a train unless, prior to boarding, the person has delivered all firearms and ammunition, if any, to the operator of the train. *See*, MONT. CODE ANN. § 45-8-339 (2009).

State law also prohibits possession, carry, or storage of weapons in school buildings (other than home schools), unless advance permission has been obtained from the trustees of the school district. The definition of "weapon" includes, but is not limited to, "any type of firearm, a knife with a blade 4 or more inches in length, a sword, a straight razor, a throwing star, nun-chucks, or brass or other metal knuckles." *See*, MONT. CODE ANN. § 45-8-361 (2009).

Knife Carry:

Montana prohibits the carry of concealed weapons, with or without a permit, in state or local government offices, banks and financial institutions, and alcohol-serving establishments. *See*, MONT. CODE ANN. § 45-8-328 (2009).

In addition, state law prohibits the carry or possession of weapons in schools (other than home schools), including knives with blades four or more inches in length, swords, and straight razors. *See*, MONT. CODE ANN. § 45-8-361 (2009).

40.3 Selected City Ordinances

The state legislature has preempted municipalities and other political subdivisions from regulating firearms to any extent greater than state law. Thus, firearms regulation is uniform throughout the state.

The city ordinances below relate to knife carry:

Billings – Possession or carry of weapons at city council meetings prohibited. The definition of "weapon" includes dirks, daggers, swords, and razors (except safety razors). *See*, BILLINGS, MONT., CITY CODE § 18-204 (2009).

40.4 State Resources

Montana Highway Patrol
2550 Prospect Ave.
Helena, MT 59620-1419
Phone: (406) 444-7000
Fax: (406) 444-4169
Website: http://www.doj.mt.gov/enforcement/highwaypatrol/

Montana Attorney General
P.O. Box 201401
Helena, MT 59620-1401
Phone: (406) 444-2026
Fax: (406) 444-3549
Website: http://doj.mt.gov/default.asp

41 Nebraska – The Cornhusker State

Area: 76,872 sq.mi. (Rank: 15th)   Population: 1,783,432 (Rank: 38th)
Violent Crime Rate (per 100,000 residents): 303.7 (Rank: 21st Safest)
State Motto: *Equality Before the Law*

Firearms Carry Summary:

Carry considerations	Status
Restaurants and bars	Concealed allowed in restaurants, but cannot consume alcohol. *See*, NEB. REV. STAT. § 69-2441(5) (2009)
Churches / Places of worship	Prohibited. *See*, NEB. REV. STAT. § 69-2441(1) (2009)
State parks / forests	Concealed carry with permit allowed, unless posted otherwise
Vehicle carry	Loaded handguns and rifles allowed in plain view, otherwise unloaded and securely cased; shotguns must be unloaded
LE notification if stopped?	Required
Retreat requirement for self-defense	Required, except in home. *See*, NEB. REV. STAT. § 28-1409 (2009)
Preemption law	Limited preemption for those with permits. *See*, NEB. REV. STAT. § 18-1703 (2009)
Open Carry	Allowed, but local government may regulate / prohibit
Military-pattern semi-auto restrictions	Not restricted
NFA weapons	NFA-friendly, compliance with federal law only

Reciprocity / Recognition

Nebraska **recognizes** *permits from the following states:*

Alaska	Arizona	Arkansas	Colorado
Connecticut	Florida	Idaho	Hawaii
Kansas	Kentucky	Louisiana	Michigan
Minnesota	Missouri	Nevada	New Jersey
New Mexico	North Carolina	North Dakota*	Ohio
Oklahoma	Oregon	Rhode Island	South Carolina
Tennessee	Utah	Virginia	West Virginia
Wyoming	Dist. of Columbia		

<u>Note</u>: North Dakota – Class One permit only

*Nebraska **recognizes** permits from the following states only for those who are 21 years or age or older:*

California	Iowa	Maine	Montana
North Dakota*	Texas		

Note: North Dakota – Class Two permit only

*Nebraska permits **are recognized by** the following states:*

Alaska	Arizona	Arkansas	Colorado*
Florida*	Idaho	Indiana	Kansas
Kentucky	Louisiana	Michigan*	Missouri
Montana	Nevada	North Carolina	North Dakota
Oklahoma	South Dakota	Tennessee	Texas
Utah	Vermont	Virginia	

Note: In the reciprocity / recognition tables above, states with an asterisk (*) require the permit holder to both have a permit from, and be a resident of, the recognized state in order for reciprocity / recognition of the permit.

Knife Carry Summary:

Note: Blade length limits, if any, in parentheses.

Knife Type	Open Carry	Concealed Carry	Notes
Folding	Yes	Yes (≤ 3½")	
Fixed Blade	Yes	No	
Dirks, Daggers, Stilettos	No	No	
Automatics	No	No	
Balisongs	Yes	Yes (≤ 3½")	

41.1 Discussion

Firearms Carry:

Travelers to the Cornhusker State will find a somewhat restrictive legal environment for carry of loaded firearms for self protection. Nebraska issues conceal carry permits on a "shall issue" basis to its residents, and currently recognizes the permits of over thirty other states. For those possessing a recognized permit, the state's preemption law prohibits local governments from regulating concealed carry of loaded handguns. For those without recognized permits, however, the lack of full preemption may be of concern for the law-abiding traveler, as local governments can regulate transport, possession or carry within their jurisdictions.

Nebraska requires a recognized permit in order to carry loaded handguns in a concealed manner. Open carry, however, is legal under state law and does not require a permit. Unfortunately, cities and towns can regulate or prohibit open carry of firearms in their jurisdictions, and can regulate or prohibit concealed carry for those without recognized permits.

Travelers in vehicles may transport loaded handguns and rifles provided that the firearms are in plain view, or securely cased and stored in the trunk of the vehicle if the traveler does not possess a recognized permit. Shotguns must be transported in an unloaded condition, and either in plain view or securely cased. Travelers with firearms traveling through designated game deserves should transport their firearms unloaded and securely cased.

Holders of recognized concealed carry permits may carry loaded handguns concealed while in a vehicle. For those without recognized permits, handguns may only be stored in glove compartments or center consoles if the gun is unloaded *and* the glove compartment or center console *is locked.* Otherwise the handgun should be transported unloaded and stored in the trunk of the vehicle, or unloaded and in a locked gun case if the vehicle does not have a trunk.

Knife Carry:

Travelers to Nebraska should be prepared to encounter a fairly restrictive legal environment for knife carry, particularly as it relates to concealed carry in urban areas. Nebraska state law contains a general prohibition against concealed carry of weapons, and the Nebraska Supreme Court has upheld and broadly interpreted the law, and companion municipal ordinances, to apply to a wide variety of knives and situations. For example, the Nebraska Supreme Court has ruled that the person carrying concealed need not carry in public, but can be prosecuted (and convicted) for concealed carry while on private property as a guest in another's home.[110] Given this broad

---

[110] *See, State v. Conklin*, 545 N.W.2d 101, 108 (Neb. 1996) (affirming conviction and upholding constitutionality of Omaha's concealed weapon ordinance). The court,

criminal statute, visitors to the Cornhusker State should exercise caution in the kinds and types of knives they carry. Although state law incorporates a three and a half inch blade length limit in the definition of "knife" applicable to the concealed weapon statute, the overall definition is sufficiently broad as to encompass virtually any type of knife, with any blade length. Thus, while the summary table above lists a three and a half inch blade length limit, the law-abiding traveler should be aware that individuals have been prosecuted, and convicted, for carrying concealed knives with blade lengths as short as three inches.[111]

Note that while open carry of knives does not trigger the concealed weapon statute, such carry, especially in urban environments, will often result in unwanted law enforcement attention.

While the state does not appear to have a switchblade prohibition, given the dim view the state courts have taken to ordinary folding pocketknives, the carry of automatic knives by the casual traveler is likely to engender a negative response from law enforcement and the courts. Carry of knives such as balisongs, which have a reputation as martial arts weapons, should be avoided for similar reasons.

No state-wide statutory prohibitions on off-limits locations for otherwise legal knife carry appear to exist, although travelers should be aware that cities and towns may pass their own ordinances restricting knife carry.

41.2 Places Off-Limits While Carrying

Firearms Carry:

Nebraska prohibits carry of concealed handguns in any police, sheriff, or Nebraska State Patrol station or office, detention facility such as a prison or jail, courtroom or building which contains a courtroom, polling place on election day, meeting of the governing body of a county, public school district, municipality, or other political subdivision, and meeting of the Legislature or legislative committee. *See*, NEB. REV. STAT. § 69-2441 (2009).

---

however, left for another day the question of whether the Omaha concealed weapon ordinance, or inferentially, the analogous state statute, would apply to persons in their own homes. *Id.*

[111] *See, id.* at 108 (upholding conviction for concealed carry of folding knife with three inch blade).

State law also prohibits concealed carry of handguns in any financial institution, professional or semiprofessional athletic event, building, grounds, vehicle, or sponsored activity or athletic event of any public, private, denominational, or parochial elementary, vocational, or secondary school, a private postsecondary career school, a community college, or a public or private college, junior college, or university. *See, id.*

Concealed carry is also prohibited in any place of worship, hospital, emergency room, or trauma center, political rally or fundraiser. *See, id.*

State law prohibits concealed carry in any "establishment having a license issued under the Nebraska Liquor Control Act that derives over one-half of its total income from the sale of alcoholic liquor", such as a bar or tavern. Note that state law prohibits consumption of alcohol while carrying. *See, id.*

Businesses and employers may also prohibit concealed carry on their premises. *See, id.*

Knife Carry:

No state law limitation, outside of schools. Towns and cities, however, may pass their own local ordinances restricting or prohibiting carry.

State law does incorporate penalties for students who possess or carry dangerous weapons on school grounds. *See*, NEB. REV. STAT. §§ 79-267, 79-283 (2009). Towns and cities may pass additional local ordinances prohibiting or otherwise restricting knife carry by non-students on school grounds.

41.3 Selected City Ordinances

Nebraska has enacted a limited preemption law that prohibits municipalities from regulating concealed handgun carry for those with recognized carry permits. Travelers without a recognize permit should be aware that some localities may regulate carry (open or concealed) of firearms.

The city ordinances below relate to knife carry:

Beatrice – Carry of concealed weapons, the definition of which includes bowie knives, dirks, and any "knife with dirk blade attachment" prohibited. *See*, BEATRICE, NEB. CODE OF ORDINANCES § 17-111 (2009). An exception exists for the carry of concealed handguns if the carrier possesses a valid concealed handgun permit. An affirmative defense (not an exception) also exists for use in lawful business, or for lawful personal protection. *See, id.*

Omaha – Carry of concealed weapons expressly forbidden. *See*, OMAHA, NEB., MUNICIPAL CODE §§ 20-192, 20-206 (2010). City mayor may prohibit carry in public (open or concealed) of weapons, including knives and razors, during time of declared emergency. *See, id.* at § 8-85.

North Platte – Carry of weapons, whether open or concealed, prohibited in or on city parks, pathways, and recreation facilities. See, NORTH PLATTE, NEB., CODE OF ORDINANCES § 38-5 (2005).

41.4 State Resources

Nebraska State Patrol
P.O. Box 94907
Lincoln, NE 68509
Phone: (402) 471-4545
Website: http://statepatrol.nebraska.gov/

Nebraska Attorney General
2115 State Capitol
Lincoln, NE 68509
Phone: (402) 471-2682
Fax: (402) 471-3297
Website: http://www.ago.state.ne.us/

42 Nevada – The Silver State

Area: 109,826 sq.mi. (Rank: 7th)   Population: 2,600,167 (Rank: 35th)
Violent Crime Rate (per 100,000 residents): 724.5 (Rank: 49th Safest)
State Motto: *All for Our Country*

Firearms Carry Summary:

Carry considerations	Status
Restaurants and bars	Concealed allowed with permit in restaurants
Churches / Places of worship	Allowed
State parks / forests	Concealed allowed with permit, otherwise must be unloaded. *See,* NEV. ADMIN. CODE ch. 407 § 105 (2009)
Vehicle carry	Concealed handguns with permit allowed, otherwise must be in plain view; long guns must be unloaded
LE notification if stopped?	Not required
Retreat requirement for self-defense	Required
Preemption law	Yes; certain local governments can require registration
Open Carry	Allowed, no permit required
Military-pattern semi-auto restrictions	Not restricted
NFA weapons	NFA-friendly, compliance with federal law only

Reciprocity / Recognition

*Nevada **recognizes** permits from the following states:*

Alaska	Arkansas	Kansas	Louisiana
Michigan	Missouri	Nebraska	New Mexico
North Carolina	Ohio	Rhode Island	Tennessee
West Virginia			

*Nevada permits **are recognized by** the following states:*

Alaska	Arizona	Arkansas	Idaho
Indiana	Kansas	Kentucky	Louisiana
Michigan*	Minnesota	Missouri	Montana
Nebraska	Oklahoma	South Dakota	Tennessee
Texas	Utah	Vermont	

Note: In the reciprocity / recognition tables above, states with an asterisk (*) require the permit holder to both have a permit from, and be a resident of, the recognized state in order for reciprocity / recognition of the permit.

Knife Carry Summary:

Note: Blade length limits, if any, in parentheses.

Knife Type	Open Carry	Concealed Carry	Notes
Folding	Yes	Yes	
Fixed Blade	Yes	Yes	No concealed machetes
Dirks, Daggers, Stilettos	Yes	No	
Automatics	Yes (< 2")	Yes (< 2")	
Balisongs	Yes (< 2")	Yes (< 2")	See note[112]

42.1 Discussion

Firearms Carry:

Travelers to Nevada will find a fairly friendly legal environment for firearms carry, provided the traveler has a recognized permit. State law allows the open carry of firearms without a permit, although travelers should be aware that open carry is not common in the urban areas of the state, and will likely result in unwanted attention from law-enforcement.

Nevada issues concealed carry permits on a "shall issue" basis to both residents and nonresidents, and will recognize the carry permits of other states whose laws are similar to Nevada's. Unfortunately, Nevada currently recognizes only a relative handful of other states' permits. Thus, those travelers wishing to carry concealed who do not possess a currently recognized permit, will need to acquire a Nevada nonresident permit.

Travelers in vehicles may carry loaded handguns on their person so long as the handguns are carried openly and in plain view.

---

[112] The statutory definition of "switchblade" under state law includes any "knife having the appearance of a pocket knife, any blade of which is 2 or more inches long and which can be released automatically by a flick of a button, pressure on the handle or other mechanical device, or is released by any type of mechanism." See, NEV. REV. STAT. § 202.350 (2009). This definition will likely support a finding that a balisong is a statutory switchblade, and thus subject to the switchblade restrictions.

Handguns may also be transported in the vehicle's glove compartment or center console. Handguns cannot be concealed upon one's person without a recognized permit.

Long guns may be transported in vehicles if in an unloaded condition and in plain view. Note that the term "unloaded" under Nevada law is a term of art and simply requires that the chamber of the firearm be empty; a long gun's magazine may be loaded, only the firing chamber of the gun must be empty.

The state Legislature has preempted local governments from regulating the possession and transportation of firearms. The state has allowed those localities with ordinances in effect prior to June 13, 1989 and which require residents to register their firearms, to keep those ordinances in effect, provided they conform to certain specified conditions. These ordinances apply to residents of the state, and do not affect travelers.

Knife Carry:

Visitors to the Silver State will find a fairly knife-friendly legal environment. Ordinary folding pocket knives should pose no problem and may be carried openly or concealed. Fixed bladed knives may also be carried openly or concealed, although state law prohibits dirks, daggers, and machetes from being carried concealed. As such, large fixed bladed knives, such as bowies, should probably not be carried concealed, lest such knives fall under the "machete" prohibition. As in most states, visitors to urban areas will likely encounter increased law enforcement attention if openly carrying any large knife. In addition, visitors to the state's numerous casinos should be aware that those establishments may impose their own restrictions on knife carry on their property.

State law prohibits possession, and hence carry of any kind, of automatic knives with blades two inches or longer. Note that knives such as balisongs, while not specifically listed as prohibited, may fall under switchblade prohibition, as balisongs do in some states. In addition, the statutory definition of a switchblade is fairly broadly worded, and will likely support a finding that a balisong falls under the switchblade definition.

State law prohibits possession of belt-buckle knives, defined as "any knife which is made an integral part of a belt buckle[.]"[113] The statute

---

[113] *See*, NEV. REV. STAT. § 202.350 subsection 1(a) (2009).

also redundantly prohibits concealed carry of same.[114] (Obviously, if you can't legally possess an item, you can't legally carry it either.)

Nevada prohibits carry, whether open or concealed, of dirks, daggers, or switchblades, in or on schools or colleges. In addition, municipal governments may pass their own ordinances restricting or prohibiting knife carry.

42.2 Places Off-Limits While Carrying

Firearms Carry:

Nevada prohibits carrying concealed firearms on the premises of a public building, such as a terminal, that is located on the property of a public airport. *See*, NEV. REV. STAT. § 202.3673 (2009).

In addition, state law prohibits firearms carry in public buildings either equipped with metal detectors or signs prohibiting firearms at each entrance, with certain exceptions unlikely to apply to the typical traveler. *See, id.*

Carry of firearms and certain knives (see below) is also prohibited in private or public school property, childcare facilities, or the property of the Nevada System of Higher Education, unless the permit holder has obtained written permission from the relevant authorized individual at those locations. *See*, NEV. REV. STAT. §§ 202.265, 202.3673 (2009).

Knife Carry:

State law prohibits the carry of dirks, daggers, or switchblades on school property. *See*, NEV. REV. STAT. § 202.265 (2009). Note that municipalities may pass their own local ordinances further restricting or prohibiting carry. For example, Reno prohibits carry of weapons in municipal courthouses. *See*, RENO, NEV. MUNICIPAL CODE § 8.12.160 (2009).

---

[114] *See*, NEV. REV. STAT. § 202.350 subsection 1(d) (2009).

42.3 Selected City Ordinances

The state legislature has preempted municipalities and other political subdivisions from regulating firearms to any extent greater than state law. Thus, firearms regulation is uniform throughout the state.

The city ordinances below relate to knife carry:

Las Vegas – Loitering while carrying concealed dangerous or deadly weapon prohibited. The definition of dangerous or deadly weapon includes dirks, daggers, switchblades, straight razors, ice picks or similar stabbing instruments, any knife with a blade three inches or longer, or any "cutting, stabbing or bludgeoning weapon or device capable of inflicting grievous bodily harm[.]" *See*, LAS VEGAS, NEV., MUNICIPAL CODE § 10.70.020 (2010).

Reno – Possession of switchblade knife (of any blade length), or any knife with blade length two inches or greater while violating any park or recreational facility ordinance is separate misdemeanor. *See*, RENO, NEV., ADMINISTRATIVE CODE § 8.23.140 (2009). Ordinance defines blade length measured "from the tip of the knife which is customarily sharpened to the unsharpened extension of the blade which forms the hinge connecting the blade to the handle." *See, id.* Possession of weapons in Reno Municipal courthouse prohibited. *See, id.* at § 8.12.160.

42.4 State Resources

Nevada Department of Public Safety
555 Wright Way
Carson City, NV 89711-0900
Phone: (775) 684-4808
Fax: (775) 684-4809
Website: http://dps.nv.gov/

Attorney General of Nevada
Office of the Attorney General
100 North Carson St.
Carson City, NV 89701-4717
Phone: (775) 684-1100
Fax: (775) 684-1108
Website: http://ag.state.nv.us/

43 New Hampshire – The Granite State

Area: 8,968 sq.mi. (Rank: 44th)   Population: 1,315,809 (Rank: 41st)
Violent Crime Rate (per 100,000 residents): 157.2 (Rank: 3rd Safest)
State Motto: *Live Free or Die!*

Firearms Carry Summary:

Carry considerations	Status
Restaurants and bars	Allowed
Churches / Places of worship	Allowed
State parks / forests	Allowed
Vehicle carry	Loaded handguns allowed with permit, otherwise must be unloaded; long guns must be unloaded
LE notification if stopped?	Not required
Retreat requirement for self-defense	Required, except in home. *See,* N.H. REV. STAT. ANN. § 627:4 (2009)
Preemption law	Yes. *See,* N.H. REV. STAT. ANN. § 159:26 (2009)
Open Carry	Allowed, no permit required
Military-pattern semi-auto restrictions	Not restricted
NFA weapons	NFA-friendly, compliance with federal law only

Reciprocity / Recognition

*New Hampshire **recognizes** resident permits (only) from the following states (Note: Permit holder must have a permit from, and be a resident of, the recognized state):*

Alabama	Alaska	Arizona	Colorado
Florida	Georgia	Idaho	Indiana
Kentucky	Louisiana	Michigan	Missouri
Mississippi	North Carolina	North Dakota	Oklahoma
Pennsylvania	Tennessee	Utah	Wyoming

*New Hampshire permits **are recognized by** the following states:*

Alabama	Alaska	Arizona	Colorado*
Florida*	Georgia	Idaho	Indiana
Kentucky	Louisiana	Michigan*	Mississippi
Missouri	North Carolina	North Dakota	Oklahoma
Pennsylvania	South Dakota	Tennessee	Utah
Vermont	Wyoming		

Note: In the reciprocity / recognition tables above, states with an asterisk (*) require the permit holder to both have a permit from, and be a resident of, the recognized state in order for reciprocity / recognition of the permit.

Knife Carry Summary:

Note: Blade length limits, if any, in parentheses.

Knife Type	Open Carry	Concealed Carry	Notes
Folding	Yes	Yes	
Fixed Blade	Yes	Yes	
Dirks, Daggers, Stilettos	Yes	Yes	
Automatics	Yes	Yes	
Balisongs	Yes	Yes	

43.1 Discussion

Firearms Carry:

Nestled in the northeast corner of the country, New Hampshire prides itself on its dedication to personal liberties. New Hampshire patriots like Daniel Webster and Revolutionary War hero Gen. John Stark, whose message addressed to a reunion of his comrades of the war that gave us our Nation included the words "Live Free Or Die; Death Is Not The Worst of Evils." The state's motto, "Live Free or Die," reflects a fiercely independent and freedom-loving streak that persists to this day. This respect for personal freedoms is notably reflected in the state's liberal firearms laws, unusual for an Eastern state. Indeed, the state's liberal firearms laws stand in stark contrast to those of Massachusetts, its neighbor to the south.

Open carry of loaded firearms is legal throughout the state, and does not require a permit, unless in a vehicle. New Hampshire's strong preemption law prevents local governments from regulating any aspect of possession, transportation, or licensing related to firearms of firearms components.[115]

State law requires a recognized permit to carry a loaded handgun in a vehicle, or concealed on one's person. New Hampshire issues

---

[115] *See,* N.H. REV. STAT. ANN. § 159:26 (2009).

such permits to residents and nonresidents on a "shall issue" basis, and will recognize another state's permits, if that other state honors New Hampshire permits, and the permit holder is a resident of the recognized state. Thus, travelers with a permit from their home state will enjoy carry privileges in New Hampshire if their home state recognizes New Hampshire permits.

Travelers without a recognized permit must transport their handguns in an unloaded condition. Those unloaded handguns may be stored anywhere in the vehicle, including the vehicle glove compartment or center console.

Travelers in a vehicle must transport long guns in an unloaded condition. Such weapons should be securely encased in commercial and cases, and stowed in the trunk or cargo storage area of the vehicle.

Knife Carry:

With respect to knives, visitors will find a permissive legal environment for knife carry. The state legislature has recently passed a law removing the prohibition on the carry of dirks, dagger, stilettos, and switchblades, so such knives are now legal to carry in the Granite State.

Ordinary fixed and folding pocket knives should pose no problem, and may be carried openly or concealed, although carry of large fixed blades should be avoided in urban areas, as such carry will likely result in unwanted law enforcement attention. There is no statutorily defined blade length limit.

Apart from courthouses, no state-wide statutory prohibitions on off-limits locations for otherwise legal knife carry exist, although travelers should be aware that cities and towns may pass their own ordinances restricting knife carry. New Hampshire does not preempt its cities and towns from regulating knife carry, unlike the case for firearms, where the state has prohibited cities and towns from enacting their own firearms carry restrictions, ensuring uniform state-wide firearms laws. As such, towns and cities may enact ordinances regulating knife carry in such areas as school property within their jurisdictions.

43.2 Places Off-Limits While Carrying

Firearms Carry:

Unlike many other states that specify voluminous lists of off-limits locations for firearms carry, New Hampshire prohibits carry of firearms and other deadly weapons in few places, namely courthouses and court rooms and other areas used by courts. *See*, N.H. REV. STAT. ANN. § 159:19 (2009).

Visitors to the New Hampshire State House should be aware that a recent rule change by the legislative committee responsible for the statehouse physical plant prohibits firearms carry in the statehouse, with or without a permit. As this book goes to press, legislative efforts are underway to reverse this rule change.

Knife Carry:

New Hampshire prohibits the carry of firearms and other deadly weapons, the definition of which includes knives, in courthouses. *See*, N.H. REV. STAT. ANN. § 159:19 (2009).

43.3 Selected City Ordinances

The state legislature has preempted municipalities and other political subdivisions from regulating firearms to any extent greater than state law. Thus, firearms regulation is uniform throughout the state.

The city ordinances below relate to knife carry:

Manchester – Carry of "dangerous weapons" on school grounds prohibited. The definition of "dangerous weapons" specifically includes knives. MANCHESTER, N.H., CODE § 130.41 (1999).

43.4 State Resources

Department of Safety
New Hampshire State Police
33 Hazen Drive
Concord, NH 03305
Phone: (603) 271-3575
Fax: (603) 271-2527
Website: http://www.nh.gov/safety/divisions/nhsp/

Attorney General of New Hampshire
New Hampshire Department of Justice
33 Capitol Street
Concord, NH 03301
Phone: (603) 271-3658
Fax: (603) 271-2110
Website: http://doj.nh.gov/

44 New Jersey – The Garden State

Area: 7,417 sq.mi. (Rank: 46th)   Population: 8,682,661 (Rank: 11th)
Violent Crime Rate (per 100,000 residents): 326.5 (Rank: 22nd Safest)
State Motto: *Liberty and Prosperity*

Firearms Carry Summary:

Carry considerations	Status
Restaurants and bars	Allowed with NJ permit
Churches / Places of worship	Allowed with NJ permit
State parks / forests	Prohibited without NJ permit
Vehicle carry	Transport of firearms of any kind requires a NJ-issued permit
LE notification if stopped?	Not required
Retreat requirement for self-defense	Required, except in home. *See*, N.J. REV. STAT. § 2C:3-4 (2009).
Preemption law	No, municipalities explicitly allowed to regulate.
Open Carry	Prohibited
Military-pattern semi-auto restrictions	Highly restricted, "assault firearms" and normal-capacity (more than 15 rounds) magazines prohibited from entry into state
NFA weapons	Prohibited

Reciprocity / Recognition

New Jersey **does _not_ recognize** permits from any other state.

New Jersey permits **are recognized by** the following states:

Alaska	Arizona	Idaho	Indiana
Kansas	Kentucky	Michigan*	Missouri
Montana	Nebraska	Oklahoma	South Dakota
Tennessee	Texas	Utah	Vermont

Note: In the reciprocity / recognition tables above, states with an asterisk (*) require the permit holder to both have a permit from, and be a resident of, the recognized state in order for reciprocity / recognition of the permit.

Knife Carry Summary:

Note: Blade length limits, if any, in parentheses.

Knife Type	Open Carry	Concealed Carry	Notes
Folding	Yes	Yes	See note[116]
Fixed Blade	Yes	No	See note[117]
Dirks, Daggers, Stilettos	No	No	
Automatics	No	No	
Balisongs	No	No	

44.1 Discussion

Firearms Carry:

Travelers to the Garden State will find a decidedly hostile legal environment for firearms carry. New Jersey requires a permit to merely purchase or possess a firearm in the home. Carry, either openly or concealed, of a loaded handgun in public or while traveling in a vehicle is strictly prohibited without a New Jersey-issued carry permit. Such permits are issued on a highly discretionary basis to both residents and (theoretically) nonresidents. New Jersey does not recognize the permits of any other state.

As is the case with most restrictive "may issue" states, those who are famous, wealthy, or well-connected are likely in a better position to meet the subjective criteria to be issued a New Jersey handgun carry permit. Funny how that works.

Transport of firearms in a vehicle also requires the appropriate permit. Limited exceptions exist for persons traveling directly to a place for hunting, firearms exhibition, repair facility, or shooting range. The firearms must be transported in unloaded condition, securely cased in a commercial gun case, and stored in the locked trunk of a vehicle.[118] If the vehicle has no trunk, then the gun case must be locked and stored in the cargo area of the vehicle. Any ammunition should be stored separately in its own locked case.

---

[116] New Jersey law prohibits the carry of weapons to use unlawfully against another. *See*, N.J. STAT. § 2C:39-4(d) (2009). Travelers should avoid carry of "tactical" knives or knives with aggressive, weapon-like appearances.

[117] While the relevant statutes do not explicitly discuss concealment, travelers should be aware that concealment is often one of the factors considered in determining whether a knife is carried as a weapon for unlawful use against another (which is prohibited under state law). *See, e.g.*, N.J. STAT. §§ 2C:39-4(d), 2C:39-5(d) (2009).

[118] *See*, N.J. REV. STAT. § 2C:39-6(g) (2009)

Travelers without the appropriate New Jersey-issued permit(s) who are merely transiting the state, will need to rely on the federal McClure-Volkmer interstate transport provisions for safe passage through the state.

Note that New Jersey bans possession of "assault firearms", i.e., military pattern semiautomatic firearms, as well as magazines capable of holding more than fifteen rounds of ammunition. Naturally, possession of machine guns by "mere" citizens is also prohibited.

Travelers should be aware that state law limits possession of hollow point ammunition ("hollow nose" or "dum dum" ammo in the state's parlance). Residents may possess such ammunition in their homes or on their own land. Limited exceptions exist, including for those engaged in lawful hunting. Visitors to the state, however, should be aware that state law is decidedly biased against possession of such ammunition by non-law-enforcement personnel.

Travelers should also be aware that state law explicitly allows municipalities to regulate and/or prohibit firearms use in their separate jurisdictions. Thus, depending on their location in the state, visitors to New Jersey may face additional, or differing, firearms-related legal requirements.

Knife Carry:

As is the case with firearms, visitors to the Garden State will find a generally hostile legal environment for knife carry. The statutory definition of weapon encompasses virtually all knives, and state law requires that possession of any knife "under circumstances not manifestly appropriate for such lawful uses as it may have is" a crime.[119] Thus, the law-abiding traveler with even a folding pocket knife had better have a good, plausible reason for carrying that utility tool with a sharpened edge, and the proffered reason had better match the type of knife being carried. That all black, "tactical" knife with the large tanto point blade will be a hard sell as an all-around utility knife and apple peeler. Similarly, a fixed bladed hunting or fishing knife should be fine if you're actually out hunting or fishing, with the appropriate hunting or fishing licenses, but will likely get you in trouble if carried in the city.

---

[119] See, N.J. STAT. § 2C:39-5(d) (2009).

Dirks, daggers, stilettos and automatic knives (switchblades and gravity knives) are *per se* weapons under New Jersey law, and are, for all practical purposes, prohibited. Technically, possession may be possible with an "explainable lawful purpose,"[120] but should you rely on this caveat, you (or the lawyer you're paying for) will likely be doing your explaining to a jury. Good luck.

Given this generally hostile legal environment, travelers should also be wary of carrying balisongs, as these knives may fall under the switchblade prohibition, as balisongs do in some states. In addition, balisongs are often associated with, and perceived as being, martial arts weapons, and thus may be prohibited under one of more of the state's weapon statutes.

Finally, New Jersey prohibits the carry of weapons on school, college, or other educational institution property.

44.2 Places Off-Limits While Carrying

Firearms Carry:

New Jersey prohibits the carry of firearms, regardless of whether you have a New Jersey issued carry permit, on the buildings or grounds of schools, colleges, universities, or other educational institutions, without written authorization from the governing officer of the respective institution. *See*, N.J. REV. STAT. § 2C:39-5(e) (2009).

Knife Carry:

New Jersey state law prohibits the carry of weapons, the definition of which likely includes virtually all knives, on school, college or other educational institution grounds. *See*, N.J. STAT. § 2C:39-5 (2009).

44.3 Selected City Ordinances

The state legislature has preempted municipalities and other political subdivisions from regulating firearms to any extent greater than state law. Thus, firearms regulation is uniform throughout the state.

---

[120] *See, id.* at § 2C:39-3.

The city ordinances below relate to knife carry:

Hamilton – Possession of any weapon "potentially harmful to wildlife and dangerous to human safety" prohibited in public parks or recreation areas. *See*, HAMILTON TOWNSHIP, N.J., CODE OF ORDINANCES § 98-1 (2005).

Randolph – Carry of weapons in public parks or recreation areas prohibited. *See*, RANDOLPH TOWNSHIP, N.J., REV. ORDINANCES § 34-34 (2009).

44.4 State Resources

New Jersey State Police
P O Box 7068
West Trenton, NJ 08628
Phone: (609) 882-2000
Fax: (609) 292-3508
Website: http://www.njsp.org/index.html

Attorney General of New Jersey
Department of Law & Public Safety
Hughes Justice Complex
Trenton, NJ 08625-0080
Phone: (609) 292-4925
Fax: (609) 292-3508
Website: http://www.state.nj.us/lps/

45 New Mexico – Land of Enchantment

Area: 121,356 sq.mi. (Rank: 5th)   Population: 1,984,356 (Rank: 36th)
Violent Crime Rate (per 100,000 residents): 649.9 (Rank: 43rd Safest)
State Motto: *Crescit Eundo (It Grows as It Goes)*

Firearms Carry Summary:

Carry considerations	Status
Restaurants and bars	Prohibited, even with permit until July 1, 2010; new law effective July 1, 2010 allows concealed carry with recognized permit in restaurants that serve beer and wine only, but cannot consume alcohol
Churches / Places of worship	Allowed
State parks / forests	Chamber unloaded carry allowed
Vehicle carry	Open or concealed carry allowed
LE notification if stopped?	Not required
Retreat requirement for self-defense	Required
Preemption law	Yes. *See*, N.M. Const. Art. 2 § 6
Open Carry	Allowed
Military-pattern semi-auto restrictions	Not restricted
NFA weapons	NFA-friendly, compliance with federal law only

Reciprocity / Recognition

New Mexico recognizes permits from the following states:

Alaska	Arizona	Colorado	Delaware
Florida	Kentucky	Michigan	Minnesota
Missouri	Montana	North Carolina	North Dakota
Ohio	Oklahoma	South Carolina	Tennessee
Texas	Virginia	Wyoming	

New Mexico permits are recognized by the following states:

Alaska	Arizona	Colorado*	Florida*
Idaho	Indiana	Kansas	Kentucky
Michigan*	Minnesota	Missouri	Montana
Nebraska	Nevada	Oklahoma	South Dakota
Tennessee	Texas	Utah	Vermont
Virginia	Wyoming		

Note: In the reciprocity / recognition tables above, states with an asterisk (*) require the permit holder to both have a permit from, and be a resident of, the recognized state in order for reciprocity / recognition of the permit.

Knife Carry Summary:

Note: Blade length limits, if any, in parentheses.

Knife Type	Open Carry	Concealed Carry	Notes
Folding	Yes	Yes	
Fixed Blade	Yes	Yes	See note[121]
Dirks, Daggers, Stilettos	No	No	
Automatics	No	No	
Balisongs	No	No	See note[122]
Sword Canes	No	No	

45.1 Discussion

Firearms Carry:

Travelers to New Mexico will find a generally friendly legal environment for firearms carry. New Mexico requires a recognized permit to carry a concealed, loaded handgun on one's person. Such permits are issued on a "shall issue" basis to qualified residents twenty-one years or older. New Mexico does not issue carry permits to nonresidents, but does currently recognize the carry permits of twenty other states.

Open carry of firearms is legal without a permit and increasingly common, particularly in the more rural areas of the state. Such carry is legal most places in the state, except locations such as schools, universities, and the like.

---

[121] State law prohibits carry of certain *per se* deadly weapons in public, including such large fix bladed knives as bowie knives, butcher knives, and sword canes. *See,* N.M. Stat. § 30-7-2 (2009). Law-abiding travelers should exercise caution when carrying any large fix blade, lest they run afoul of the cited statute (or a judge or jury's interpretation thereof).

[122] The New Mexico Court of Appeals has ruled that butterfly knives (balisongs) are switchblades under the law, and thus fall under the state's switchblade prohibition. *See,* State v. Riddall, 811 P.2d 576, 582 (N.M. Ct. App. 1991).

New Mexico law treats a person's vehicle as an extension of his or her home, and as such no permit is needed to carry a loaded firearm either openly or concealed in one's vehicle for personal protection. The loaded firearm may be carried on one's person, stored in the glove compartment or center console, or pretty much anywhere else in the vehicle.

New Mexico's strong preemption law is embedded directly in its state constitution, and prohibits municipalities and counties from regulating "in any way, an incident of the right to keep and bear arms."[123]

Knife Carry:

Visitors to New Mexico will find a legal environment that is fairly, and somewhat surprisingly, restrictive of knife carry. This is somewhat surprising, given the large, lightly populated rural nature of this beautiful Western state.

With respect to knives, ordinary folding pocket knives should pose no problem, and may be carried openly or concealed. There is no statutorily defined blade length limit. Dirks, daggers, stilettos, and automatic knives (switchblades), however, are prohibited. The state's courts have held that balisongs (butterfly knives) are statutory switchblades, and thus fall under the switchblade prohibition. Thus, balisongs are prohibited.

In addition, while fixed blades may be carried openly or concealed, state law prohibits carry of certain *per se* deadly weapons in public, including such large fix-bladed knives as bowie knives, butcher knives, and sword canes. Thus travelers should exercise care when carrying knives that may fall under a prohibited category.

State law prohibits carry of deadly weapons on school premises. In addition, local court rules in some judicial districts prohibit knife carry in courts and courthouses.

45.2 Places Off-Limits While Carrying

Firearms Carry:

New Mexico prohibits the carry of firearms, whether openly or concealed, and whether loaded or unloaded, in establishments that sell alcoholic beverages for on-premises consumption. Violation of

---

[123] *See*, N. M. CONST. Art. 2 § 6.

this prohibition is a felony. *See*, N.M. STAT. § 30-7-3 (2009). [**Note:**
On July 1, 2010 a new law takes effect – see below] A person who
possesses a recognized carry permit may carry a concealed
handgun into an establishment such as a liquor store that sells
alcoholic beverages that are <u>not</u> for consumption on the premises.
See, id.

Note: On July 1, 2010, carry of concealed handguns by holders of
recognized carry permits in restaurants that are licensed to serve
beer and wine only for on-premises consumption becomes legal.
Restaurants may prohibit such carry, however, by conspicuously
posting a notice to that effect, or by verbal notification. *See*, N.M.
STAT. § 30-7-3 (2010) (effective July 1, 2010). Note that you may not
consume alcohol while carrying.

State law prohibits carry of firearms and other deadly weapons on
school premises, school buses, and other public property, including
parking areas, being used for school-sanctioned activities. Violation
of this prohibition is a felony. Various exceptions exist for school
sanctioned activities involving firearms, as well as an exception for
possession of such weapons in a private vehicle by a person over
nineteen years of age. *See*, N.M. STAT. § 30-7-2.1. Carry of
concealed firearms is also prohibited in preschools. *See*, N.M. STAT.
§ 29-19-8.

State law prohibits firearms carry on university premises, the
definition of which includes community colleges and technical-
vocational schools, and other public property, including parking
areas, being used for university-sanctioned activities. Violation of
this prohibition is a petty misdemeanor, and universities are required
to conspicuously post notices that state it is unlawful to carry a
firearm on university premises. As is the case for schools, various
exceptions exist for university sanctioned activities involving firearms,
as well as an exception for possession of such weapons in a private
vehicle by a person over nineteen years of age. *See*, N.M. STAT. §
30-7-2.4.

New Mexico also prohibits the carrying of firearms in a courthouse or
court facility, regardless of whether the carrier possesses a
recognized permit or not, without the permission of the presiding
judicial officer. *See*, N.M. STAT. § 29-19-11.

State law prohibits the carrying of firearms and other deadly weapons
on board buses if the weapons are readily accessible. *See*, N.M.
STAT. § 30-7-13.

Travelers should be aware that state law specifically provides that concealed carry permits are not valid on tribal lands, unless authorized by the governing body of the tribe or Indian nation. *See,* N.M. STAT. § 29-19-10.

Knife Carry:

New Mexico prohibits the carry of firearms and other deadly weapons in schools and on school grounds, or at school-sanctioned events, with certain limited exceptions for, e.g., firearms-related programs. State law also prohibits the readily accessible possession of firearms and other deadly weapons on buses.

Note that local court rules for various courts may also prohibit carry of deadly weapons, including knives, into courts or courthouses in those judicial districts. *See, e.g.,* DIST. CT. (2D JUDICIAL DIST.), LOCAL R. 2-108.

45.3 Selected City Ordinances

The state legislature has preempted municipalities and other political subdivisions from regulating firearms to any extent greater than state law. Thus, firearms regulation is uniform throughout the state.

The city ordinances below relate to knife carry:

No relevant ordinances imposing additional restrictions *beyond* that embodied in state law. A number of municipalities have enacted local ordinances that mimic state law with respect to knife and deadly weapon offenses. *See, e.g.,* ALAMOGORDO, N.M., CODE OF ORDINANCES § 11-05-350 (2005) (Unlawful carrying of deadly weapon); CARLSBAD, N.M., CODE OF ORDINANCES § 32-2 (2000) (List of petty misdemeanors includes unlawful carry of deadly weapon); FARMINGTON, N.M., CITY CODE § 18-5-43 (2006) (Switchblades prohibited).

45.4 State Resources

New Mexico Department of Public Safety
P.O. Box 1628
Santa Fe, NM 87504-1628
Phone: (505) 841-8053
Website: http://www.dps.nm.org/

Attorney General of New Mexico
407 Galisteo Street
Santa Fe, NM 87501
Phone: (505) 827-6000
Fax: (505) 827-5826
Website: http://www.nmag.gov/

46 New York – The Empire State

Area: 47,214 sq.mi. (Rank: 30th)   Population: 19,490,297 (Rank: 3rd)
Violent Crime Rate (per 100,000 residents): 398.1 (Rank: 27th Safest)
State Motto: *Excelsior (Ever Upwards)*

Firearms Carry Summary:

Carry considerations	Status
Restaurants and bars	Allowed with permit
Churches / Places of worship	Allowed with permit
State parks / forests	Generally prohibited; limited exceptions for lawful hunting
Vehicle carry	Handgun possession or transport requires NY permit; long guns must be unloaded and securely cased
LE notification if stopped?	Not required
Retreat requirement for self-defense	Required, except in home. *See*, N.Y. PENAL LAW § 35.15 (2009)
Preemption law	Limited preemption; New York City heavily regulates ownership and possession. *See*, N.Y. PENAL LAW § 400 subd. 6 (2009)
Open Carry	Prohibited
Military-pattern semi-auto restrictions	Restricted to pre-Sept. 1994 "assault weapons"
NFA weapons	Prohibited

Reciprocity / Recognition

New York **does _not_ recognize** permits from any other state.

New York permits **are recognized by** the following states:

Alaska	Arizona	Idaho	Indiana
Kentucky	Michigan*	Missouri	Montana
Oklahoma	South Dakota	Tennessee	Texas
Utah	Vermont		

Note: In the reciprocity / recognition tables above, states with an asterisk (*) require the permit holder to both have a permit from, and be a resident of, the recognized state in order for reciprocity / recognition of the permit.

Knife Carry Summary:

Note: Blade length limits, if any, in parentheses.

New York (excluding New York City)

Knife Type	Open Carry	Concealed Carry	Notes
Folding	Yes	Yes	See note[124]
Fixed Blade	Yes	Yes	See note[124]
Dirks, Daggers, Stilettos	No	No	See note[124]
Automatics	No	No	
Balisongs	Yes	Yes	See notes[124, 125]
Sword Canes	No	No	

New York City

Knife Type	Open Carry	Concealed Carry	Notes
Folding	No	Yes (< 4")	See note[124]
Fixed Blade	No	Yes (< 4")	See note[124]
Dirks, Daggers, Stilettos	No	No	
Automatics	No	No	
Balisongs	No	Yes (< 4")	See notes[124, 125]
Sword Canes	No	No	

---

[124] State law prohibits carry of weapons with intent to use unlawfully against another, and creates a legal presumption that a dangerous knife is being carried for unlawful use against another. *See*, N.Y. PENAL LAW § 265.01 (2009). Whether a knife is a "dangerous knife" under the statute depends on several factors, including whether the knife is designed or adapted as a weapon, or whether the circumstances surrounding the possession of the knife evince an intention to use the same unlawfully against another. *See*, In the Matter of Jamie D., 466 N.Y.S.2d 286 (N.Y. 1983). Cautious travelers should avoid carry of any knife with overly aggressive or weapon-like appearance.

[125] While a few cases have addressed the issue of whether a balisong, or butterfly knife, is a gravity knife under the state's gravity knife statute and have held that a butterfly knife is not a gravity knife under the statute, the state's highest court has, to date, not taken a position on the issue. *See*, e.g., People v. Zuniga, 303 A.D.2d 773; 759 N.Y.S.2d 86 (N.Y. App. Div. 2003) (holding butterfly knife not gravity knife and dismissing indictment); People v. Dolson, 142 Misc.2d 779, 538 N.Y.S.2d 393 (N.Y. Co. Ct., 1989) (holding butterfly knife not gravity knife under statute and reversing conviction). As a result, cautious travelers should avoid carry of balisongs at this time, especially in NYC, given the aggressive enforcement and prosecution environment. Don't be a test case!

46.1 Discussion

Firearms Carry:

Travelers to the Empire State will find a generally hostile legal environment for firearms carry or transport. New York requires a permit to possess or carry handguns. Such permits are issued on a discretionary "may issue" basis to residents, and the issuing authority may place whatever restrictions on the permit's scope as it sees fit. New York does not recognize the permits of any other state.

As is the case with other discretionary issue states, wide variation exists in permit issuance probabilities and criteria. Some areas of the state reportedly are quite fair and reasonable in their permit issuance criteria, while others, particularly those in the metropolitan counties near New York City, are much less likely to issue permits to ordinary, law-abiding residents. And New York City is its own little anti-gun kingdom within the state, issuing extremely few carry permits relative to its 8 million inhabitants. As always, those who are famous, wealthy, or well-connected politically, will likely enjoy a decided advantage over those not so fortuitously endowed when it comes to being able to secure a carry permit.

The state will also issue permits on a discretionary basis to nonresidents that work in the state whose employment requires them to be able to carry a handgun, such as armored car personnel, bank security guards, and the like.

New York prohibits open carry of handguns, with or without a New York-issued permit.

Travelers may transport non-military pattern rifles and shotguns into the state without a permit, provided that the firearms are unloaded and securely cased in commercial gun cases. New York has its own "assault weapons" ban similar in scope to the now-expired federal ban, which prohibits possession of any semiautomatic, cosmetically impaired firearm of military pattern, as well as magazines capable of holding more than ten rounds of ammunition, not lawfully possessed or manufactured before September 13, 1994. Naturally, possession or private ownership of actual machine guns is also prohibited.

Travelers with handguns wishing to transit the state will need to rely on the McClure-Volkmer provisions of federal law governing interstate transportation of firearms. They must be on a continuous, uninterrupted journey through the state, their firearms must be

214 | THE TRAVELER'S GUN & KNIFE LAW BOOK

unloaded, securely cased, and stowed in the locked trunk of the vehicle, or if the vehicle has no trunk, then the gun case must be locked. Any ammunition should be transported in a separate, locked case. In addition, the traveler must be able to legally possess the firearms and ammunition being transported at both the origin and destination of the journey.

Visitors to New York City should realize that possession of any firearm is strictly prohibited without a New York City-issued license. Handgun licenses issued by other New York cities and counties are not valid in New York City, unless they contain a special endorsement granting validity issued by the New York City police Commissioner.

Those traveling by air should also be aware of reports of a number of arrests or threatened arrests of nonresidents without the appropriate New York-issued permits, and in at least one case of confiscation of the traveler's firearms, when those nonresidents attempted to check their unloaded and cased firearms at New York City area airports, despite apparently complying with the mandates of the federal interstate transport provisions. *Caveat viator* – Let the traveler beware.

Knife Carry:

Visitors to the Empire State will find important differences in the legal climate for knife carry, depending on whether their travels take them to New York City or to locations outside the Big Apple.

In New York City, open carry of any knife is prohibited, and thus travelers to NYC should ensure that any knife they carry, including folding pocket knives, are completely concealed from ordinary observation, including the pocket clip. In addition, carry of any knife with a blade four inches or longer is prohibited. The city has also enacted a prohibition on the possession of box cutters in public by anyone under the age of twenty-one, and on school premises by anyone under the age of twenty-two, with certain limited exceptions. The N.Y.C. Administrative Code defines box cutters as any "knife consisting of a razor blade, retractable, non-retractable, or detachable in segments, attached to or contained within a plastic or metal housing, including utility knives, snap-off knives, and box cart cutters."[126] Travelers should note that, as is the case in every other state, the city's more restrictive knife carry ordinances simply

---

[126] *See*, N.Y.C. ADMIN. CODE § 10-134.1 (2005).

supplement, rather than supercede, state law. Thus, for example, the switchblade prohibition under state law also applies in New York City, despite the fact that the city does not have its own separate switchblade prohibition.

Travelers should further be aware that NYC has reportedly been very aggressive in its interpretation and enforcement of the state's gravity knife statute, which defines a "gravity knife" as any knife with a locking blade released from the handle by gravity or the application of centrifugal force.[127]   Thus, knives that can be "flipped open" by holding the handle *or the blade* with a flick of the wrist, technically could be held to be a "gravity knife" under the statute. This insidious interpretation of the statute encompasses virtually all folding pocket knives without closed-position locks. While the typical knife collector or average pocket knife user would hardly consider the ordinary folding pocket knife with a locking blade to be a gravity knife, as that term is generally understood, such is the risk one runs in New York City.

Note that a number of other states and jurisdictions have similar gravity knife prohibitions, yet few prosecutions appear to exist in those other states for carry of ordinary pocket knives with locking blades under the gravity knife statutes of those other states. If you carry a folding pocket knife in NYC, be careful!

Outside of New York City, and under New York state law, no statutorily defined blade length limit exists. Ordinary folding pocket knives may be carried openly or concealed. Similarly, ordinary fix bladed knives may be carried openly or concealed. In any event, regardless of the type of knife, the knife must not be carried with intent to use unlawfully against another. Furthermore, under state law, carry of "any dagger, dirk, stiletto, dangerous knife or any other weapon, instrument, …, made or adapted for use primarily as a weapon, is presumptive evidence of intent to use the same unlawfully against another."[128] That is, the law *presumes* that knives such as daggers, dirks and stilettos are carried as weapons for unlawful use. Carry of other "dangerous kni[ves]," such as hunting knives, not primarily designed or specially adapted as weapons, may still violate state law if the circumstances surrounding such carry leads a fact-finder, such as a jury, to conclude that the knife was being carried as a weapon for unlawful use.[129]

---

[127] *See*, N.Y. PENAL LAW § 265.00 subdiv.5 (2009).

[128] *See*, N.Y. PENAL LAW § 265.15 subdiv.4 (2009).

[129] *See,* In the Matter of Jamie D., 466 N.Y.S.2d 286 (N.Y. 1983). In this case, the Court of Appeals of New York, the state's highest court, ruled that "the circumstances of its possession, although there has been no modification of the implement, may

With regard to balisongs, or butterfly knives, while a few cases have addressed the issue of whether such knives are gravity knives under the state's gravity knife statute and have held that butterfly knives are not statutory gravity knives, travelers should be aware that the state's highest court has, to date, *not* taken a position on the issue. As a result, cautious travelers should avoid carry of balisongs at this time, especially given the public, and possibly judicial, perception of balisongs as martial arts weapons.

46.2 Places Off-Limits While Carrying

Firearms Carry:

New York prohibits carry of firearms in schools, colleges and universities, and school buses unless written authorization has been obtained from the educational institution. *See,* N.Y. PENAL LAW § 265.01 (2009). In addition, state agencies may prohibit possession or carry of firearms in buildings, facilities or public lands under their control. For example, visitors should be aware that the New York Department of Environmental Conservation generally prohibits firearms possession on the public lands under their control, with limited exceptions for lawful hunting.

Knife Carry:

New York City prohibits carry of box cutters in public places by anyone under twenty-one years of age, and in schools by anyone under the age of twenty-two. Certain limited exceptions and affirmative defenses exist. *See,* N.Y.C. ADMIN. CODE § 10-134.1 (2005).

46.3 Selected City Ordinances

No knife law preemption, limited firearms licensing law preemption only. *See,* N.Y. PENAL LAW § 400.00(6) (2009).

The city ordinances below relate to knife carry:

New York City – Unlawful to carry knife with blade four inches or longer. *See,* N.Y.C. ADMIN. CODE § 10-133 (2009). Open carry of

permit a finding that on the occasion of its possession it was essentially a weapon rather than a utensil." *Id.* at 288.

knives prohibited. *See, id.* Carry of box cutters on school premises by person under twenty-two years of age prohibited; carry of box cutters in public place by person under twenty-one years of age prohibited (certain limited exceptions and affirmative defenses apply). *See, id.* at § 10-134.1.

46.4 State Resources

New York State Police
Public Information Office
1220 Washington Avenue
Albany, NY 12226
Phone: (518) 457-2180
Website: http://www.troopers.state.ny.us/

Attorney General of New York
The Capitol
Albany, NY 12224-0341
Phone: (800) 771-7755
Phone: (518) 474-7330
Website: http://www.oag.state.ny.us/home.html

47 North Carolina – The Tar Heel State

Area: 48,711 sq.mi. (Rank: 29th)   Population: 9,222,414 (Rank: 10th)
Violent Crime Rate (per 100,000 residents): 467.3 (Rank: 33rd Safest)
State Motto: *Esse Quam Videri (To Be, Rather Than to Seem)*

Firearms Carry Summary:

Carry considerations	Status
Restaurants and bars	Prohibited
Churches / Places of worship	Allowed, except at funerals. *See,* N.C. GEN. STAT. § 14-277.2 (2009)
State parks / forests	Prohibited. *See,* N.C. ADMIN. CODE tit. 15A, r. 12b.0901 (2010)
Vehicle carry	Loaded firearms allowed if in plain view
LE notification if stopped?	Required
Retreat requirement for self-defense	Required, except in home. *See,* N.C. GEN. STAT. § 14-51.1 (2009)
Preemption law	Yes, but localities can prohibit in public buildings and grounds, public parks and recreation areas. *See,* N.C. GEN. STAT. § 14-409.40 (2009)
Open Carry	Allowed without permit
Military-pattern semi-auto restrictions	Not restricted
NFA weapons	Local permit required in addition to compliance with federal law

Reciprocity / Recognition

*North Carolina **recognizes** permits from the following states:*

Alabama	Alaska	Arizona	Arkansas
Colorado	Delaware	Florida	Georgia
Idaho	Indiana	Kansas	Kentucky
Louisiana	Michigan	Mississippi	Missouri
Montana	Nebraska	North Dakota	New Hampshire*
Ohio	Oklahoma	Pennsylvania	South Carolina
South Dakota	Tennessee	Texas	Utah
Virginia	Washington	West Virginia	Wyoming

Note: North Carolina recognizes New Hampshire resident permits only.

*North Carolina permits **are recognized by** the following states:*

Alabama	Alaska	Arizona	Arkansas
Colorado*	Delaware	Florida*	Georgia
Idaho	Indiana	Kansas	Kentucky

Louisiana	Michigan*	Mississippi	Missouri
Montana	North Dakota	Nebraska	Nevada
New Hampshire*	New Mexico	Ohio	Oklahoma
Pennsylvania	South Carolina*	South Dakota	Tennessee
Texas	Utah	Vermont	Virginia
Washington	West Virginia	Wyoming	

Note: In the reciprocity / recognition tables above, states with an asterisk (*) require the permit holder to both have a permit from, and be a resident of, the recognized state in order for reciprocity / recognition of the permit.

Knife Carry Summary:

Note: Blade length limits, if any, in parentheses.

Knife Type	Open Carry	Concealed Carry	Notes
Folding	Yes	Yes	
Fixed Blade	Yes	No	
Dirks, Daggers, Stilettos	Yes	No	
Automatics	Yes	No	
Balisongs	Yes	No	

47.1 Discussion

Firearms Carry:

Travelers to the Tar Heel State will find a generally friendly legal environment for firearms carry. Carry of concealed handguns in public or in a vehicle requires a recognized permit. North Carolina issues such permits to qualified residents on a "shall issue" basis, and currently recognizes the carry permits of over thirty other states.

Open carry in the Tar Heel State is legal without a permit, although visitors should be aware that municipalities may regulate "the display of firearms on the streets, sidewalks, alleys, or other public property[.]"[130]

Travelers in vehicles without recognized permits may carry loaded firearms, provided that the guns are in plain view and clearly visible. Loaded handguns may not be concealed on one's person without a

---

[130] *See*, N.C. GEN. STAT. §§ 160A-189 (cities); 153A-129 (counties).

recognized permit. Loaded long guns should be in gun racks or otherwise visible from outside the vehicle. Otherwise they should be transported in an unloaded condition, securely cased and stowed in the trunk or the vehicle's cargo area.

Note that North Carolina law requires that a person carrying a concealed weapon with a recognized permit must, if stopped by a law enforcement officer, inform the officer that the person holds a valid permit and is carrying a concealed handgun. The person must display both the permit and proper identification upon request of the officer.[131]

North Carolina's preemption law prohibits local governments from regulating the possession, ownership, storage, transfer, sale, purchase, licensing, or registration of firearms. Local governments may, however, prohibit the possession of firearms in public-owned buildings and associated grounds and parking areas (but cannot prohibit the storage of firearms within a motor vehicle on those grounds or areas), and in public parks and recreation areas. As noted above, municipalities may also regulate the open display of firearms in public within their jurisdictions.

Knife Carry:

Visitors to the Tar Heel State will find a fairly friendly legal environment for knife carry. State law prohibits concealed carry of any knife other than an ordinary pocket knife, but otherwise permits open carry of a wide variety of other knives. Ballistic knives, however, are strictly prohibited, and may not be possessed even by law enforcement. There is no statutorily defined blade length limit under state law, although municipalities may impose their own restrictions in this regard, as well as the types of knives that may be carried. For example, some municipalities prohibit possession of automatic knives (switchblades), which are otherwise legal under state law. Other municipalities have enacted blade length limit restrictions, and placed restrictions on carry in public city government buildings.

Under state law, knives may not be carried on educational institution property, with certain limited exceptions not generally applicable to visitors to the state. In addition, state law prohibits carry of deadly weapons on state government property or in courthouses. Finally, state law prohibits possession of deadly weapons by anyone

---

[131] *See*, N.C. GEN. STAT. § 14-415.11(a) (2009).

participating in, affiliated with, or present as a spectator at parades, funeral processions, picket lines, or demonstrations at private health care facilities or public places under the control of the state or any municipality.

47.2 Places Off-Limits While Carrying

Firearms Carry:

North Carolina prohibits carrying firearms, whether openly or concealed, on school property, including school buildings and school buses, school campuses, grounds, recreational areas and athletic fields. *See*, N.C. GEN. STAT. § 269.2 (2009).

Firearms carry is also prohibited at events or assemblies that charge admission, such as concerts, and at establishments where alcoholic beverages are served. 269.3

State law also forbids carry of firearms in or on the grounds of the State Capitol Building, Executive Mansion, Western Residence of the Governor, or in any building housing any court of the General Court of Justice. *See*, N.C. GEN. STAT. § 269.4 (2009).

North Carolina prohibits carry of dangerous weapons at parades, funeral processions, picket lines, demonstrations at private health care facilities, or demonstrations at public places owned or under the control of the state or any of its political subdivisions. Rifles or guns carried in pickup truck racks at holiday parades or funeral processions are presumed to not violate this prohibition. *See*, N.C. GEN. STAT. § 277.2 (2009).

State law prohibits carry of concealed handguns in law enforcement or correctional facilities, buildings housing only state or federal offices, or offices of the state or federal government located in buildings not exclusively occupied by same. Financial institutions and any other premises conspicuously posted to prohibit concealed handguns are also included in this prohibition. *See*, N.C. GEN. STAT. § 415.11(c) (2009). State owned highway rest areas and rest stops are not included in the prohibition. *See, id.*

North Carolina prohibits consumption of alcohol while carrying a concealed handgun. *See, id.*

The state's administrative code prohibits carry in parks. *See*, N.C. ADMIN. CODE tit. 15A r. 12b.0901 (2010).

Knife Carry:

North Carolina prohibits the carry, whether openly or concealed, of bowie knives, dirks, daggers, switchblades, razors and razor blades, or "any sharp-pointed or edged instrument" in schools or on school property. *See,* N.C. GEN. STAT. § 14-269.2(d) (2009). Certain limited exceptions do exist for instructional supplies and use, food preparation, and maintenance. *See, id.* State law also prohibits any form of carry of deadly weapons in state government buildings, and in courthouses. *See,* N.C. GEN. STAT. § 14-269.4 (2009).

State law prohibits possession of deadly weapons by anyone participating in, affiliated with, or present as a spectator at parades, funeral processions, picket lines, or demonstrations at private health care facilities or public places under the control of the state or any municipality. *See,* N.C. GEN. STAT. § 14-277.2 (2009).

Note that municipalities may pass their own local ordinances prohibiting or otherwise restricting knife carry within their jurisdictions.

47.3 Selected City Ordinances

The state legislature has preempted municipalities and other political subdivisions from regulating firearms to any extent greater than state law. Thus, firearms regulation is uniform throughout the state.

The city ordinances below relate to knife carry:

Cary – Carry, whether openly or concealed, of any knife with blade three inches or greater prohibited in city parks. Exception exists for use in public exhibitions and with permit from director of parks and recreation. *See,* CARY, N.C., CODE OF ORDINANCES § 24-10 (2006).

Charlotte – Possession or carry of any kind of knife with blade greater than three and a half inches on city property prohibited. Exception exists for knives used solely for food preparation, instruction, or maintenance, and for razors and razor blades used solely for personal shaving. *See,* CHARLOTTE, N.C., CODE OF ORDINANCES § 15-14 (2009)

Durham – Possession of dangerous weapons on or in city government property, including parks and recreation facilities, prohibited. The definition of dangerous weapon includes bowie knives, dirks, daggers, razors, and switchblades. *See*, DURHAM, N.C., CODE OF ORDINANCES § 46-22 (2009). An exception exists for possession of a concealed handgun by a person holding a valid carry permit. *See, id.* Possession of firearms or dangerous weapons on any public street temporarily closed for street fair, concert, art display, bike race or similar event. An exception exists for possession of a concealed handgun by a person holding a valid carry permit. *See, id.* at § 46-24. Possession of firearm of other dangerous weapon on public mass transportation vehicle prohibited, with exception for possession of a concealed handgun by a person holding a valid carry permit. *See, id.* at § 46-25.

Winston-Salem – Possession of switchblades prohibited. *See*, WINSTON-SALEM, N.C., CODE OF ORDINANCES § 38-12 (2009).

47.4 State Resources

North Carolina State Highway Patrol
512 N. Salisbury Street
Raleigh, NC 27699-4702
Phone: (919) 733-7952
Website: http://www.nccrimecontrol.org/

Office of the Attorney General
North Carolina Department of Justice
9001 Mail Service Center
Raleigh, NC 27699-9001
Phone: (919) 716-6400
Fax: (919) 716-6750
Website: http://www.ncdoj.com/

48 North Dakota – The Peace Garden State

Area: 68,976 sq.mi. (Rank: 17th)   Population: 641,481 (Rank: 48th)
Violent Crime Rate (per 100,000 residents): 166.5 (Rank: 4th Safest)
State Motto: *Liberty and Union, Now and Forever, One and Inseparable*

Firearms Carry Summary:

Carry considerations	Status
Restaurants and bars	Prohibited
Churches / Places of worship	Prohibited
State parks / forests	Concealed with permit allowed
Vehicle carry	Loaded firearm carry allowed with permit; otherwise, must be unloaded and in plain view or securely cased.
LE notification if stopped?	Not required
Retreat requirement for self-defense	Required, except in home. *See,* N.D. CENT. CODE § 12.1-05-07 (2009)
Preemption law	Limited preemption. *See,* N.D. CENT. CODE § 62.1-01-03 (2009)
Open Carry	Loaded open carry generally prohibited; *unloaded* open carry allowed during daylight hours; other exceptions for hunting, target shooting. *See,* N.D. CENT. CODE § 62.1-03-01 (2009)
Military-pattern semi-auto restrictions	Not restricted
NFA weapons	NFA-friendly, compliance with federal law only

Reciprocity / Recognition

*North Dakota **recognizes** permits from the following states:*

Alabama	Alaska	Arizona	Arkansas
Colorado	Delaware	Florida	Georgia
Idaho	Indiana	Kentucky	Louisiana
Michigan	Missouri	Montana	Nebraska
New Hampshire	New Mexico	North Carolina	Oklahoma
Pennsylvania	South Dakota	Tennessee	Texas
Utah	Vermont	Virginia	West Virginia
Wyoming			

North Dakota permits **are recognized by** *the following states:*

Alabama	Alaska	Arizona	Arkansas
Colorado*	Delaware	Florida*	Georgia
Idaho	Indiana	Kentucky	Louisiana
Michigan*	Missouri	Montana	North Carolina
Nebraska	New Hampshire*	New Mexico	Oklahoma
Pennsylvania	South Dakota	Tennessee	Texas
Utah	Vermont	Virginia	West Virginia
Wyoming			

Note: In the reciprocity / recognition tables above, states with an asterisk (*) require the permit holder to both have a permit from, and be a resident of, the recognized state in order for reciprocity / recognition of the permit.

Knife Carry Summary:

Note: Blade length limits, if any, in parentheses.

Knife Type	Open Carry	Concealed Carry	Notes
Folding	Yes	Yes (< 5")	See note[132]
Fixed Blade	Yes	Yes (< 5")	See note[132]
Dirks, Daggers, Stilettos	Yes	No	
Automatics	Yes	No	
Balisongs	Yes	No	See note[133]

48.1 Discussion

Firearms Carry:

Visitors who appreciate wide, open spaces will find much to admire during their visit to the Peace Garden State. Those traveling with

---

[132] While the definition of "dangerous weapon" under state law includes knives with blades five inches or longer, the North Dakota Supreme Court has held that a knife with weapon-like features and a blade two and three-quarter inches long was in fact a "dangerous weapon", and upheld a conviction for concealed carry of a dangerous weapon on this basis. *See*, State v. Vermilya, 423 N.W.2d 153, 155 (N.D. 1988). Thus, careful travelers would do well to avoid carrying "tactical" folders and fixed bladed with overly aggressive, weapon-like features, even those with blades less than the statutory five inches in length, lest they run afoul of such a determination.

[133] State law includes "martial arts weapon" under the definition of "dangerous weapon." *See*, N.D. CENT. CODE § 62.1-01-01 (2009). Travelers should note that balisongs (butterfly knives) are often perceived as martial arts weapons, and thus cautious travelers would be wise to avoid carrying any balisong concealed, even those with blades less than five inches long, without a recognized concealed weapon permit.

firearms will find a few quirks in North Dakota law that they should be aware of to help assure a legally uneventful visit.

North Dakota requires a permit to carry a concealed firearm or dangerous weapon either concealed on one's person, or in a vehicle. Such permits are issued on a "shall issue" basis to residents and nonresidents. In addition, North Dakota currently recognizes that carry permits of twenty-six other states.

In contrast to other Western states, open carry of loaded handguns is generally prohibited in public areas, although notable exceptions allow such carry while in the field and engaged in hunting, trapping, or target shooting.[134] State law allows the open carry of unloaded handguns during the daytime, defined as between the hours of one hour before sunrise to one hour after sunset. Outside this time window, state law requires that handguns be transported in unloaded and securely cased condition. In addition, the state's preemption law nevertheless allows municipalities to regulate carry in their jurisdictions.

Those without a recognized permit traveling in a vehicle may transport firearms provided that the firearms are unloaded and either in plain view and easily discernible to casual observation, or securely cased in commercial gun cases and stored in the trunk of the vehicle. If the vehicle has no trunk, then the gun case should be locked and stored in the vehicle's cargo compartment. Note that handguns may not be transported in vehicle glove compartments or center consoles without a recognized permit.

Knife Carry:

Visitors to North Dakota will no doubt be moved by its rugged beauty, and will appreciate the state's generally knife friendly legal environment. Under state law, a wide variety of knives may be legally carried openly, including automatic knives, daggers, stilettos, etc. Concealed carry of knives deemed dangerous weapons, however, is prohibited without a recognized concealed weapons permit. The definition of "dangerous weapon" includes automatic knives such as switchblades and gravity knives, machetes, scimitars, stilettos, swords and daggers, and any knife with a blade five inches or longer.[135] Note that while such knives are *per se* dangerous weapons, other knives not specifically enumerated, or with blades

---

[134] *See*, N.D. CENT. CODE § 62.1-03-01 (2009).
[135] *See*, N.D. CENT. CODE § 62.1-01-01 (2009).

less than five inches may also qualify as dangerous weapons if, for example, the knife is designed (or marketed) or specially adapted or modified for use as a weapon, with little or no other non-weapon uses. For instance, the Supreme Court of North Dakota has held, in affirming a conviction under the state's concealed weapon statute, that a straight razor with a two and three-quarter inch blade and certain weapon-like features that made the razor unsuitable for shaving, was a dangerous weapon under the statute.[136]

The definition of dangerous weapon also specifically includes any "martial arts weapon."[137] As such, balisongs (butterfly knives), which are often associated with, and perceived as martial arts weapons, could quite likely be deemed a dangerous weapon, and thus should not be carried concealed without a recognized permit. In addition, balisongs may be deemed to be statutory switchblades, as balisongs are in some states, and so would be subject to the same restrictions as switchblades, which require a recognized permit for concealed carry.

Fortunately, North Dakota is a "shall issue" state for concealed weapons permits, and both issues permits to non-residents, as well as recognizes a number of other states' permits. Those travelers with recognized permits may carry firearms and dangerous weapons concealed, subject to North Dakota law.

State law prohibits carry of firearms or dangerous weapons in establishments selling alcoholic beverages, or on gaming sites. Note that towns and cities may enact their own ordinances further restricting or prohibiting knife carry, and some of the larger cities have in fact done so.

48.2 Places Off-Limits While Carrying

Firearms Carry:

North Dakota prohibits possession of firearms and dangerous weapons in establishments engaged in the retail sale of alcoholic beverages, and at gaming sites. *See*, N.D. CENT. CODE § 62.1-02-04 (2009).

State law also prohibits possession of firearms at public gatherings, which term is expansively defined to include athletic or sporting events, schools or school functions, churches or church functions,

---

[136] *See*, State v. Vermilya, 423 N.W.2d 153 (N.D. 1988).
[137] *See*, N.D. CENT. CODE § 62.1-01-01 (2009).

political rallies or functions, musical concerts, publicly owned parks that prohibit hunting, and publicly owned or operated buildings. The statute specifies that the term "public gathering" does not apply to a state or federal park. *See*, N.D. CENT. CODE § 62.1-02-05 (2009).

Knife Carry:

North Dakota state law prohibits the carry of firearms and other dangerous weapons, the definition of which includes a broad variety of knives, such as switchblades, gravity knives, machetes, stilettos, swords, daggers, etc., and any knife with a blade five inches or longer, in liquor establishments or gaming sites. *See*, N.D. CENT. CODE § 62.1-02-04 (2009).

Note that local towns and cities may pass their own local ordinances prohibiting or restricting knife possession or carry in their jurisdictions.

State law prohibits firearm or weapon possession by students on school property or at school functions. *See*, N.D. CENT. CODE § 15.1-19-10 (2009). No state law limitation appears to exist for non-students. Towns and cities, however, may pass their own local ordinances prohibiting carry on school grounds by non-students.

48.3 Selected City Ordinances

The state legislature has preempted municipalities and other political subdivisions from regulating firearms to any extent greater than state law. Thus, firearms regulation is uniform throughout the state.

The city ordinances below relate to knife carry:

Minot – Possession of unsheathed or uncased knives prohibited in public, in places selling alcoholic beverages, places of public accommodations or public assembly, or on private property without permission of the property owner. *See*, MINOT, N.D., CODE OF ORDINANCES § 23-66 (2010). Possession of *per se* weapons other than firearms prohibited in public, in places selling alcoholic beverages, or on private property without permission of the property owner. The ordinance defines "weapon" as "any device or substance which is designed or subsequently modified to disable, to wound, or to kill a human being which device or substance as designed or subsequently modified is not customarily used for any other purpose." *See, id.* at § 23-67.

48.4 State Resources

Bureau of Criminal Investigation
P.O. Box 1054
Bismarck, ND 58502-1054
Phone: (701) 328-5500
Fax: (701) 328-5510
Website: http://www.ag.state.nd.us/BCI/BCI.htm

Office of the Attorney General
600 E. Boulevard Ave Dept 125
Bismarck, ND 58505
Phone: (701) 328-2210
TTY: (800) 366-6888
TDD: (701) 328-3409
Fax: (701) 328-2226
Website: http://www.ag.state.nd.us/

49 Ohio – The Buckeye State

> Area: 40,948 sq.mi. (Rank: 35th)   Population: 11,485,910 (Rank: 7th)
> Violent Crime Rate (per 100,000 residents): 348.2 (Rank: 26th Safest)
> State Motto: *With God, All Things Are Possible*

Firearms Carry Summary:

Carry considerations	Status
Restaurants and bars	Prohibited
Churches / Places of worship	Prohibited, unless place of worship explicitly allows. *See,* OHIO REV. CODE § 2923.126(B)(6) (2009)
State parks / forests	Concealed with permit allowed
Vehicle carry	Loaded handguns allowed with permit; otherwise firearms unloaded, actions open and in plain view, or securely cased
LE notification if stopped?	Required. *See,* OHIO REV. CODE § 2923.126(A) (2009)
Retreat requirement for self-defense	Required, except in home or vehicle. *See,* OHIO REV. CODE § 2901.09 (2009)
Preemption law	Yes. *See,* OHIO REV. CODE § 9.68 (2009)
Open Carry	Allowed, no permit required
Military-pattern semi-auto restrictions	Not restricted
NFA weapons	State law imposes "safe storage" requirement, in addition to compliance with federal law

Reciprocity / Recognition

*Ohio **recognizes** permits from the following states:*

Alaska	Arizona	Arkansas	Delaware
Florida	Idaho	Kentucky	Michigan
Missouri	Nebraska	North Carolina	Oklahoma
South Carolina	Tennessee	Utah	Virginia
Washington	West Virginia	Wyoming	

*Ohio permits **are recognized by** the following states:*

Alaska	Arizona	Arkansas	Delaware
Florida*	Idaho	Indiana	Kansas
Kentucky	Michigan*	Minnesota	Missouri
Montana	North Carolina	Nebraska	New Mexico

Nevada	Oklahoma	South Carolina*	South Dakota
Tennessee	Utah	Vermont	Virginia
Washington	West Virginia	Wyoming	

Note: In the reciprocity / recognition tables above, states with an asterisk (*) require the permit holder to both have a permit from, and be a resident of, the recognized state in order for reciprocity / recognition of the permit.

Knife Carry Summary:

Note: Blade length limits, if any, in parentheses.

Knife Type	Open Carry	Concealed Carry	Notes
Folding	Yes	Yes	See note[138]
Fixed Blade	Yes	No	See note[139]
Dirks, Daggers, Stilettos	Yes	No	
Automatics	No	No	
Balisongs	Yes	No	See note[140]

49.1 Discussion

Firearms Carry:

Visitors to Ohio will find a somewhat restrictive legal environment for firearms carry, particularly if traveling in a motor vehicle. Ohio requires a permit to carry a loaded handgun in a concealed manner. Such permits are issued to residents on a "shall issue" basis, and the Ohio Attorney General is empowered to enter into reciprocity agreements with other states to recognize each other's permits.

A person with a recognized permit who is traveling by vehicle may carry a loaded handgun in a holster either openly or concealed on his person. The handgun may also be stored in the vehicle's glove

---

[138] State law prohibits concealed carry of deadly weapons, so any knife carried concealed must not be either "designed or specially adapted for use as a weapon," or actually "possessed, carried, or used as a weapon" in order to be legally carried concealed. *See*, OHIO REV. CODE ANN. §§ 2923.11, 2923.12 (2009).

[139] Readers should note that while some fixed bladed knives may be deemed not to be deadly weapons, as that term is defined in Ohio law, there appear to exist numerous cases where fixed bladed knives have been ruled deadly weapons, thus resulting in convictions for carrying concealed weapons.

[140] Balisongs have been held to be deadly weapons, and hence prohibited from concealed carry. *See*, City of Columbus v. Dawson, 501 N.E.2d 677, 679 (Ohio Ct. App. 1986).

compartment or center console, or in a locked gun case. A closed case, bag, box, or other container that is in plain sight and that has a lid, cover, or other closing mechanism that must be opened for a person to gain access to the handgun.[141] Those traveling on motorcycles should be aware that these same requirements apply to carrying a handgun while on a motorcycle. Note that only handguns may be carried in a loaded condition while in a vehicle, and only with a recognized permit. Long guns must always be transported unloaded in a vehicle.

Travelers in vehicles without recognized permits must transport their firearms, whether handguns or long guns, in an unloaded condition. In addition, the firearms must be either in plain view and secured in a gun rack or holder, or in a closed package, box, or case, or with the action open or the weapon disassembled. The unloaded firearms may also be stored in the separate trunk compartment of the vehicle, such that access would require leaving the passenger compartment of the vehicle.[142]

Anyone with a recognized permit carrying a loaded handgun concealed should take special note that Ohio law requires the permit holder, if stopped by a law enforcement officer acting in an official capacity, to promptly notify the officer that he or she has a license to carry a concealed handgun, and that he or she is currently carrying a loaded handgun. This applies whether the permit holder is in the vehicle or not. In addition, state law requires that the permit holder keep his or her hands in plain sight unless otherwise directed by the officer, and to not remove, attempt to remove, grasp, hold, or touch the handgun with his or her hands or fingers during the encounter.[143] Note that state law provides serious criminal penalties for violation of these requirements.

Open carry is legal in Ohio without a permit, and the state's strong preemption law prohibits local governments from legally enacting firearm carry bans in their jurisdictions.[144]

Knife Carry:

Visitors to the Buckeye State will find a fairly restrictive legal environment for knife carry. State law prohibits carrying a concealed

---

[141] See, OHIO REV. CODE § 2923.16(E) (2009).
[142] See, OHIO REV. CODE § 2923.16(C) (2009).
[143] See, OHIO REV. CODE § 2923.126(A) (2009).
[144] See, OHIO REV. CODE § 9.68 (2009) (specifying preemption statute).

deadly weapon, defined as "any instrument, device, or thing capable of inflicting death, and designed or specially adapted for use as a weapon, or possessed, carried, or used as a weapon."[145] While the state recently enacted "shall-issue" licensing for concealed handguns, no such provision or permit exists for knives.

Most knives may be carried openly, with the exception of automatic knives such as switchblades or gravity knives, sales of which are strictly prohibited except to law enforcement personnel. Ballistic knives are included in the definition of "dangerous ordnance," and are subject to a wide range of statutory restrictions.

Ordinary folding pocket knives may be carried openly or concealed, although travelers should avoid carry of "tactical" folders with overly aggressive, weapon-like appearance or features, lest such knives be deemed deadly weapons, and hence prohibited from concealed carry. Note that "concealed" under Ohio law means either concealed on the person, or concealed ready at hand (readily accessible). While there is no statutorily defined blade length limit, readers should note that blade length often factors into whether a particular knife is determined to be a deadly weapon.

The Ohio Court of Appeals has ruled that balisongs (butterfly knives) are deadly weapons, and hence may not be carried concealed.[146]

State law prohibits possession or carry of deadly weapons in "school safety zones," courthouses and buildings containing a courtroom. In addition, "home rule" municipalities may enact their own ordinances restricting or prohibiting knife carry.

49.2 Places Off-Limits While Carrying

Firearms Carry:

Ohio prohibits the carrying of concealed handguns in a laundry list of places, including the premises of law enforcement agencies such as police stations, sheriff's offices, and state highway patrol stations; state correctional and detention facilities; airport passenger terminals; mental health institutions; school safety zones, the definition of which includes schools, school buildings, school premises, school activities, and school buses; as well as courthouses and court rooms. *See,* OHIO REV. CODE § 2923.126(B) (2009).

---

[145] *See,* OHIO REV. CODE ANN. §§ 2923.11(A), 2923.12 (2009).
[146] *See,* City of Columbus v. Dawson, 501 N.E.2d 677, 679 (Ohio Ct. App. 1986).

| THE TRAVELER'S GUN & KNIFE LAW BOOK

State law further prohibits concealed handgun carry in establishments that serve alcoholic beverages; or on the premises of any public or private college, university, or other institution of higher education, with an exception for handguns stored in locked motor vehicles; or in any place of worship, such as a church, synagogue, or mosque, unless the place of worship permits concealed handguns on its premises. *See, id.*

Child and family day care centers and homes are also off-limits to concealed handgun carriers. *See, id.*

Concealed handguns are also verboten in aircraft in or intended for operation in foreign air transportation, interstate air transportation, intrastate air transportation, or the transportation of mail. *See, id.*

State law further prohibits concealed handguns in local and state government buildings, with an exception for buildings used primarily as shelters, restrooms, motor vehicle parking facilities, or rest facilities. *See, id.*

Knife Carry:

Ohio state law prohibits the possession of deadly weapons in "school safety zones" and courthouses and buildings containing a courtroom. *See,* OHIO REV. CODE ANN. §§ 2923.122, 2923.123 (2009). Note that "home rule" municipalities may enact their own restrictions or prohibitions on knife carry.

49.3 Selected City Ordinances

The state legislature has preempted municipalities and other political subdivisions from regulating firearms to any extent greater than state law. Thus, firearms regulation is uniform throughout the state.

The city ordinances below relate to knife carry:

Cincinnati – Possession of dangerous or deadly weapons on school property or at school-sponsored activities prohibited. *See,* CINCINNATI, OHIO, MUNICIPAL CODE § 708-39 (2010). Carry of deadly or dangerous weapon in city buildings, including handguns, prohibited "notwithstanding the possession of a permit to carry a concealed handgun pursuant to Section 2923.125 of the Ohio Revised Code." *See, id.* at § 708-41. City manager empowered during "public danger or emergency" to restrict or prohibit possession or carry of weapons, including knives and razors, in public. *See, id.* at Art. XVIII, § 7.

Dayton – Carrying concealed deadly weapons prohibited. *See,* DAYTON, OHIO, CODE OF ORDINANCES § 138.02 (2009). A person violating this prohibition may assert an affirmative defense showing that the weapon was carried for defensive purposes, while the defendant was "engaged in a lawful activity, and had reasonable cause to fear a criminal attack upon himself or a member of his family or upon his home, such as would justify a prudent man in going armed[.]" *See, id.*

49.4 State Resources

Ohio State Highway Patrol
Customer Service Center West
1970 West Broad Street
Columbus, OH 43223
Phone: (877) 772-8765
Phone: (614) 995-5353
Website: http://www.statepatrol.ohio.gov/

Attorney General of Ohio
30 E. Broad St., 17th Floor
Columbus, OH 43215
Phone: (800) 282-0515
Phone: (614) 466-4320
Website: http://www.ohioattorneygeneral.gov/

50 Oklahoma – The Sooner State

Area: 68,667 sq.mi. (Rank: 19th)   Population: 3,642,361 (Rank: 28th)
Violent Crime Rate (per 100,000 residents): 526.7 (Rank: 41st Safest)
State Motto: *Labor omnia vincit (Labor Conquers All Things)*

Firearms Carry Summary:

Carry considerations	Status
Restaurants and bars	Allowed with permit in restaurants only. *See*, OKLA. STAT. tit. 21 § 1272.1 (2009)
Churches / Places of worship	Allowed with permit
State parks / forests	Allowed with permit, except in buildings. *See*, OKLA. STAT. tit. 21 § 1277(B)(4) (2009)
Vehicle carry	Loaded handguns allowed with permit. Long guns must be unloaded and in plain view or securely cased or stored in trunk.
LE notification if stopped?	Required. *See*, OKLA. STAT. tit. 21 § 1290.8 (2009)
Retreat requirement for self-defense	Not required. *See*, OKLA. STAT. tit. 21 § 1289.25 (2009)
Preemption law	Yes. *See*, OKLA. STAT. tit. 21 § 1289.24 (2009)
Open Carry	Generally prohibited
Military-pattern semi-auto restrictions	Not restricted
NFA weapons	NFA-friendly, compliance with federal law only

Reciprocity / Recognition

Oklahoma **recognizes** permits from **all other states**.

Oklahoma permits **are recognized by** the following states:

Alabama	Alaska	Arizona	Arkansas
Colorado*	Delaware	Florida*	Georgia
Idaho	Indiana	Kansas	Kentucky
Louisiana	Michigan*	Minnesota	Mississippi
Missouri	Montana	North Carolina	North Dakota
Nebraska	New Hampshire*	New Mexico	Ohio
Pennsylvania	South Carolina*	South Dakota	Tennessee
Texas	Utah	Vermont	Virginia
Washington	West Virginia	Wyoming	

Note: In the reciprocity / recognition tables above, states with an asterisk (*) require the permit holder to both have a permit from, and be a resident of, the recognized state in order for reciprocity / recognition of the permit.

Knife Carry Summary:

Note: Blade length limits, if any, in parentheses.

Knife Type	Open Carry	Concealed Carry	Notes
Folding	Yes	Yes	
Fixed Blade	Yes	Yes	See note[147]
Dirks, Daggers, Stilettos	No	No	
Automatics	No	No	
Balisongs	No	No	See note[148]
Sword Canes	No	No	

50.1 Discussion

Firearms Carry:

Visitors to the Sooner State will find a fairly friendly legal environment for firearms carry. Oklahoma requires a permit to carry a concealed firearm on one's person. Such permits are issued on a "shall issue" basis to qualified residents who are at least twenty-one years old. Fortunately for travelers, Oklahoma recognizes permits from all other states. If you have a carry permit from any state, it's valid in Oklahoma.

Visitors carrying concealed handguns should be aware that state law imposes a caliber restriction on ammunition loaded into any concealed handgun, limiting such ammunition (and thus the gun) to .45 caliber and smaller. Thus, those wishing to conceal carry their .500 magnums are out of luck in Oklahoma.[149]

---

[147] State law prohibits carry, whether openly or concealed, of bowie knives. *See,* OKLA. STAT. tit. 21 § 1272 (2009). Thus, travelers should exercise care when carrying any large, fixed bladed knife, lest they run afoul of this prohibition.

[148] Balisongs may fall under the state's prohibition on switchblades, as balisongs do in some states. Therefore, travelers would do well to avoid carrying balisongs.

[149] *See,* OKLA. STAT. tit. 21 § 1290.6 (2009) (defining and criminalizing carry of "prohibited ammunition" in concealed handguns). Note that the statute also prohibits carry in concealed handguns of ammunition with "restricted bullets", defined as "a

238 | The Traveler's Gun & Knife Law Book

Open carry of firearms in public is generally prohibited in most areas, even with a recognized carry permit. Obvious exceptions exist for those engaged in lawful hunting, target shooting, and firearms-related educational activities.

Travelers in vehicles may carry loaded handguns with a recognized permit. Those with permits may also transport a magazine or clip fed long gun with a loaded magazine inserted, but the chamber of the gun unloaded and empty. Such long gun may be transported in an exterior locked compartment of the vehicle, the vehicle's trunk, or the interior passenger compartment of the vehicle, provided the traveler has a recognized permit.[150]

Travelers in vehicles without permits must transport their firearms, whether handguns or long guns, unloaded and either in plain view, any commercial gun case that's wholly or partially visible from outside the vehicle, in a vehicle mounted gun rack, or in an exterior locked compartment or trunk of the vehicle. In addition, those without permits may transport long guns concealed behind a seat or within the interior of the vehicle, provided that the long gun is completely unloaded, meaning that the chamber is empty and no loaded magazine or clip is inserted into the weapon.[151]

Visitors carrying concealed handguns with a recognized permit should be aware that Oklahoma law requires that, upon being stopped by any law enforcement officer acting in an official capacity, they inform the officer that they are licensed to carry, and are currently carrying, a concealed handgun.[152]

Knife Carry:

Visitors to Oklahoma will find a fairly restrictive legal environment for knife carry. Ordinary folding pocket knives should pose no problem, and may be carried openly or concealed. Fixed bladed knives may be carried openly or concealed as well, although readers should note that bowie knives are specifically prohibited. As a result, visitors should avoid carry of large fix bladed knives, especially in urban areas, lest their knives be deemed bowies for purposes of

---

round or elongated missile with a core of less than sixty percent (60%) lead and having a fluorocarbon coating, which is designed to travel at a high velocity and is capable of penetrating body armor[.]" See, Okla. Stat. tit 21 § 1289.19 (2009).

[150] See, Okla. Stat. tit 21 § 1289.13 (2009).
[151] See, Okla. Stat. tit 21 § 1289.7 (2009).
[152] See, Okla. Stat. tit 21 § 1290.8 (2009).

prosecution. State law does provide an explicit exception for knives carried for bona fide hunting, fishing, or recreational uses. Thus, hunting or fishing knives may be carried openly or concealed while on a legal, bona fide hunting or fishing trip.

There is no statutorily defined blade length limit. Dirks, daggers, stilettos, and automatic knives, however, are prohibited. Note that balisongs, while not specifically prohibited, may fall under the switchblade prohibition, as balisongs do in some states. Thus, visitors should avoid carry of balisongs in the Sooner State.

Oklahoma prohibits the carry of firearms and other deadly weapons, including daggers, dirks, switchblades, sword canes, and bowie knives, in establishments that serve alcoholic beverages, and in schools or on school property. Violation of either of these prohibitions is a felony. In addition, municipalities may pass their own local ordinances prohibiting or further restricting knife carry in their jurisdictions.

50.2 Places Off-Limits While Carrying

Firearms Carry:

Oklahoma prohibits carrying of concealed handguns, with or without a permit, in a variety of places, including local or state government buildings; meetings of local or state government, including meetings of school boards; correctional and detention facilities such as prisons and jails; colleges and universities; sports arenas during professional sporting events; and gambling parlors that engage in pari-mutuel wagering. *See*, OKLA. STAT. tit 21 § 1277 (2009).

State law specifically excludes vehicle parking lots at the above locations from the prohibition against concealed firearms carry. In addition, concealed handgun carry is allowed in parks, recreational areas, and fairgrounds, although not in buildings, offices, and other structures that are specifically prohibited above that are located in such parks, recreational areas, or fairgrounds. For example, while concealed handgun carry is allowed in a state park, carry would not be allowed in state- owned or operated visitor centers in such parks. *See, id.*

State law allows those with concealed carry permits to possess handguns on college or university campuses with written permission from the college or university, which written consent must be carried along with the permit while on the college or university campus.

State law prohibits possession of firearms or other weapons in or on public or private elementary or secondary schools, including vocational-technical schools, school property, and school buses. Exceptions exist for those in vehicles picking up or dropping-off students, provided the vehicle does not remain unattended on school property, and for those participating in certified hunter education programs. *See*, OKLA. STAT. tit 21 § 1280.1 (2009).

Knife Carry:

Oklahoma prohibits the carry of firearms and other deadly weapons, including daggers, dirks, switchblades, sword canes, and bowie knives, in establishments that serve alcoholic beverages, and in schools or on school property. *See*, OKLA. STAT. tit. 21 §§ 1272.1, 1280.1 (2009). Violation of either of these prohibitions is a felony. *See, id.* at §§ 1272.2, 1280.1.

In addition, towns and cities may pass their own local ordinances prohibiting or further restricting knife carry in their jurisdictions.

50.3 Selected City Ordinances

The state legislature has preempted municipalities and other political subdivisions from regulating firearms to any extent greater than state law. Thus, firearms regulation is uniform throughout the state.

The city ordinances below relate to knife carry:

Oklahoma City – Carry of handguns and other deadly weapons, including daggers, dirks, switchblades, "spring-type" knives, sword canes, and bowie knives, prohibited in churches and religious assemblies, and any place "persons are assembled for public worship, for amusement, or for educational or scientific purposes, or into any circus, show or public exhibition of any kind, or into any ballroom, or to any social party or social gathering, or to any election, or to any political convention, or to any other public assembly[.]" *See*, OKLAHOMA CITY, OKLA., MUNICIPAL CODE § 30-303 (2009). Note that the city also prohibits the sale of switchblades and pocket knives with blades longer than four inches. *See, id.* at §§ 30-307, 30-311.

Sallisaw – Unlawful to carry concealed any bowie knife, dirk, dagger, switchblade knife. *See*, SALLISAW, OKLA., CODE OF ORDINANCES § 66-71 (2009).

50.4 State Resources

Oklahoma Department of Public Safety
P.O. Box 11415
Oklahoma City, Oklahoma 73136
Phone: (405) 425-2424
Website: http://www.dps.state.ok.us/

Attorney General of Oklahoma
313 NE 21st Street
Oklahoma City, OK 73105
Phone: (405) 521-3921
Website: http://www.oag.state.ok.us/

51 Oregon – The Beaver State

Area: 95,997 sq.mi. (Rank: 10th)   Population: 3,790,060 (Rank: 27th)
Violent Crime Rate (per 100,000 residents): 257.2 (Rank: 11th Safest)
State Motto: *She Flies With Her Own Wings*

Firearms Carry Summary:

Carry considerations	Status
Restaurants and bars	Concealed allowed with permit
Churches / Places of worship	Concealed allowed with permit
State parks / forests	Concealed allowed with permit
Vehicle carry	Loaded firearms must be carried in plain view, otherwise secured in locked case, locked glove compartment or trunk
LE notification if stopped?	Not required
Retreat requirement for self-defense	Required
Preemption law	Limited preemption; local governments can regulate carry in public without permit. *See*, OR. REV. STAT. § 166.170 *et. seq.* (2009)
Open Carry	Allowed without permit, but local governments can prohibit
Military-pattern semi-auto restrictions	Not restricted
NFA weapons	NFA-friendly, compliance with federal law only

Reciprocity / Recognition

Oregon **does _not_ recognize** permits from any other state.

Oregon permits **are recognized by** the following states:

Alaska	Arizona	Idaho	Indiana
Kentucky	Michigan*	Missouri	Montana
Nebraska	Oklahoma	South Dakota	Tennessee
Utah	Vermont		

Note: In the reciprocity / recognition tables above, states with an asterisk (*) require the permit holder to both have a permit from, and be a resident of, the recognized state in order for reciprocity / recognition of the permit.

Knife Carry Summary:

Note: Blade length limits, if any, in parentheses.

Knife Type	Open Carry	Concealed Carry	Notes
Folding	Yes	Yes	
Fixed Blade	Yes	Yes	
Dirks, Daggers, Stilettos	Yes	No	
Automatics	Yes	No	
Balisongs	Yes	No	

51.1 Discussion

Firearms Carry:

Visitors to the Beaver State will find a somewhat restrictive legal environment for firearms carry, although permissive relative to its southern neighbor, California. Oregon requires a permit to carry a handgun concealed on one's person. Such permits are issued on a "shall issue" basis to qualified residents. Unfortunately for the traveler, Oregon does not recognize the carry permits of any other state. Even more unfortunate, the state will only issue nonresident permits to those residing in contiguous states.

While state law allows the open carry of handguns without a permit, the state's limited preemption law unfortunately allows local governments to regulate, restrict and/or prohibit the carry of loaded firearms in public for those without an Oregon-issued permit. Not surprisingly, several of the less gun friendly (mostly urban) locales such as Portland have done so, and thus the cautious traveler should exercise care when open carrying a loaded firearm in the Beaver State.

Travelers without Oregon issued permits may carry loaded handguns in a vehicle if they do so in visible belt holsters, as Oregon does not consider such carry as concealed under state law. State law prohibits possession of any handgun in a vehicle that is "concealed and readily accessible". Thus, absent a permit, handguns may not be kept in unlocked glove compartments, center consoles, or unlocked cases or containers in the passenger compartment of the vehicle. Handguns transported in commercial gun cases and stored in the trunk are acceptable. For vehicles without separate trunk compartments, handguns must be secured in a locked case, or in a locked glove compartment or locked center console, and the key must not be inserted in the lock.

Long guns may be transported in a loaded condition, provided they are in plain view and visible to casual observation from outside the vehicle, such as in a gun rack. Otherwise, they may be securely cased in commercial gun cases or stored in the trunk of the vehicle. Concealment upon one's person is prohibited.

Knife Carry:

Visitors to the Beaver State will find a fairly friendly legal environment for knife carry, with a strong legal bias towards open carry. In fact, state law prohibits concealed carry of switchblades, dirks, daggers, ice picks, and similar instruments, but permits open carry of these knives. Concealed carry of folding pocket knives and ordinary fixed blades should pose no problem. There is no statutorily defined blade length limit. Note that state law makes carry or possession of any dangerous or deadly weapon with intent to use unlawfully against another a crime. In addition, note that balisongs may be considered statutory switchblades, as balisongs are in some states, and thus concealed carry would be prohibited.

The state prohibits carry or possession of dangerous weapons on or in public buildings and court facilities. The definition of public building, for purposes of this prohibition, includes hospitals, and educational institutions such as schools and colleges.

51.2 Places Off-Limits While Carrying

Firearms Carry:

Oregon prohibits possession or carry of firearms, whether loaded or unloaded, and dangerous weapons in public buildings, which term is expansively defined as including hospitals, state government Capitol area buildings, public and private schools, colleges and universities, City Halls, residences of state officials, and the grounds adjacent to each such building. Included in the definition of "public building" are those parts of buildings occupied by state or local government agencies. See, OR. REV. STAT. 166.360, 166.370 (2009). Note that this prohibition does not apply to a person who possesses an Oregon issued concealed carry permit. See, id.

Possession of firearms on school property is allowed if the firearm is unloaded and locked in a motor vehicle. *See, id.*

State law also prohibits possession or carry of firearms and dangerous weapons, with or without a permit, in court facilities in courthouses. *See, id.*

Knife Carry:

Oregon prohibits the carry of firearms and other dangerous weapons in public buildings, the definition of which includes schools and colleges, and in court facilities. *See,* OR. REV. STAT. § 166.370 (2009).

51.3 Selected City Ordinances

The state legislature has preempted municipalities and other political subdivisions from regulating firearms carry by those with Oregon-issued concealed carry permits. Note that some localities may regulate or prohibit carry by those without a permit in their jurisdictions.

The city ordinances below relate to knife carry:

Hillsboro – Concealed carry of dirk, dagger, stiletto, or any knife other than ordinary pocket knife prohibited. *See,* HILLSBORO, OR., MUNICIPAL CODE § 9.12.010 (2006).

51.4 State Resources

Oregon State Police
255 Capitol St. N.E.
Salem, OR 97310
Phone: (503) 378-3720
Fax: (503) 378-8282
Website: http://www.oregon.gov/OSP/

Attorney General of Oregon
Department of Justice
1162 Court Street NE
Salem, OR 97301-4096
Phone: (503) 378-4400
Fax: (503) 378-4017
Website: http://www.doj.state.or.us/

52 Pennsylvania – The Keystone State

Area: 44,817 sq.mi. (Rank: 32nd)   Population: 12,448,279 (Rank: 6th)
Violent Crime Rate (per 100,000 residents): 410.0 (Rank: 28th Safest)
State Motto: *Virtue, Liberty, and Independence*

Firearms Carry Summary:

Carry considerations	Status
Restaurants and bars	Allowed
Churches / Places of worship	Allowed
State parks / forests	Allowed with permit
Vehicle carry	Loaded handguns allowed with permit, otherwise must be unloaded and in securely locked case in trunk or vehicle cargo area; long guns must be unloaded and securely cased or stored in trunk
LE notification if stopped?	Not required
Retreat requirement for self-defense	Required, except in home. *See*, 18 PA. CONS. STAT. § 505 (2009)
Preemption law	Yes. *See*, 18 PA. CONS. STAT. § 6120 (2009)
Open Carry	Generally allowed; Philadelphia requires permit to open carry
Military-pattern semi-auto restrictions	Not restricted
NFA weapons	NFA-friendly, compliance with federal law only

Reciprocity / Recognition

*Pennsylvania **recognizes** permits from the following states:*

Alaska	Arizona	Arkansas	Colorado
Florida	Georgia	Idaho	Indiana
Kentucky	Louisiana	Michigan	New Hampshire
Missouri	Montana	North Carolina	North Dakota
Oklahoma	South Dakota	Tennessee	Texas
Utah	Virginia	West Virginia	Wyoming

*Pennsylvania permits **are recognized by** the following states:*

Alaska	Arizona	Arkansas	Colorado*
Florida*	Georgia	Idaho	Indiana
Kentucky	Louisiana	Michigan*	Missouri
Montana	North Carolina	North Dakota	New Hampshire*

Oklahoma	South Dakota	Tennessee	Texas
Utah	Vermont	Virginia	West Virginia
Wyoming			

Note: In the reciprocity / recognition tables above, states with an asterisk (*) require the permit holder to both have a permit from, and be a resident of, the recognized state in order for reciprocity / recognition of the permit.

Knife Carry Summary:

Note: Blade length limits, if any, in parentheses.

Knife Type	Open Carry	Concealed Carry	Notes
Folding	Yes	Yes	
Fixed Blade	Yes	Yes	
Dirks, Daggers, Stilettos	No	No	See note[153]
Automatics	No	No	
Balisongs	No	No	See note[154]

52.1 Discussion

Firearms Carry:

Visitors to the Keystone State will find a fairly friendly legal environment for firearms carry. Pennsylvania requires a permit to carry a loaded handgun either in a vehicle or concealed on one's person. Such permits are issued on a "shall issue" basis to qualified

---

[153] The state law prohibition on offensive weapons lists a number of *per se* offensive weapons, including any "dagger, knife, razor or cutting instrument, the blade of which is exposed in an automatic way by switch, push-button, spring mechanism, or otherwise." *See*, 18 PA. CONS. STAT. § 908 (2009). The Pennsylvania Supreme Court, in a decision from 1979, seems to indicate that "dagger" is modified by the automatic opening provision of the statute. *See*, Comm. v. Fisher, 400 A.2d 1284, 1286 (Pa. 1979) (citing Comm. v. Cartagena, 393 A.2d 350, 361 (Pa. 1978)). The case cited, however, does not include the term "dagger" as being modified by the automatic opening provision of the statute. *See*, Comm. v. Cartagena, 393 A.2d 350, 361 (Pa. 1978). A conservative reading of these opinions and the statute tends to lead to the conclusion that daggers are *per se* offensive weapons, and thus may not be possessed.

[154] Balisongs may fall under the switchblade prohibition, as balisongs do in some states. While at least one county court has concluded that balisongs (butterfly knives) are not prohibited offensive weapons, travelers should be aware that this lower court ruling would have binding effect only in the deciding court's jurisdiction, in this case, Bucks County. *See*, Comm. v. Miles, 7 Pa. D. & C.4th 67 (Bucks C., 1989). As such, a conservative view of the legal status of balisongs leads to listing its status as prohibited, absent a clarification in the statutory language, or an appropriate ruling from a higher court with statewide application on this issue.

residents, as well as to nonresidents who possess a permit from their home state. In addition, Pennsylvania currently recognizes the permits of twenty-four other states.

Open carry of a loaded handgun in public and not in a vehicle is legal in most of the state without a permit. Travelers should note, however, that state law requires a recognized permit for open carry of firearms in Philadelphia. Pennsylvania's preemption law forbids local governments from separately regulating firearms carry.

Pennsylvania strictly regulates the carry of loaded firearms in vehicles. Long guns must be transported in an unloaded condition, and should be securely cased or locked in the trunk of a vehicle. Those without carry permits must transport handguns in a similar unloaded and securely cased condition, and stored in the trunk or cargo compartment of the vehicle. Ammunition should be stored separately from the firearm.

Those travelers with recognized permits may, of course, carry loaded handguns either openly or concealed in the vehicle. In addition, state law provides two exceptions to the general prohibition against carry of loaded handguns in vehicles without a recognized permit. First, such carry is allowed if the person possesses "a valid and lawfully issued license *for that firearm*" issued by any state.[155] Second, loaded handgun carry in a vehicle is allowed if the traveler possesses a carry permit from another state, regardless of whether Pennsylvania currently recognizes permits from that state, if (1) that state provides a reciprocal privilege for Pennsylvania permit holders, and (2) the Pennsylvania Attorney General has determined that that state's firearms laws are similar to Pennsylvania's.[156]

Knife Carry:

Visitors to Pennsylvania will find a fairly restrictive legal environment for knife carry, perhaps reflecting a legislative compromise between the state's urban and rural areas. Ordinary fixed and folding knives may be carried openly or concealed. Note that state law prohibits

---

[155] *See*, 18 PA. CONS. STAT. § 6106(b)(11) (2009) (emphasis added). Note that most carry permits are not firearm-specific, i.e., the permit is not tied to a specific firearm.
[156] *See*, 18 PA. CONS. STAT. § 6106(b)(15) (2009). The exception reads: "Any person who possesses a valid and lawfully issued license or permit to carry a firearm which has been issued under the laws of another state, regardless of whether a reciprocity agreement exists between the Commonwealth and the state under section 6109(k), provided: (i) The state provides a reciprocal privilege for individuals licensed to carry firearms under section 6109. (ii) The Attorney General has determined that the firearm laws of the state are similar to the firearm laws of this Commonwealth." *See, id.*

concealed carry of any weapon "readily capable of lethal use" with intent to employ the weapon criminally.[157] There is no statutorily defined blade length limit. Dirks, daggers, stilettos, and automatic knives, however, are prohibited.

With regard to balisongs, readers should note that balisongs may fall under the switchblade prohibition, as balisongs do in some states. While one lower county court has held that balisongs are not prohibited offensive weapons, be aware this ruling only applies in that particular county. Given that no higher court with state-wide jurisdiction has apparently issued a published opinion on the issue of balisongs, cautious travelers would do well to avoid possession of balisongs in the state.

State law prohibits the carry of firearms and other weapons, the definition of which includes any knife, in or on elementary or secondary schools or school property, including school buses. In addition, state law prohibits the carry of firearms or dangerous weapons into court facilities. The definition of dangerous weapon applicable to this prohibition specifically includes daggers and switchblades. Note that municipalities may enact their own ordinances further restricting or prohibiting knife carry in their jurisdictions. In particular, travelers to the City of Brotherly Love should be aware that Philadelphia appears to have enacted a sweeping prohibition on "cutting weapons" in public, the penalty for violation of which is a minimum fine of at least $300, *and a minimum imprisonment* of ninety days.[158] Whether such a broad prohibition and/or penalty would in fact withstand judicial scrutiny is unclear, although you probably don't want to be the test case.

52.2 *Places Off-Limits While Carrying*

Firearms Carry:

Pennsylvania prohibits possession of weapons, the definition which includes firearms, in elementary and secondary schools, and school buses. *See*, 18 PA. CONS. STAT. § 912 (2009).

State law also prohibits possession of firearms or other dangerous weapons in courts and court facilities. *See*, 18 PA. CONS. STAT. § 913 (2009).

---

[157] *See*, 18 PA. CONS. STAT. ANN. § 907 (2009).
[158] See, PHILADELPHIA, PA., CODE § 10-820 (2010).

Knife Carry:

State law prohibits the carry of firearms and other weapons, the definition of which includes any knife, in or on elementary or secondary schools or school property, including school buses. *See,* 18 PA. CONS. STAT. § 912 (2009).

State law also prohibits the carry of firearms or dangerous weapons into court facilities. The definition of dangerous weapon applicable to this prohibition specifically includes daggers and switchblades. *See,* 18 PA. CONS. STAT. § 913 (2009).

52.3 Selected City Ordinances

The state legislature has preempted municipalities and other political subdivisions from regulating firearms to any extent greater than state law. Thus, firearms regulation is uniform throughout the state.

The city ordinances below relate to knife carry:

Philadelphia – Carry of switchblades prohibited. *See,* PHILADELPHIA, PA., CODE § 10-810 (2010). Use or possession on public streets or on public property of any "cutting weapon", defined as "[a]ny knife or other cutting instrument which can be used as a weapon that has a cutting edge similar to that of a knife" prohibited, with exception for "tool or instrument commonly or ordinarily used in a trade, profession or calling" while "actually being used in the active exercise of that trade, profession or calling." *See, id.* at § 10-820. Violation penalty is *minimum* fine of $300 *and minimum* ninety day imprisonment. *Id.* Possession of weapons, the definition of which includes knives and cutting instruments, prohibited on or within 100 feet of any school, or in any conveyance providing transportation to or form school. *See, id.* at § 10-833.

52.4 State Resources

Pennsylvania State Police
Department Headquarters
1800 Elmerton Ave.
Harrisburg, PA 17110
Phone: (717) 783-5599
Website: http://www.psp.state.pa.us/

Attorney General of Pennsylvania
16th Floor, Strawberry Square
Harrisburg, PA 17120
Phone: (717) 787-3391
Fax: (717) 787-8242
Website: http://www.attorneygeneral.gov/

53 Rhode Island – The Ocean State

> Area: 1,045 sq.mi. (Rank: 50th)   Population: 1,050,788 (Rank: 43rd)
> Violent Crime Rate (per 100,000 residents): 249.4 (Rank: 9th Safest)
> State Motto: *Hope*

Firearms Carry Summary:

Carry considerations	Status
Restaurants and bars	Allowed with permit
Churches / Places of worship	Allowed with permit
State parks / forests	Prohibited; exceptions for lawful hunting, etc.
Vehicle carry	Long guns must be unloaded, and should be securely cased. Handguns carry allowed with non-R.I. permit if solely traveling through state on uninterrupted journey, otherwise must be unloaded, secured in locked case and stored in trunk or cargo area.
LE notification if stopped?	Not required
Retreat requirement for self-defense	Required, except in home.
Preemption law	Yes. *See*, R.I. GEN. LAWS § 11-47-58 (2009)
Open Carry	Prohibited without AG-issued permit
Military-pattern semi-auto restrictions	Not restricted
NFA weapons	Prohibited

Reciprocity / Recognition

*Rhode Island **does not recognize** permits from any other state.*

*Rhode Island permits **are recognized by** the following states:*

Alaska	Arizona	Idaho	Indiana
Kentucky	Michigan*	Missouri	Nebraska
Oklahoma	South Dakota	Tennessee	Texas
Utah	Vermont		

Note: In the reciprocity / recognition tables above, states with an asterisk (*) require the permit holder to both have a permit from, and be a resident of, the recognized state in order for reciprocity / recognition of the permit.

Knife Carry Summary:

Note: Blade length limits, if any, in parentheses.

Knife Type	Open Carry	Concealed Carry	Notes
Folding	Yes	Yes (≤ 3")	
Fixed Blade	Yes	Yes (≤ 3")	
Dirks, Daggers, Stilettos	Yes	Yes (≤ 3")	
Automatics	Yes	Yes (≤ 3")	
Balisongs	No	No	

53.1 Discussion

Firearms Carry:

Travelers to the Ocean State will find a fairly restrictive legal environment for firearms carry in this small northeastern state. Rhode Island requires a permit to carry a loaded handgun on one's person or in a vehicle. The state issues such permits on a discretionary basis to residents and nonresidents. Rhode Island does not recognize the carry permits of any other state.

State law prohibits carry, with or without a permit, of loaded long guns in a vehicle. Long guns must be transported in an unloaded condition.[159] Given the state's generally restrictive attitude towards firearms, the prudent traveler would be wise to also securely case all long guns and stow them in the trunk of the vehicle. If the vehicle has no trunk, then the gun case should be locked and stored in the vehicle cargo area.

No permit is required to transport a handgun from your home or place of business to or from a bona fide target range, provided that the handgun is unloaded, and either broken down and in plain view, or secured in a gun case.[160]

Rhode Island provides an exception to handgun carry in a vehicle for travelers who are merely passing through and transiting the state. Those travelers with carry permits from any state may carry a handgun in their vehicle under this exception. Note that for the

---

[159] *See*, R.I. GEN. LAWS § 11-47-51 (2009).
[160] *See*, R.I. GEN. LAWS § 11-47-10 (2009).

254 | THE TRAVELER'S GUN & KNIFE LAW BOOK

exception to apply, the traveler must be transiting the state in a continuous, uninterrupted journey, with no intent to remain in Rhode Island.[161]   A quick stop for gas would likely be acceptable, but stopping to sightsee and the like probably would not.

For those travelers without permits who do not fall within the above exception, handguns must be unloaded, securely cased and stored in the trunk of a vehicle. If the vehicle has no trunk, the case should be locked and stored in the vehicle's cargo area.   Any ammunition should be separately cased and stored apart from the gun.

Knife Carry:

Visitors to the Ocean State will find a fairly permissive legal environment for knife carry, at least on paper. State law technically allows open carry of a wide spectrum of knives, and concealed carry of knives with blades three inches or shorter. Rhode Island is one of the few states that specifies how blade length is measured for purposes of the statute, to wit, "from the end of the handle where the blade is attached to the end of the blade[.]"[162]   The Rhode Island Supreme Court has ruled that violation of the statutory blade limit for concealed carry does not require any showing of intent to use the knife unlawfully, and that mere concealed possession is sufficient for conviction.[163]

Technically, state law allows carry of dirks, daggers, stilettos, bowie knives and "sword-in-canes" (sword canes), so long as the wearer harbors no intent to use such knife unlawfully against another.[164]   In practice, however, a visitor openly wearing a large dagger or bowie knife in this small, mostly urban Eastern state will likely encounter concerned, apprehensive looks from citizens, and considerable unwanted law enforcement attention.

In addition, readers should note that state law prohibits possession of so-called "Kung-Fu" weapons, and balisongs, which are often associated with, and perceived by the public as, martial arts weapons, may fall under this statutory ban on possession. Some limited exceptions and affirmative defenses exist, but are unlikely to apply to the typical traveler.

---

[161] See, R.I. GEN. LAWS § 11-47-8 (2009).
[162] See, R.I. GEN. LAWS § 11-47-42 (2009).
[163] See, State v. Johnson, 414 A.2d 477, 480 (R.I. 1980).
[164] See, R.I. GEN. LAWS § 11-47-42 (2009).

State law prohibits possession of firearms or other weapons on school grounds, or at school-sponsored events or while riding school-provided transportation. The penalty for violation of this prohibition is a felony, with a minimum prison sentence of one year, or a hefty fine. Note that municipalities may enact their own restrictions on knife carry beyond those in state law, although few appear to have done so.

53.2 Places Off-Limits While Carrying

Firearms Carry:

Rhode Island prohibits the carry of firearms on school grounds, at school sponsored events, or while riding school provided transportation such as school buses. A conviction for violation of this prohibition carries a one-year mandatory minimum sentence. Exceptions exist for officially recognized and school sanctioned activities involving firearms, such as firearms instruction and firearms safety courses. *See*, R.I. GEN. LAWS § 11-47-60 (2009).

Knife Carry:

Rhode Island prohibits the carry of firearms and other weapons on school grounds, or at school-sponsored events or while riding school-provided transportation. *See*, R.I. GEN. LAWS § 11-47-60 (2009).

53.3 Selected City Ordinances

The state legislature has preempted municipalities and other political subdivisions from regulating firearms. Thus, firearms regulation is uniform throughout the state.

The city ordinances below relate to knife carry:

Newport – Possession of switchblades prohibited. *See*, NEWPORT, R.I., CODIFIED ORDINANCES § 9.16.030 (2010). Display of "any deadly weapon, or instrument or thing which by its appearance may be considered a deadly weapon, in any public place in a manner calculated or likely to alarm or frighten another or others" prohibited. *See, id.* at § 9.04.050.

53.4 State Resources

Rhode Island State Police
311 Danielson Pike
Scituate, RI 02857-1907
Phone: (401) 444-1000
Fax: (401) 444-1105
Website: http://www.risp.state.ri.us/

Attorney General of Rhode Island
150 South Main Street
Providence, RI 02903
Phone: (401) 274-4400
Fax: (401) 222-1331
Website: http://www.riag.state.ri.us/

54 South Carolina – The Palmetto State

Area: 30,109 sq.mi. (Rank: 40th)   Population: 4,479,800 (Rank: 24th)
Violent Crime Rate (per 100,000 residents): 729.7 (Rank: 50th Safest)
State Motto: *Dum Spiro Spero (While I Breathe, I Hope)*

Firearms Carry Summary:

Carry considerations	Status
Restaurants and bars	Prohibited even with permit. *See*, S.C. CODE § 16-23-465 (2009)
Churches / Places of worship	Prohibited without permission of church or place of worship. *See*, S.C. CODE § 23-31-215 (2009)
State parks / forests	Allowed with permit; exceptions also exist for lawful hunting. *See*, S.C. CODE § 51-3-145 (2009)
Vehicle carry	Loaded handguns may be carried in closed glove compartment or center console; loaded long guns allowed except in hunting area during hunting season
LE notification if stopped?	Required. *See*, S.C. CODE § 23-31-215(K) (2009)
Retreat requirement for self-defense	Not required. *See*, S.C. CODE § 16-11-440 (2009)
Preemption law	Yes. *See*, S.C. CODE §§ 23-31-510, 23-31-520 (2009)
Open Carry	Generally prohibited
Military-pattern semi-auto restrictions	Not restricted
NFA weapons	Compliance with federal law only

Reciprocity / Recognition

South Carolina **recognizes** resident permits (only) from the following states (Note: Permit holder must have a permit from, and be a resident of, the recognized state):

Alaska	Arizona	Arkansas	Florida
Kansas	Kentucky	Louisiana	Michigan
Missouri	North Carolina	Ohio	Oklahoma
Tennessee	Texas	Virginia	West Virginia
Wyoming			

*South Carolina permits **are recognized by** the following states:*

Alaska	Arizona	Arkansas	Florida*
Idaho	Indiana	Kansas	Kentucky
Louisiana	Michigan*	Missouri	Montana
North Carolina	Nebraska	New Mexico	Ohio
Oklahoma	South Dakota	Tennessee	Texas
Utah	Vermont	Virginia	West Virginia
Wyoming			

Note: In the reciprocity / recognition tables above, states with an asterisk (*) require the permit holder to both have a permit from, and be a resident of, the recognized state in order for reciprocity / recognition of the permit.

Knife Carry Summary:

Note: Blade length limits, if any, in parentheses.

Knife Type	Open Carry	Concealed Carry	Notes
Folding	Yes	Yes	
Fixed Blade	Yes	Yes	
Dirks, Daggers, Stilettos	Yes	No	
Automatics	Yes	Yes	Some localities restrict
Balisongs	Yes	Yes	Some localities restrict

54.1 Discussion

Firearms Carry:

Travelers to the Palmetto State will find a generally hospitable legal environment for firearms carry. South Carolina requires a permit to carry a concealed handgun on or about one's person. The state issues such permits on a "shall issue" basis to qualified residents, and to qualified nonresidents who own real property in the state. South Carolina will recognize the permits of other states that require permit holders to pass a criminal background check, along with a course in firearms training and safety. Note that a permit holder must be a resident of the recognized state in order for his permit to be valid in South Carolina. Currently, South Carolina recognizes permits from sixteen other states.

A traveler without a recognized carry permit may nevertheless carry a loaded handgun in a vehicle, provided that the handgun is stored in a closed glove compartment, center console, or trunk of the vehicle. In addition, handguns may be transported securely cased in commercial gun cases and stored in the trunk or vehicle cargo area.[165] Travelers with recognized permits may of course carry loaded handguns concealed on their person while in a vehicle.

For those without recognized permits traveling on motorcycle, loaded handguns may be transported in a closed saddlebag or similar closed accessory container.

Travelers should be aware that state law requires those with recognized permits carrying concealed handguns inform any law enforcement officer that stops or contacts them in an official capacity of the fact that they are permit holders. In addition, the law requires that upon the officer's request for identification or a driver's license, a permit holder carrying a handgun must present his or her permit along with the other requested identification.

Loaded long guns may be transported in a vehicle except in state parks and wildlife management areas and the like during hunting season, when such guns must be unloaded and securely cased when in the vehicle.

For those without recognized permits, state law allows licensed hunters and fishermen to carry loaded handguns while engaged in hunting or fishing, or going to or from such activities either on foot or in a vehicle.[166]

Knife Carry:

Visitors to the Palmetto State will find a generally permissive legal environment for knife carry under state law. Carry, whether open or concealed, of most knives is generally permitted under state law. Note, however, that state law prohibits concealed carry of deadly weapons "usually used for the infliction of personal injury."[167] Thus, knives designed or specially adapted as weapons, such as daggers and swords, will likely fall under this prohibition. The statute, however, exempts from its scope dirks, knives and razors unless they are used with intent to commit, or in furtherance of, a crime.[168]

---

[165] See, S.C. CODE § 16-23-20 (2009).
[166] See, id.
[167] See, S.C. CODE § 16-23-460 (2009).
[168] Id.

State law prohibits carry of firearms and other weapons, the definition of which includes knives with blades over two inches long, on elementary or secondary school grounds. Although this prohibition seems straightforward, readers should be aware that the statute contains a catchall provision that, in at least one case, has been used to declare that possession of a razor with a one inch blade was a prohibited weapon.[169]

As is the case in most states, municipalities may enact their own local ordinances prohibiting or further restricting knife carry within their jurisdictions, and a number of cities and towns have done so. For example, the city of Columbia, the state capitol, prohibits carry of any kind of a number of types of knives, including dirks, butcher knives, and razors, as well as possession of switchblades.[170]

54.2 Places Off-Limits While Carrying

Firearms Carry:

South Carolina prohibits the carrying of concealable firearms, with or without a permit, in a variety of places, including law enforcement offices and facilities such as police, sheriff, and highway patrol stations; correctional and detention facilities; courthouses and court rooms; polling places on election days; local government offices and meeting places; school or college athletic events not related to firearms; and preschool and daycare facilities. *See*, S.C. CODE § 23-31-215(M) (2009).

State law also prohibits the carry of concealable firearms in a church or other place of worship without the express permission of the church or place of worship. Carry is also forbidden in hospitals, medical clinics, doctors' offices and other facilities where medical services or procedures are performed without the employer's express authorization. *See, id.*

State law prohibits carry of firearms in schools, colleges, universities and other postsecondary educational institutions without the express permission of the institution. This prohibition does not apply to those with recognized carry permits, so long as the weapons remain in an

---

[169] *See, In the Interest of Dave G.*, 477 S.E.2d 470, 324 S.C. 347 (S.C. Ct. App. 1996) (affirming conviction for possession of razor blade with one inch blade on school property, and upholding trial judge factual determination that razor was "weapon, device or object" capable of "inflicting bodily injury or death.").
[170] *See*, COLUMBIA, S.C., CODE OF ORDINANCES §§ 14-102, 14-103 (2009).

attended or locked vehicle and are secured in a closed glove compartment, center console, vehicle trunk, or securely cased in a commercial gun case stored in the vehicle's cargo or luggage compartment. *See*, S.C. CODE § 16-23-420.

Carry of firearms is also prohibited in publicly owned buildings without the express permission of the authority in charge of the premises. This does not apply to interstate highway rest areas, provided the person has a recognized carry permit. *See, id.*

South Carolina prohibits carry of firearms into any establishment that sells alcoholic beverages for on premises consumption. Violation of this prohibition is a misdemeanor punished by a fine of up to $2,000 and/or up to three years in prison, in addition to revocation of the violator's carry permit. *See*, S.C. CODE § 16-23-465.

As is the case elsewhere, private businesses and employers can prohibit the carry of concealed weapons on their premises. *See*, S.C. CODE § 23-31-220. State law requires that businesses wishing to do so must conspicuously post signs to that effect at each entrance. The design, size, text and placement of such signs is specified by statute. *See*, S.C. CODE § 23-31-235.

State law requires that those carrying concealed firearms on a recognized permit may not carry such weapons into the private residence or dwelling of another without the express permission of the owner or person in legal control of the premises. Violation of this requirement is a misdemeanor that carries a minimum $1000 fine, revocation of the violator's carry permit for five years, and the possibility of up to a year in prison. *See*, S.C. CODE § 23-31-225.

Knife Carry:

State law prohibits the carry of firearms and other weapons, the definition of which includes knives with blades over two inches long, on elementary or secondary school property. *See*, S.C. CODE § 16-23-430 (2009). Readers should be aware that the statute contains a catchall provision that, in at least one case, has been used to declare that a razor blade under the two inch limit, to be a prohibited weapon.[171]

In addition, municipalities may pass their own local ordinances prohibiting or otherwise restricting knife carry within their jurisdictions.

---

[171] *See, In the Interest of Dave G.*, 477 S.E.2d 470, 471-72 (S.C. Ct. App. 1996).

54.3 Selected City Ordinances

The state legislature has preempted municipalities and other political subdivisions from regulating firearms to any extent greater than state law. Thus, firearms regulation is uniform throughout the state.

The city ordinances below relate to knife carry:

Charleston – Possession of martial arts weapons prohibited. *See*, CHARLESTON, S.C., CODE § 21-211 (2009). Concealed carry of "any ice pick, razor, knife, dagger or stiletto, the blade of which exceeds three (3) inches in length" prohibited. *See, id.* at § 21-215.

Columbia – Carry, whether open or concealed, of any "dirk, butcher knife, case knife, sword or spear, ..., razors or other weapons of offense" prohibited. *See*, COLUMBIA, S.C., CODE OF ORDINANCES § 14-102 (2009). Possession of switchblades within the city prohibited. *See, id.* at § 14-103. Possession, purchase, sale or transfer of firearms, ammunition, or "dangerous weapon of any kind" outside one's own premises prohibited during declared state of emergency when curfew has been imposed. See, id. at § 7-35.

Myrtle Beach – Carry, whether open or concealed, of dirks, razors, "or other deadly weapons used for the infliction of injury to person or property" prohibited. *See*, MYRTLE BEACH, S.C., CODE OF ORDINANCES § 14-102 (2009). Possession of firearms, ammunition, or "dangerous weapon of any kind" outside one's own premises prohibited during declared state of emergency when a curfew has been imposed. See, id. at § 8-1.

54.4 State Resources

South Carolina Law Enforcement Division
P.O. Box 21398
Columbia, SC 29221-1398
Phone: (803) 896-7099
Website: http://www.sled.sc.gov/

South Carolina Attorney General
1000 Assembly Street, Room 519
Columbia, SC 29201
Phone: (803) 734-3970
Website: http://www.scattorneygeneral.org/

55 South Dakota – The Mount Rushmore State

Area: 75,885 sq.mi. (Rank: 16th)   Population: 804,194 (Rank: 46th)
Violent Crime Rate (per 100,000 residents): 201.4 (Rank: 5th Safest)
State Motto: *Under God the People Rule*

Firearms Carry Summary:

Carry considerations	Status
Restaurants and bars	Allowed with permit in restaurants only.[172]
Churches / Places of worship	Allowed
State parks / forests	Allowed
Vehicle carry	Loaded handgun in plain sight allowed without permit, or unloaded and cased; loaded long guns allowed
LE notification if stopped?	Not required
Retreat requirement for self-defense	Required
Preemption law	Yes. See, S.D. Codified Laws §§ 7-18A-36 (counties); 8-5-13 (townships); 9-19-20 (municipalities) (2009)
Open Carry	Allowed, no permit required
Military-pattern semi-auto restrictions	Not restricted
NFA weapons	NFA-friendly, compliance with federal law only

Reciprocity / Recognition

South Dakota **recognizes** permits from **all other states**.

South Dakota permits **are recognized by** the following states:

Alaska	Arizona	Arkansas	Colorado*
Florida*	Georgia	Idaho	Indiana
Kentucky	Louisiana	Maine*	Michigan*
Mississippi	Missouri	Montana	North Carolina
North Dakota	Oklahoma	Pennsylvania	Tennessee
Texas	Utah	Vermont	Virginia

---

[172] *See*, S.D. CODIFIED LAWS § 23-7-8.1 (2009), which states in relevant part that "[t]he holder of a permit may carry a concealed pistol anywhere in South Dakota except in any licensed on-sale malt beverage or alcoholic beverage establishment that derives over one-half of its total income from the sale of malt or alcoholic beverages."

West Virginia   Wyoming

Note: In the reciprocity / recognition tables above, states with an asterisk (*) require the permit holder to both have a permit from, and be a resident of, the recognized state in order for reciprocity / recognition of the permit.

Knife Carry Summary:

Note: Blade length limits, if any, in parentheses.

Knife Type	Open Carry	Concealed Carry	Notes
Folding	Yes	Yes	
Fixed Blade	Yes	Yes	
Dirks, Daggers, Stilettos	Yes	Yes	
Automatics	Yes	Yes	See note[173]
Balisongs	Yes	Yes	See note[174]

55.1 Discussion

Firearms Carry:

Visitors to the Mount Rushmore State will find a friendly legal environment for firearms carry. South Dakota requires a permit to carry a concealed handgun. Such permits are issued on a "shall issue" basis to qualified residents. Travelers will be pleased to know that South Dakota recognizes carry permits from every other state. Thus, if you have a carry permit, it's valid for carry in South Dakota.

Open carry in South Dakota is legal without a permit and generally accepted, a reflection of the state's lightly populated rural character and wide-open spaces.

Travelers with permits may carry loaded handguns either openly or concealed while traveling in a vehicle.

---

[173] Effective July 1, 2006, possession of ballistic knives is no longer prohibited. *See*, S.D. CODIFIED LAWS § 22-14-19 (2005) (repealed effective July 1, 2006).
[174] Effective July 1, 2006, possession of butterfly/balisong knives by minors is no longer prohibited. *See*, S.D. CODIFIED LAWS § 22-14-29 (2005) (repealed effective July 1, 2006).

A traveler without a permit may carry loaded handguns in the vehicle so long as the handguns are in plain view and not concealed. With respect to firearms, state law defines "concealed" as meaning "totally hidden from view," and that so long as "any part of the firearm is capable of being seen, it is not concealed" under South Dakota law.[175] For those without permits, handguns may also be transported in an unloaded condition and stored in the trunk of the vehicle, closed glove compartment or center console. The unloaded handgun may also be securely cased in a commercial gun case of a size large enough so that it cannot be concealed on one's person.

Long guns may be transported in the vehicle either loaded or unloaded. During hunting season or when traveling through game or wildlife preserves and refuges, long guns should be unloaded and securely cased and/or stored in the vehicle's trunk.

If traveling via motorcycle or off-road vehicle, firearms must be unloaded and securely cased unless the traveler possesses a permit.

Knife Carry:

Visitors to South Dakota will find a permissive legal environment for knife carry. State law permits open or concealed carry of most knives. State law makes it a felony, however, to carry a concealed dangerous weapon, the definition of which includes any knife, with intent to commit a felony. There is no statutorily defined blade length limit. The legislature has repealed, effective July 1, 2006, two knife-related statutes prohibiting possession of ballistic knives, and prohibiting possession of butterfly or balisong knives by persons under the age of eighteen.

Apart from courthouses and schools, no other state-wide statutory prohibitions on off-limits locations for otherwise legal knife carry exist, although cities and towns may pass their own ordinances restricting knife carry. South Dakota does not preempt its cities and towns from regulating knife carry, unlike the case for firearms, where the state

---

[175] See, S.D. CODIFIED LAWS § 22-1-2. In addition, in September 2004 the state's Attorney General issued a formal opinion concluding that "... it is my opinion that Legislature did not intend to require a license or a permit to carry a handgun in a vehicle if any part of the firearm is capable of being seen. Therefore the criminal sanctions in SDCL 22-14-9 do not apply unless the handgun is truly "concealed." If the firearm is "concealed" within a motor vehicle and thus completely incapable of being seen, the carrier must either have a license or permit or comply with the provisions of SDCL 22-14-10." See, Att'y Gen. Opinion re: "Handguns in vehicles" dated Sept. 17, 2004.

has prohibited local governments from enacting their own firearms carry restrictions, ensuring uniform state-wide firearms laws. As such, local governments may enact their own ordinances prohibiting or otherwise restricting knife carry within their jurisdictions.

55.2 Places Off-Limits While Carrying

Firearms Carry:

South Dakota prohibits the carry of firearms on elementary and secondary school premises, and school vehicles such as school buses. Exceptions exist for school sanctioned activities involving firearms, such as firearms training. *See*, S.D. CODIFIED LAWS § 13-32-7 (2009).

State law prohibits possession of firearms, with or without a permit, in county courthouses, the definition of which includes the state capitol. *See*, S.D. CODIFIED LAWS § 22-14-23.

State law also prohibits carry of firearms in establishments such as bars and taverns that derive more than one half of their total income from the sale of alcoholic beverages. *See*, S.D. CODIFIED LAWS § 23-7-8.1.

Knife Carry:

South Dakota prohibits the carry of firearms and other dangerous weapons on elementary or secondary school premises. *See*, S.D. CODIFIED LAWS § 13-32-7 (2009). State law also prohibits possession of firearms and dangerous weapons in county courthouses. *See, id.* at § 22-14-23.

55.3 Selected City Ordinances

The state legislature has preempted municipalities and other political subdivisions from regulating firearms to any extent greater than state law. Thus, firearms regulation is uniform throughout the state.

The city ordinances below relate to knife carry:

Aberdeen – Concealed carry of daggers, bowie knives, dirks, and other dangerous and deadly weapons prohibited. *See*, ABERDEEN, S.D., REVISED ORDINANCES § 19-76 (2008). Possession in licensed alcoholic beverage establishments of any "sharp or dangerous weapon" prohibited, except a folding pocket knife (kept in closed position) with blade less than three inches. *See, id.* § 4-4.

Rapid City – Concealed carry of "any knife with a blade exceeding 3 inches in length, or any sharp or dangerous weapon such as is usually employed in attack or defense of the person" prohibited. *See,* RAPID CITY, S.D., CODE OF ORDINANCES § 9.28.030 (2010). Carry, whether open or concealed, of any weapon or "sharp or dangerous object," other than a folding knife carried in the closed position with a blade less than three inches in length, prohibited in all alcoholic beverage establishments except those solely selling beer for off-premises consumption. *See, id.* at § 9.28.040.

Sioux Falls – Concealed carry of daggers, bowie knives, razors, dirks and other dangerous and deadly weapons prohibited. *See,* SIOUX FALLS, S.D., REVISED ORDINANCES § 26-51 (2010). Drawing of deadly weapons, including knives, so that weapon "may be used against or upon another person" prohibited, except for self-defense purpose. *See, id.* at § 26-52. Carry in "threatening or menacing manner, without authority of law, any pistol, revolver, dagger, razor, dangerous knife, stiletto, …, or other dangerous weapon" prohibited. *See, id.* at § 26-25.

55.4 State Resources

South Dakota Department of Public Safety
118 West Capitol Avenue
Pierre, South Dakota 57501
Phone: (605) 773-3178
Fax: (605) 773-3018
Website: http://dps.sd.gov/

Attorney General of South Dakota
1302 E Hwy 14, Suite 1
Pierre SD 57501-8501
Phone: (605) 773-3215
TTY: (605) 773-6585
Fax: (605) 773-4106
Website: http://www.state.sd.us/attorney/index.asp

56 Tennessee – The Volunteer State

Area: 41,217 sq.mi. (Rank: 34th)   Population: 6,214,888 (Rank: 17th)
Violent Crime Rate (per 100,000 residents): 722.4 (Rank: 48th Safest)
State Motto: *Agriculture and Commerce*

Firearms Carry Summary:

Carry considerations	Status
Restaurants and bars	Currently prohibited, even with permit – see footnote[176]
Churches / Places of worship	Allowed with permit
State parks / forests	Concealed with permit allowed
Vehicle carry	Loaded handguns allowed with permit, otherwise must be unloaded and cased; long guns unloaded and cased; if traveler has permit, long guns may be transported with empty chamber but loaded magazine
LE notification if stopped?	Not required
Retreat requirement for self-defense	Not required. *See*, TENN. CODE. ANN. § 39-11-611 (2009)
Preemption law	Yes.
Open Carry	Allowed with permit
Military-pattern semi-auto restrictions	Not restricted
NFA weapons	NFA-friendly, compliance with federal law only

Reciprocity / Recognition

Tennessee **recognizes** permits from **all other states**.

Tennessee permits **are recognized by** the following states:

Alabama	Alaska	Arizona	Arkansas
Colorado*	Delaware	Florida*	Georgia
Idaho	Indiana	Kansas	Kentucky

---

[176] In November 2009, the Chancery Court of Davidson County, Tenn., ruled that the state's recently enacted July 2009 law (passed over the governor's veto) allowing permit holders to carry in restaurants that serve alcohol was unconstitutionally vague, thus effectively putting the law on hold. As such, carry is currently prohibited in restaurants that serve alcohol. A renewed legislative effort to fix the court's objection has resulted in the legislature passing a new amended law in May 2010 to allow carry in restaurants that serve alcohol. At press time that law had not yet taken effect. The governor may veto it, as he did the last law, requiring a legislative override. Even if the new law takes effect, the anti-gun, anti-self-defense crowd may file another lawsuit to try to stop it.

Louisiana	Michigan*	Minnesota	Mississippi
Missouri	Montana	North Carolina	Nebraska
North Dakota	New Hampshire*	New Mexico	Nevada
Ohio	Oklahoma	Pennsylvania	South Carolina*
South Dakota	Texas	Utah	Vermont
Virginia	West Virginia	Wyoming	

Note: In the reciprocity / recognition tables above, states with an asterisk (*) require the permit holder to both have a permit from, and be a resident of, the recognized state in order for reciprocity / recognition of the permit.

Knife Carry Summary:

Note: Blade length limits, if any, in parentheses.

Knife Type	Open Carry	Concealed Carry	Notes
Folding	Yes (< 4")	Yes (< 4")	
Fixed Blade	Yes (< 4")	Yes (< 4")	
Dirks, Daggers, Stilettos	Yes (< 4")	Yes (< 4")	
Automatics	No	No	
Balisongs	Yes (< 4")	Yes (< 4")	See note[177]

56.1 Discussion

Firearms Carry:

Travelers to the Volunteer State will find a fairly friendly legal environment for firearms carry. Tennessee requires a permit to carry a handgun either openly or concealed on one's person. Such permits are issued on a "shall issue" basis to qualified residents. In addition, Tennessee recognizes the carry permits of all other states.

Those without permits traveling in the vehicle must transport their firearms, both handguns and long guns, in an unloaded condition and either in plain view, or securely cased in commercial gun cases. Any ammunition should be stored separately, apart from the guns. Storage of handguns in glove compartments or center console storage areas is not permitted without a recognized permit.

---

[177] State law prohibits possession of switchblades. *See*, TENN. CODE § 39-17-1302(7) (2009). Note that balisongs may fall under the switchblade prohibition, as balisongs do in some states. As such, cautious travelers would be wise to avoid carry of balisongs.

For travelers with permits, loaded handguns may be carried either openly or concealed while in a vehicle. Long guns in a vehicle, however, must be transported with at least the firearms' chambers unloaded and empty, although magazines may remain loaded.[178]

Tennessee has preempted local county and municipal governments from regulating most aspects of firearms carry and possession. The state allows local governments to prohibit handguns in parks and other recreational areas within their jurisdictions. In addition, local ordinances enacted before April 1986 have been grandfathered, and any such ordinances are still in effect.[179]

Knife Carry:

Visitors to the Volunteer State will find a fairly permissive legal environment for knife carry. State law prohibits carry with any intent to go armed, that is, with the intent to use the knife carried as a weapon, of any knife with a blade greater than four inches in length. Fixed and folding knives, with blades four inches or less, may be carried openly or concealed. Switchblades are prohibited. Note that balisongs may fall under the switchblade prohibition, as balisongs do in some states. As such, cautious travelers would be wise to avoid carry of balisongs in this state.

State law prohibits carry of any "bowie knife, hawk bill knife, ice pick, dagger, ..., switchblade knife, ... or any other weapon of like kind" on public or private school grounds. The statute defines "weapon of like kind" as encompassing "razors and razor blades, except those used solely for personal shaving, and any sharp pointed or edged instrument," and provides limited exceptions for instructional, food preparation, and maintenance uses.[180] In addition, Tennessee prohibits possession of weapons, including switchblades, in court facilities.[181]

As in many states, local governments may enact their own ordinances prohibition or otherwise restricting the carry of knives within their jurisdictions.

---

[178] See, TENN. CODE § 39-17-1307 (2009)
[179] See, TENN. CODE § 39-17-1314 (2009).
[180] See, TENN. CODE § 39-17-1309 (2009).
[181] See, TENN. CODE § 39-17-1306 (2009).

56.2 Places Off-Limits While Carrying

Firearms Carry:

Tennessee prohibits the possession or carry of firearms, whether openly or concealed, in school buildings, school buses, campus grounds, school recreational areas and athletic fields, or any other school, college or university property. A nonstudent adult may possess firearms within a private vehicle if the firearms are not handled while the vehicle is on school property. See, TENN. CODE. ANN. § 39-17-1309 (2009).

State law prohibits possession or carry of firearms with the "intent to go armed" in public parks, playgrounds, civic centers and building facilities, areas and property owned, used or operated by the state, or by county or municipal governments, for recreational purposes. This prohibition does not generally apply to those possessing recognized carry permits, unless the property is owned or under the control of a county or municipal government, and that particular local government has decided to ban firearms in that location. State law requires posting notice of such firearms bans in prominent locations. See, TENN. CODE. ANN. § 39-17-1311 (2009).

Carry of firearms is prohibited in courts and courthouses in any locations where judicial proceedings are under way. See, TENN. CODE. ANN. § 39-17-1306 (2009).

In 2009, Tennessee passed a law allowing those with recognized carry permits to carry in establishments that serve alcoholic beverages for on premises consumption. See, TENN. CODE. ANN. § 39-17-1305 (2009). Unfortunately, in November 2009 a Tennessee court ruled that statute unconstitutional. Thus, absent a ruling from a higher court in Tennessee, or passage of a revised statute, at this time carry of firearms into places that serve alcohol is prohibited, even if one has a recognized carry permit.

Knife Carry:

Tennessee prohibits carry of any kind, "with the intent to go armed", of firearms, or any "bowie knife, hawk bill knife, ice pick, dagger, …, switchblade knife, … or any other weapon of like kind" on public or private school grounds. The term "weapon of like kind" encompasses "razors and razor blades, except those used solely for personal shaving, and any sharp pointed or edged instrument," with

272 | THE TRAVELER'S GUN & KNIFE LAW BOOK

limited exceptions for instructional, food preparation, and maintenance uses. *See*, TENN. CODE § 39-17-1309 (2009).

State law also prohibits possession of weapons, including switchblades, in court facilities. *See*, TENN. CODE § 39-17-1306 (2009).

56.3 Selected City Ordinances

The state legislature has preempted municipalities and other political subdivisions from regulating most aspects of firearms carry, transport and possession. Thus, firearms regulation is mostly uniform throughout the state, although some pre-April 1986 local ordinances may still be in effect.

The city ordinances below relate to knife carry:

Memphis – Carry of any kind with intent to go armed of any razor, dirk, bowie knife, or "other knife of like form, shape or size", pocket knife with blade over four inches in length, sword cane, ice pick, or Spanish stiletto prohibited. *See*, MEMPHIS, TENN., CODE OF ORDINANCES § 10-32-2 (2009). Unlawful to engage in "cruising," defined as "driving a motor vehicle past a traffic control point in the area designated as a no cruising zone more than three times in one hour," while also, among other prohibited acts, "[c]arrying in any manner whatever, with the intent to go armed, any razor; dirk; bowie knife or other knife of like form, shape or size; pocket knife with any blade over four inches in length; sword cane; ice pick; ...; Spanish stiletto." *See, id.* at § 11-16-50.

Knoxville – Carry, whether open or concealed, with the intent to go armed, of "any razor, dirk, bowie knife or other knife of like form, shape or size, sword cane, icepick, slingshot, blackjack, brass knuckles, [or] Spanish stiletto" prohibited. *See*, KNOXVILLE, TENN., CODE OF ORDINANCES § 19-104 (2009). Sales of dirks, bowie knives, sword canes, and Spanish stilettos prohibited. *See, id.* at § 19-105. Sale to minor of bowie knives, dirks, hunting knives, or switchblades, except for hunting purposes, prohibited. *See, id.* at § 19-106. Carry of switchblades by minor (person under 18 years old) prohibited. *See, id.* at § 19-107.

56.4 State Resources

Tennessee Department of Safety
P.O. Box 945
Nashville, TN 37202
Phone: (615) 251-8590
Fax: (615) 532-3056
Website: http://www.state.tn.us/safety/

Tennessee Attorney General
P.O. Box 20207
Nashville, TN 37202-0207
Phone: (615) 741-3491
Fax: (615) 741-2009
Website: http://www.tn.gov/attorneygeneral/

57 Texas – The Lone Star State

Area: 261,797 sq.mi. (Rank: 2nd)	Population: 24,326,974 (Rank: 2nd)
Violent Crime Rate (per 100,000 residents): 507.9 (Rank: 39th Safest)	
State Motto: *Friendship*	

Firearms Carry Summary:

Carry considerations	Status
Restaurants and bars	Allowed with permit in restaurants only. *See*, TEX. PENAL CODE ANN. § 46.035 (2009)
Churches / Places of worship	Prohibited
State parks / forests	Allowed with permit
Vehicle carry	Concealed loaded handguns allowed; loaded long guns allowed
LE notification if stopped?	Required. *See*, TEX. GOV'T CODE ANN. § 411.205 (2009)
Retreat requirement for self-defense	Not required. *See*, TEX. PENAL CODE ANN. §§ 9.31, 9.32 (2009)
Preemption law	Yes.
Open Carry	Prohibited, even with permit
Military-pattern semi-auto restrictions	Not restricted
NFA weapons	NFA-friendly, compliance with federal law only

Reciprocity / Recognition

*Texas **recognizes** permits from the following states:*

Alabama	Alaska	Arizona	Arkansas
California	Colorado	Connecticut	Delaware
Florida	Georgia	Hawaii	Iowa
Idaho	Indiana	Kansas	Kentucky
Louisiana	Maryland	Massachusetts	Michigan
Mississippi	Missouri	Montana	North Carolina
North Dakota	Nebraska	New Jersey	New York
New Mexico	Nevada	Oklahoma	Pennsylvania
Rhode Island	South Carolina	South Dakota	Tennessee
Utah	Virginia	Washington	Wyoming

*Texas permits **are recognized by** the following states:*

Alabama	Alaska	Arizona	Arkansas
Colorado*	Delaware	Florida*	Georgia
Idaho	Indiana	Kansas	Kentucky
Louisiana	Michigan*	Minnesota	Mississippi
Missouri	Montana	North Carolina	North Dakota
Nebraska	New Mexico	Oklahoma	Pennsylvania
South Carolina*	South Dakota	Tennessee	Utah
Vermont	Virginia	Wyoming	

Note: In the reciprocity / recognition tables above, states with an asterisk (*) require the permit holder to both have a permit from, and be a resident of, the recognized state in order for reciprocity / recognition of the permit.

Knife Carry Summary:

Note: Blade length limits, if any, in parentheses.

Knife Type	Open Carry	Concealed Carry	Notes
Folding	Yes (≤ 5½")	Yes (≤ 5½")	
Fixed Blade	Yes (≤ 5½")	Yes (≤ 5½")	See note[182]
Dirks, Daggers, Stilettos	No	No	
Automatics	No	No	
Balisongs	No	No	See note[183]

57.1 Discussion

Firearms Carry:

Travelers to Texas will find a somewhat restrictive legal environment for firearms carry. Visitors to the Lone Star State may find this somewhat peculiar, given the image of Texas in popular culture. It may come as a surprise, for example, that Texas prohibits open carry

---

[182] State law specifically prohibits bowie knives, regardless of blade length. *See*, TEX. PENAL CODE § 46.02 (2009).

[183] Balisongs likely fall under the switchblade prohibition, as balisongs do in some states, as a number of appellate decisions have referred to a balisong as an "illegal knife". *See, e.g., Ex Parte Turner*, No. 08-02-00355-CR, (Tex. Ct. App. 2003) (stating and describing butterfly knife as "illegal weapon"); *Walbey v. State*, 926 S.W.2d 307, 310 (Tex. Crim. App. 1996) (describing prior arrest for possession of "illegal butterfly knife" and ice pick).

of handguns under most circumstances, even with a recognized carry permit. Yet unfortunately, that is indeed the case.

Texas requires a permit to carry a concealed handgun on one's person. Such permits are issued on a "shall issue" basis to qualified residents and nonresidents. Fortunately for the traveler, the Lone Star State does recognize the carry permits of forty other states.

Travelers with recognized permits who are carrying concealed handguns should be aware that state law requires, if stopped by a law enforcement officer for an official purpose who requests identification (such as a drivers license), that the permit holder automatically and without separate request display both the requested identification and the permit holder's carry permit.[184]

A traveler without a recognized permit may generally not carry a handgun either openly or concealed. State law does provide a "bona fide journey" exception for travelers, although as is the case with many such fact-specific exceptions, considerable room exists for adverse law enforcement action against someone claiming this exemption. State law does, of course, provide exceptions for handgun carry when involved in such activities as lawful hunting and target shooting.

A law-abiding traveler without a recognized permit may nevertheless carry a loaded handgun in a vehicle, so long as the handgun is carried concealed. Long guns may also be carried in a loaded condition anywhere in the vehicle either in plain view, or securely cased in commercial gun cases.

State law preempts local governments from regulating firearms carried by those with recognized permits. Local governments may, however, regulate and/or prohibit firearms carry in places like public parks, parades, and political rallies in their jurisdictions for those *without* recognized handgun carry permits.

Knife Carry:

Visitors to the Lone Star State will find a fairly restrictive legal environment for knife carry. Readers may find this perhaps somewhat surprising, given the modern public image and history ("Remember the Alamo!") of Texas, and the grand, rugged scale of the largest of the lower 48 states.

---

[184] *See,* TEX. GOV'T CODE § 411.205 (2009).

Nevertheless, with respect to knives, Texas law prohibits carry of daggers, dirks, stilettos, automatic knives (switchblades), and large fixed bladed knives such as bowie knives. The state law definition of an "illegal knife" includes any knife with a blade over five and a half inches. Granted, this is one of the largest statutory blade length limits in the country, and will no doubt help uphold the public perception that things are big in Texas! Note, however, that the state's appellate courts have held that the five and a half inch limit refers to the entire blade, including any unsharpened portion, and not just to the sharpened edge.[185]

Balisongs, while not specifically listed as a prohibited item, likely fall under the switchblade prohibition, as balisongs do in a number of states. Indeed, a number of appellate court decisions have referred to balisongs in a conclusory fashion as an "illegal knife" type.

State law prohibits carry of switchblades and illegal knives in a wide variety of locations, such as school and educational institution premises, polling places on election day, court facilities, racetracks, and the secured areas of airports. State law also prohibits such carry within 1,000 feet of a place of execution on the day a death sentence is to be carried out, provided the person carrying has received notice of such prohibition.

Finally, readers should be aware that local governments may enact their own ordinances prohibiting or otherwise restricting knife carry in their jurisdictions beyond the restrictions embodied in state law, although most towns and cities, including such large cities as Dallas, do not appear to have done so to any significant extent.

57.2 Places Off-Limits While Carrying

Firearms Carry:

Texas prohibits possession or carry of firearms, with or without a permit, in a variety of places, including on the premises of schools and other educational institutions, activities sponsored by schools or

---

[185] *See, e.g., Rainer v. State*, 763 S.W.2d 615 (Tex. Ct. App. 1989) (affirming conviction for unlawful carry of illegal knife, hunting knife with sharpened edge less than five and a half inches, but with entire blade exceeding five and a half inches); *McMurrough v. State*, 995 S.W.2d 944, 946 (Tex. Ct. App. 1999) (discussing blade length measurement and stating that term "blade" includes both sharpened and unsharpened portion of knife, excluding handle).

278 | THE TRAVELER'S GUN & KNIFE LAW BOOK

educational institutions, and school buses, without the written authorization of the school or educational institution. Firearms carry is also forbidden at polling places, courts and court houses without written authorization of the court, racetracks, and the secured areas of airports (obviously, federal law also prohibits carry in the secure areas of airports). *See*, TEX. PENAL CODE ANN. § 46.03 (2009).

In addition, Texas prohibits carry of firearms within 1,000 feet of places of execution, on the day of execution. *See, id.*

State law prohibits carry of firearms, with or without a permit, in establishments such as bars and taverns that derive 51% or more of their income from the sale of alcoholic beverages for on-premises consumption. The law requires that such establishments must post prominent signs to notify patrons that carrying of firearms is prohibited in that establishment. *See*, TEX. PENAL CODE ANN. § 46.035 (2009).

Handgun carry is also prohibited at school, college, or professional sporting events unless the permit holder is a participant in the event and the event requires the use of a handgun. *See, id.*

State law also prohibits carry of handguns on the premises of any correctional facility such as a prison or jail; on the premises of any hospital or nursing home, unless the permit holder has written authorization from the hospital or nursing home administration; and in any amusement park. *See, id.*

Those wishing to protect themselves and their loved ones during religious worship will find themselves out of luck in Texas, because state law prohibits handgun carry even with a recognized permit in churches, synagogues, or other places of religious worship. *See, id.*

Rounding out the list of places where handgun carry is prohibited are any meetings of any governmental entity. *See, id.*

Knife Carry:

Texas prohibits the carry of firearms, switchblades, and illegal knives such as daggers, dirks, stilettos, bowie knives and knives with blades exceeding five and a half inches in length, on school and educational institution premises, polling places on election day, court facilities, racetracks, and the secured areas of airports. *See*, TEX. PENAL CODE § 46.03 (2009). State law also prohibits such carry within 1,000 feet of a place of execution on the day a death sentence is to be carried out, provided the person carrying has received notice of such prohibition. *See, id.*

Note that local governments may enact their own ordinances prohibiting or otherwise restricting knife carry in their jurisdictions beyond the restrictions embodied in state law, although most towns and cities, including such large cities as Dallas, do not appear to have done so to any significant extent.

57.3 Selected City Ordinances

The state legislature has preempted municipalities and other political subdivisions from regulating firearms to any extent greater than state law. Thus, firearms regulation is uniform throughout the state.

The city ordinances below relate to knife carry:

Corpus Christi – Carry in public of any straight razor, razor blade, knife having a blade measured from the handle of three inches or longer, any fixed blade, switchblade, ice pick, bowie knife, dirk, dagger, spear, machete, hand sickle, or stiletto prohibited. *See,* CORPUS CHRISTI, TEX., CODE OF ORDINANCES § 33-73 (2010). Certain limited exceptions apply, including an exception for persons "traveling", which under state law means in a private motor vehicle not engaged in criminal activity. *See, id.* at § 33-74, and TEX. PENAL CODE ANN. § 46.15 (2009). Carry of any knife or dagger manufactured or sold for offensive or defensive purposes prohibited on Corpus Christi International Airport property. *See,* CORPUS CHRISTI, TEX., CODE OF ORDINANCES § 9-38 (2010). Exception exists for passengers checking such items in checked baggage. *See, id.*

Laredo – Unlawful to carry illegal knife at any public park, public meeting, political rally, parade, or non-weapons-related school, college, or professional athletic event. *See,* LAREDO, TEX., CODE OF ORDINANCES § 21-152 (2008).

San Antonio – Carry in public of knife with locking blade *less than* five and a half inches prohibited. *See,* SAN ANTONIO, TEX., CODE OF ORDINANCES § 21-17 (2010). Exceptions exist for hunting, fishing, or "lawful sporting activity", for occupational use, and while traveling, which under state law means in a private motor vehicle not engaged in criminal activity. *See, id.,* and TEX. PENAL CODE ANN. § 46.15 (2009). Carry of knives in public by persons less than seventeen years of age prohibited. *See,* SAN ANTONIO, TEX., CODE OF ORDINANCES § 21-155 (2010). Carry of weapons, the definition of which includes illegal knives, and knives, prohibited in city-owned buildings, parking garages, or parking areas. *See*, SAN ANTONIO, TEX., CODE OF ORDINANCES § 21-157 (2010).

Texarkana – Carry of deadly weapons, including firearms, and "knives, switchblades, swords, or other weapons that could endanger other passengers" prohibited on public transit vehicles, facilities and locations. *See*, TEXARKANA, TEX., CODE OF ORDINANCES § 15-66 (2010).

57.4 State Resources

Texas Department of Public Safety
P.O. Box 4087
Austin, Texas 78773-0001
Phone: (800) 224-5744
Phone: (512) 424-7293
Website: http://www.txdps.state.tx.us/

Attorney General of Texas
P. O. Box 12548
Austin, TX 78711-2548
Phone: (512) 463-2100
Fax: (512) 475-2994
Website: http://www.oag.state.tx.us/

58 Utah – The Beehive State

Area: 82,144 sq.mi. (Rank: 12th)   Population: 2,736,424 (Rank: 34th)
Violent Crime Rate (per 100,000 residents): 221.8 (Rank: 6th Safest)
State Motto: *Industry*

Firearms Carry Summary:

Carry considerations	Status
Restaurants and bars	Allowed
Churches / Places of worship	Generally allowed, but church or place of worship can prohibit. *See,* UTAH CODE § 76-10-530 (2009)
State parks / forests	Concealed allowed with permit
Vehicle carry	Loaded handguns allowed concealed or in plain view; long guns must be unloaded and cased
LE notification if stopped?	Not required
Retreat requirement for self-defense	Not required. *See,* UTAH CODE § 76-2-402 (2009)
Preemption law	Yes. *See,* UTAH CODE §§ 53-5a-102, 76-10-500 (2009)
Open Carry	Allowed with permit
Military-pattern semi-auto restrictions	Not restricted
NFA weapons	NFA-friendly, compliance with federal law only

Reciprocity / Recognition

Utah **recognizes** permits from **all other states**.

Utah permits **are recognized by** the following states:

Alabama	Alaska	Arizona	Arkansas
Colorado*	Delaware	Florida*	Georgia
Idaho	Indiana	Kentucky	Louisiana
Michigan*	Minnesota	Mississippi	Missouri
Montana	North Carolina	North Dakota	Nebraska
New Hampshire*	Ohio	Oklahoma	Pennsylvania
South Dakota	Tennessee	Texas	Vermont
Virginia	Washington	West Virginia	Wyoming

Note: In the reciprocity / recognition tables above, states with an asterisk (*) require the permit holder to both have a permit from, and be a resident of, the recognized state in order for reciprocity / recognition of the permit.

Knife Carry Summary:

Note: Blade length limits, if any, in parentheses.

Knife Type	Open Carry	Concealed Carry	Notes
Folding	Yes	Yes	See note[186]
Fixed Blade	Yes	No	See note[187]
Dirks, Daggers, Stilettos	Yes	No	
Automatics	Yes	No	
Balisongs	Yes	No	

58.1 Discussion

Firearms Carry:

Visitors to the Beehive State will find a friendly legal environment for firearms carry. Utah requires a permit to carry a firearm concealed on one's person or in a vehicle. Such permits are issued to qualified residents on any "shall issue" the basis. In addition, Utah recognizes the carry permits of all other states.

The open carry of loaded firearms in public requires a carry permit. In Utah, a firearm is not considered "loaded" if the firing chamber is empty *and* firing the gun requires *at least two* separate physical actions.[188] Thus, a semiautomatic pistol with an empty chamber may

[186] Readers should note that case law exists where knives with blades as short as four inches were found to be dangerous weapons. *See, State v. Kirkwood,* 2002 UT App. 128 (2002) (affirming conviction and upholding jury finding of knife with four inch blade as dangerous weapon). Travelers would be wise to avoid carry of large folders or "tactical" type folders with overly aggressive appearances or weapon-like features.

[187] Case law exists where courts have found fixed bladed knives with five and a half to six inch blades to be dangerous weapons. *See, State v. Archambeau,* 820 P.2d 920 (Utah Ct. App. 1991) (affirming conviction, upholding constitutionality of statutory definition of "dangerous weapon" as applied to defendant, and determination of knife with five and a half inch blade, and bowie knife with six inch blade as dangerous weapons). As such, travelers should avoid concealed carry of large fixed bladed knives without a valid, recognized concealed carry permit.

[188] *See,* UTAH CODE § 76-10-502 (2009), which states: "(1) For the purpose of this chapter, any pistol, revolver, shotgun, rifle, or other weapon described in this part shall be deemed to be loaded when there is an unexpended cartridge, shell, or projectile in the firing position.

(2) Pistols and revolvers shall also be deemed to be loaded when an unexpended cartridge, shell, or projectile is in a position whereby the manual operation of any mechanism once would cause the unexpended cartridge, shell, or projectile to be fired.

(3) A muzzle loading firearm shall be deemed to be loaded when it is capped or primed and has a powder charge and ball or shot in the barrel or cylinders."

be carried with a loaded magazine inserted, as (1) the firing chamber is empty, and (2) firing the gun would require two separate actions: the chambering of a round, and the pressing of the trigger. Similarly, long guns with empty chambers may be transported with magazines containing ammunition. Muzzleloading firearms are considered loaded if capped or primed.

A traveler may carry loaded handguns with or without a permit if traveling in a vehicle. Such handguns may be carried either openly or concealed anywhere in the vehicle, such as in the vehicle's glove compartment or center console, as well as on the traveler's person. Long guns, however, must be transported in an unloaded condition and should be securely cased.

Utah's strong preemption law prohibits local governments from separately regulating most aspects of firearms and firearms carry.

Knife Carry:

Visitors to Utah will find a fairly permissive legal environment for knife carry, with a strong legal bias for open, versus concealed, carry. State law permits open carry of a wide range of knives. State law, however, prohibits concealed carry of dangerous weapons without a recognized permit. Fortunately, Utah is a "shall-issue" state and recognizes all other states' concealed weapons permits.

Even without a recognized permit, concealed carry of ordinary folding pocket knives is permitted, although travelers should exercise caution and should probably avoid carrying "tactical" type knives with aggressive weapon-like features or appearances, lest such knives be deemed "dangerous weapons", and thus prohibited items. There is no statutorily defined blade length limit. Concealed carry of dirks, daggers, stilettos, and automatic knives, without a recognized permit, is prohibited. Note that balisongs, while not specifically prohibited, may fall under the switchblade prohibition, as balisongs do in some states. In addition, balisongs are often associated with the martial arts, and perceived as martial arts weapons. Any of these otherwise prohibited knives may be carried concealed with a valid, recognized permit.

State law prohibits carry of dangerous weapons on school premises, and in the secured areas of airports. Utah does not preempt its cities and towns from regulating knife carry, unlike the case for firearms, where the state has prohibited cities and towns from enacting their own firearms carry restrictions, ensuring uniform state-wide firearms laws. As such, local governments may enact their own ordinances prohibiting or otherwise restricting knife carry within their jurisdictions.

58.2 Places Off-Limits While Carrying

Firearms Carry:

Utah prohibits the carry of firearms, with or without a permit, in any secure area of a facility that prohibits firearms and posts notice of the prohibition; the secure areas of airports; mental health facilities; correctional facilities; and courthouses. *See*, UTAH CODE §§ 76-8-311.1 (secure areas); 76-10-529 (airports); 76-8-311.3 (correctional and mental health facilities); 78A-2-203 (courts).

Churches and other places of worship may also prohibit the carry of firearms with or without permit on their premises. *See*, UTAH CODE § 76-10-530 (2009).

State law prohibits possession or carry of firearms on school premises. This prohibition does not apply to those with carry permits, or those who have permission from the responsible school administrator. In addition, firearms are allowed for approved firearms-related activities, and may be stored in private vehicles parked on school premises. *See*, UTAH CODE § 76-10-505.5 (2009).

Knife Carry:

Utah prohibits the carry of firearms and dangerous weapons on school premises, and in the secure areas of airports. *See*, UTAH CODE §§ 76-10-505.5, 76-10-529 (2009).

58.3 Selected City Ordinances

The state legislature has preempted municipalities and other political subdivisions from regulating firearms. Thus, firearms regulation is uniform throughout the state.

The city ordinances below relate to knife carry:

Moab – Carry, without written consent of peace officer, of "dagger, stiletto, knife, dirk or other concealed deadly weapon" prohibited. *See*, MOAB, UTAH, CITY CODE § 9.28.020 (2009).

58.4 State Resources

Utah Department of Public Safety
4501 South 2700 West
Salt Lake City, Utah 84114
Phone: (801) 965-4461
Website: http://publicsafety.utah.gov/

Attorney General of Utah
Utah State Capitol Complex
350 North State Street, Suite 230
Salt Lake City, UT 84114-2320
Phone: (801) 366-0300
Fax: (801) 538-1121
Website: http://attorneygeneral.utah.gov/

59 Vermont – The Green Mountain State

Area: 9,250 sq.mi. (Rank: 43th)   Population: 621,270 (Rank: 49th)
Violent Crime Rate (per 100,000 residents): 135.9 (Rank: 2nd Safest)
State Motto: *Freedom and Unity*

Firearms Carry Summary:

Carry considerations	Status
Restaurants and bars	Allowed
Churches / Places of worship	Allowed
State parks / forests	Allowed; some exceptions for certain state game refuges
Vehicle carry	Loaded handguns allowed; long guns must be unloaded
LE notification if stopped?	Not required
Retreat requirement for self-defense	Required
Preemption law	Yes.
Open Carry	Allowed and generally accepted
Military-pattern semi-auto restrictions	Not restricted
NFA weapons	Mostly NFA-friendly, although silencers prohibited; otherwise compliance with federal law only

Reciprocity / Recognition

Vermont **recognizes** permits from **all other states**.(Vermont does not require a permit to carry concealed or openly).

Vermont does not issue permits (and none is needed to carry in Vermont), and thus there is no permit for another state to recognize. Vermont residents who can lawfully possess firearms, however, may carry concealed handguns in Alaska and Vermont, because those states do not require a permit to carry concealed handguns. After July 29, 2010, such residents may also carry concealed handguns without a permit in Arizona.

Knife Carry Summary:

Note: Blade length limits, if any, in parentheses.

Knife Type	Open Carry	Concealed Carry	Notes
Folding	Yes	Yes	

Knife Type	Open Carry	Concealed Carry	Notes
Fixed Blade	Yes	Yes	
Dirks, Daggers, Stilettos	Yes	Yes	
Automatics	Yes (< 3")	Yes (< 3")	
Balisongs	Yes (< 3")	Yes (< 3")	See note[189]

59.1 Discussion

Firearms Carry:

Visitors to the Green Mountain State will find a friendly legal environment for firearms carry. Vermont, like Alaska, requires no permit to carry loaded firearms in public, either openly or concealed.

Thus, loaded handguns may be carried openly or concealed on one person while on foot, or in a vehicle. Loaded handguns may also be transported in vehicle glove compartments, center consoles, or other storage containers. When in a vehicle, however, long guns must be transported in an unloaded condition and either in plain view, or stored in the trunk or commercial gun cases.

The state's strong preemption law prohibits local governments from regulating most aspects of firearms, including the ownership, transportation, and carrying of firearms.

Knife Carry:

Visitors to the Green Mountain State will find a permissive legal environment for knife carry, a fitting complement to the similarly permissive legal environment for firearms carry. State law allows open or concealed carry of a wide array of knives, from folders to daggers. There is no statutorily defined blade length limit, except for switchblades, which must have blades less than three inches to be legal. Cautious travelers should be aware of the possibility that balisongs may be deemed statutory switchblades, as balisongs are in some states, and thus subject to the less-than-three-inch blade restriction.

---

[189] Balisongs may be deemed statutory switchblades, as balisongs are in some states, and thus subject to the less-than-three-inch blade restriction.

Apart from schools and courthouses, no state-wide statutory prohibitions on off-limits locations for otherwise legal knife carry appear to exist, although cities and towns may pass their own ordinances restricting knife carry. Like most states, Vermont does not preempt its cities and towns from regulating knife carry, unlike the case for firearms, where the state has prohibited cities and towns from enacting their own firearms carry restrictions, ensuring uniform state-wide firearms laws. Thus, cities and towns may pass their own restrictions on knife carry, although few appear to have done so.

59.2 Places Off-Limits While Carrying

Firearms Carry:

Vermont prohibits carry firearms and dangerous weapons in schools and school buses, unless possession has been authorized by the school. See, VT. STAT. ANN. tit. 13, § 4004 (2009). State law also prohibits firearms carry in courthouses. See, VT. STAT. ANN. tit. 13, § 4016.

State law prohibits carrying of dangerous or deadly weapons in any state institution for state institution grounds, such as prisons, state-run mental health facilities, and the like. See, VT. STAT. ANN. tit. 13, § 4003.

The state may also regulate and/or prohibit the carrying of firearms in state owned or operated buildings or properties (including those leased to the state). See, VT. STAT. ANN. tit. 29, § 152.

State law prohibits possession of firearms in the Bomoseen State Game Refuge. See, VT. STAT. ANN. tit. 10, § 5226.

Knife Carry:

Vermont prohibits the carry of firearms and other dangerous or deadly weapons in schools, school buses, state institutions, and courthouses. See, VT. STAT. ANN. tit 13 §§ 4004 (schools), 4003 (state institutions), 4016 (courthouses) (2009).

59.3 Selected City Ordinances

The state legislature has preempted municipalities and other political subdivisions from regulating most aspects of firearms, including firearms carry and transport. Thus, firearms regulation of these areas is uniform throughout the state.

The city ordinances below relate to knife carry:

No relevant ordinances. An examination of ordinances for a number of municipalities shows no knife-related ordinances with restrictions greater than those embodied in state law.

59.4 State Resources

Vermont State Police
103 South Main Street
Waterbury, VT 05671-2101
Phone: (802) 244-7345
Website: http://www.dps.state.vt.us/vtsp/

Attorney General of Vermont
109 State Street
Montpelier, VT 05609-1001
Phone: (802) 828 3171
Fax: (802) 828 3187
Website: http://www.atg.state.vt.us/

60 Virginia – Old Dominion

Area: 39,594 sq.mi. (Rank: 37th)   Population: 7,769,089 (Rank: 12th)
Violent Crime Rate (per 100,000 residents): 255.9 (Rank: 10th Safest)
State Motto: *Sic Semper Tyrannis (Thus Always to Tyrants)*

Firearms Carry Summary:

Carry considerations	Status
Restaurants and bars	Open handgun carry allowed; new law effective July 1, 2010 allows concealed carry with permit, but carrier cannot consume alcohol.
Churches / Places of worship	Prohibited
State parks / forests	Concealed with permit allowed
Vehicle carry	Loaded handguns and long guns allowed in plain view, or stored in trunk
LE notification if stopped?	Not required
Retreat requirement for self-defense	Required
Preemption law	Yes. *See*, VA. CODE § 15.2-915 (2009)
Open Carry	Allowed and generally accepted
Military-pattern semi-auto restrictions	(Mostly) Not restricted; certain semi-auto shotguns prohibited ("streetsweeper", etc.)
NFA weapons	State registration required in addition to compliance with federal law

Reciprocity / Recognition

*Virginia **recognizes** permits from the following states:*

Alaska	Arizona	Arkansas	Delaware
Florida	Kentucky	Louisiana	Michigan
Minnesota	Mississippi	Missouri	Montana
North Carolina	North Dakota	Nebraska	New Mexico
Ohio	Oklahoma	Pennsylvania	South Carolina
South Dakota	Tennessee	Texas	Utah
Washington	West Virginia	Wyoming	

*Virginia permits **are recognized by** the following states:*

Alaska	Arizona	Arkansas	Delaware
Florida*	Idaho	Indiana	Kentucky
Louisiana	Michigan*	Mississippi	Missouri
Montana	North Carolina	North Dakota	Nebraska
New Mexico	Ohio	Oklahoma	Pennsylvania

| South Carolina* | South Dakota | Tennessee | Texas |
| Utah | Vermont | West Virginia | Wyoming |

Note: In the reciprocity / recognition tables above, states with an asterisk (*) require the permit holder to both have a permit from, and be a resident of, the recognized state in order for reciprocity / recognition of the permit.

Knife Carry Summary:

Note: Blade length limits, if any, in parentheses.

Knife Type	Open Carry	Concealed Carry	Notes
Folding	Yes	Yes	See note[190]
Fixed Blade	Yes	No	See note[191]
Dirks, Daggers, Stilettos	Yes	No	
Automatics	No	No	
Balisongs	No	No	See note[192]

60.1 Discussion

Firearms Carry:

Visitors to Virginia will find a generally friendly legal environment for firearms carry. State law requires a permit to carry a concealed handgun. Such permits are issued on a "shall issue" basis to qualified residents and nonresidents. In addition, Virginia will recognize permits from states whose standards of issuance are similar to Virginia's. Currently, Virginia recognizes permits from twenty-seven other states.

---

[190] Case law has sometimes taken an expansive view of the catch-all provision of the concealed carry statute. For example, a folding knife with a three and a half inch locking blade, with certain additional "weapon-like" features, has been held to be a prohibited weapon under the statute. *See*, Ohin v. Comm., 622 S.E.2d 784, 787 (Va. Ct. App. 2005). Travelers would be wise to avoid carry of "tactical" folders with overly aggressive or weapon-like appearances.

[191] State law specifically prohibits concealed carry of such large fixed bladed knives as bowie knives and machetes. *See*, VA. CODE § 18.2-308(A)(ii) (2009). Travelers should exercise caution when carrying fixed blades concealed, especially large fixed blades or those with aggressive, weapon-like appearances or features.

[192] Readers should be aware that balisongs may fall under the switchblade prohibition, as balisongs do in some states. As such, travelers should avoid carry of balisongs.

Open carry of a loaded handgun is legal in Virginia without a permit, and increasingly accepted.

State law prohibits the carry in public in certain cities and counties[193] of loaded semiautomatic centerfire rifles or pistols with magazines holding more than twenty rounds of ammunition, or that are designed to accommodate silencers or that are equipped with folding stocks. In addition, carry of loaded shotguns capable of holding more than seven rounds is also prohibited in these cities and counties. Exceptions exist for lawful hunting or lawful recreational shooting at established shooting ranges. This prohibition also does not apply to those holding valid concealed handgun permits.[194]

A traveler in a vehicle who does not possess a recognized permit may carry a loaded handgun so long as the firearm is carried openly, i.e., in plain view. Long guns may similarly be carried loaded provided that they are in plain view such as in a visible gun rack or encased in a commercial gun case that is in plain view in the vehicle.

Virginia's strong preemption law prohibits local governments from regulating any aspect of firearms possession, transport, or carry in public, although local governments may regulate firearms possession on the premises of local jails and detention facilities.

Knife Carry:

Visitors to Virginia will encounter a legal environment that strongly favors open, versus concealed, carry of knives. Ordinary folding pocket knives may be carried concealed. State law prohibits concealed carry of a variety of knives, such as dirks, machetes, razors, and such large fixed bladed knives as bowie knives. In addition, as a practical matter, state law bans possession of automatic knives, specifically switchblades and ballistic knives.[195]

---

[193] See, VA. CODE § 18.2-287.4 (2009). The prohibition applies to carry of loaded long guns on or about the person "on any public street, road, alley, sidewalk, public right-of-way, or in any public park or any other place of whatever nature that is open to the public in the Cities of Alexandria, Chesapeake, Fairfax, Falls Church, Newport News, Norfolk, Richmond, or Virginia Beach or in the Counties of Arlington, Fairfax, Henrico, Loudoun, or Prince William."

[194] See, id.

[195] See, VA. CODE § 18.2-311 (2009). This statute prohibits the possession of any switchblade "with the intent of selling, bartering, giving, or furnishing," and defines *mere possession* as prima facie evidence of such intent. This means that the law presumes that your mere possession of a switchblade signifies your intent to violate VA. CODE § 18.2-311. Thus, while technically possession without the required intent may be legal, as a practical matter, mere possession of a switchblade would likely land

There is no statutorily defined blade length limit. While state law technically allows carry of some fixed blades, travelers should be aware that the state's courts have taken a sometimes expansive view of the catch-all provision of the statute that bans "weapon[s] of like kind."[196] Furthermore, recent court decisions have interpreted the catch-all provision to include folding knives with blades as short as three and a half inches, but with "weapon-like" features and appearance. Thus, travelers should exercise caution when carrying any concealed blade, especially folders or fixed blades with overly "tactical," weapon-like appearances or features.

Readers should be aware that balisongs may fall under the switchblade prohibition, as balisongs do in some states. As such, carry of balisongs is not advised.

Virginia prohibits the carry of firearms and other dangerous weapons, including knives other than a folding pocket knife with a blade less than three inches, on elementary, middle, or high school property. This prohibition includes school buses, and school-sponsored events. Certain limited exceptions exist, such as for possession in a motor vehicle. State law prohibits carry of firearms, bowie knives, daggers and other dangerous weapons at places of worship while religious meetings or services are underway "without good and sufficient reason," although this phrase is not defined. Carry of firearms and dangerous weapons is also prohibited in courthouses. Finally, state law prohibits carry of firearms and dangerous weapons into air carrier airport terminals, with certain obvious exceptions for passengers traveling and checking or claiming such weapons into, or from, checked luggage.

Note that municipal governments may enact their own ordinances prohibiting or otherwise further restricting knife carry in their jurisdictions, although few cities or towns, with perhaps the notable exception of Richmond[197], appear to have enacted ordinances with restrictions substantially greater than those embodied in state law.

---

you in legal trouble. While the legal presumption in § 18.2-311 regarding mere possession may be rebuttable, mere possession will likely support a charge (a Class 4 misdemeanor per the statute) of violating § 18.2-311, and, absent other defenses or challenges, you (via your attorney(s)) would likely have to overcome this legal presumption in order to avoid a conviction under this statute. Don't be a test case!

[196] See, VA. CODE § 18.2-308(A)(v) (2009).

[197] See, selected city ordinances cited, Section 60.3, infra.

60.2 Places Off-Limits While Carrying

Firearms Carry:

Virginia prohibits the carry of firearms in schools, including school grounds and buildings, and school buses. Violation of this prohibition is a felony. Unloaded firearms securely cased in locked containers may be stored in a vehicle on school grounds. For purposes of this exemption, a locked vehicle trunk qualifies as a locked container. In addition, a holder of a recognized carry permit may possess a concealed handgun while in a motor vehicle in a parking lot, traffic circle, or other area of vehicle ingress or egress from the school. *See*, VA. CODE § 18.2-308.1 (2009).

State law prohibits possession or carry of firearms in courthouses. *See*, VA. CODE § 18.2-283.1 (2009).

State law allows local or regional jails and juvenile detention facilities to prohibit firearms carry on their premises. *See*, VA. CODE § 15.2-915 (2009).

Virginia prohibits carrying of firearms or dangerous weapons into churches or other places of religious worship. *See*, VA. CODE § 18.2-283 (2009). While the statute specifies that such carry is prohibited without "good and sufficient reason", the cautious traveler should realize that as a practical matter the burden of proof of such "good and sufficient reason" will be up to the traveler should you be arrested for violation of this prohibition.

Virginia prohibits the carrying of concealed firearms into establishments that serve alcoholic beverages for on-premises consumption. *See*, VA. CODE § 18.2-308(J3) (2009). Travelers wishing to carry in such establishments must do so with the firearm openly visible. **Note:** Effective July 1, 2010, carry of concealed firearms by those with a recognized permit in establishments that serve alcohol for on-premises consumption is also allowed. The carrier of the concealed firearm, however, may not consume alcohol. *See*, VA. CODE § 18.2-308(J3) (2010) (effective July 1, 2010).

Travelers should be aware that some Virginia universities may prohibit the carry or possession of firearms on their campuses, regardless of whether the traveler is a student or not, and regardless of whether the traveler holds a recognized permit or not. For example, Virginia Commonwealth University prohibits the possession of firearms on its campus without written authorization from the university president, regardless of whether a person holds a recognized permit or not. *See*, 8 VA. ADMIN. CODE § 90-10-50 (2009).

State law prohibits the carrying of firearms in airport terminals, including both secure and nonsecure areas of such terminals. Passengers may carry unloaded and securely cased firearms to or from such terminals for the purpose of checking or retrieving such firearms as baggage for air travel. *See*, VA. CODE § 18.2-287.01 (2009).

Knife Carry:

Virginia prohibits the carry of firearms and other dangerous weapons, including knives other than a folding pocket knife with a blade less than three inches, on elementary, middle, or high school property, including school buses, and at school-sponsored events. *See*, VA. CODE § 18.2-308.1 (2009). Certain limited exceptions exist, such as for possession in a motor vehicle. *See, id.* State law prohibits carry of firearms, bowie knives, daggers and other dangerous weapons at places of worship while religious meetings or services are underway "without good and sufficient reason." *See, id.* at § 18.2-283. Carry of firearms and dangerous weapons is also prohibited in courthouses. *See, id.* at § 18.2-283.1. Finally, state law prohibits carry of firearms and dangerous weapons into air carrier airport terminals, with certain exceptions for passengers traveling and checking or claiming such weapons into, or from, checked luggage. *See, id.* at § 18.2-287.01.

60.3 Selected City Ordinances

The state legislature has preempted municipalities and other political subdivisions from regulating firearms to any extent greater than state law. Thus, firearms regulation is uniform throughout the state.

The city ordinances below relate to knife carry:

Fairfax – Concealed carry of "dirk bowie knife, switchblade knife, razor," or "any weapon of like kind" prohibited. *See*, FAIRFAX, VA., CODE OF ORDINANCES § 54-171 (2009). An exception exists for those with valid concealed carry permits. *See, id.*

Richmond – Unlawful to possess any "clasp knife" (generally, folding knife with locking blade) with blade greater than three and a quarter inches in length. *See*, RICHMOND, VA., CODE OF ORDINANCES § 66-347 (2008). Concealed carry of any "dirk, bowie knife, switchblade knife, ballistic knife, razor," or "any weapon of like kind[,]" prohibited. *See, id.* at § 66-349. Unlawful to furnish dirk, switchblade or bowie knife to any minor, having "good cause to believe" such person is a minor. *See, id.* at § 66-351.

60.4 State Resources

Virginia State Police
P.O. Box 27472
Richmond, VA 23261
Phone: (804) 674-2000
Fax: (804) 674-2936
Website: http://www.vsp.state.va.us/

Attorney General of Virginia
900 East Main Street
Richmond, VA 23219
Phone: (804) 786-2071
Fax: (804) 786-1991
Website: http://www.oag.state.va.us/

61 Washington – The Evergreen State

Area: 66,544 sq.mi. (Rank: 20th)	Population: 6,549,224 (Rank: 13th)
Violent Crime Rate (per 100,000 residents): 331.2 (Rank: 23rd Safest)	
State Motto: *Alki (By and By)*	

Firearms Carry Summary:

Carry considerations	Status
Restaurants and bars	Allowed in restaurants only
Churches / Places of worship	Allowed
State parks / forests	Concealed allowed with permit
Vehicle carry	Loaded handguns allowed with permit; otherwise, all firearms must be unloaded and securely cased
LE notification if stopped?	Not required
Retreat requirement for self-defense	Required
Preemption law	Yes. *See*, WASH. REV. CODE § 9.41.290 (2009)
Open Carry	Allowed, but relatively uncommon
Military-pattern semi-auto restrictions	Not restricted
NFA weapons	Possession prohibited

Reciprocity / Recognition

*Washington **recognizes** permits from the following states:*

Arkansas	Florida	Louisiana	Michigan
Mississippi	Missouri	North Carolina	Ohio
Oklahoma	Utah		

*Washington permits **are recognized by** the following states:*

Alaska	Arizona	Arkansas	Florida*
Idaho	Indiana	Kentucky	Louisiana
Michigan*	Mississippi	Missouri	Montana
North Carolina	Ohio	Oklahoma	South Dakota
Tennessee	Texas	Utah	Virginia
Vermont			

Note: In the reciprocity / recognition tables above, states with an asterisk (*) require the permit holder to both have a permit from, and be a resident of, the recognized state in order for reciprocity / recognition of the permit.

Knife Carry Summary:

Note: Blade length limits, if any, in parentheses.

Knife Type	Open Carry	Concealed Carry	Notes
Folding	Yes	Yes	See note[198]
Fixed Blade	Yes	Yes	See note[198]
Dirks, Daggers, Stilettos	Yes	No	See note[199]
Automatics	No	No	
Balisongs	No	No	

61.1 Discussion

Firearms Carry:

Travelers to the Evergreen State find a moderately friendly legal environment for firearms carry. Washington requires a permit to carry a handgun concealed on one's person, or in a vehicle. Such permits are issued on a "shall issue" basis to qualified residents and nonresidents. Unfortunately, Washington currently recognizes that carry permits of only a relative handful of other states.

Open carry of a loaded handgun or long gun in public (and outside of a vehicle) is legal without a permit, although such carry tends to be uncommon, particularly in the more urban areas of the state.

State law provides an exception to concealed handgun carry to persons engaged in lawful outdoor recreational activities such as hunting, fishing, camping, hiking, and horseback riding. Travelers should note, however, that the exception will only apply if "considering all of the attendant circumstances, including but not limited to whether the person has a valid hunting or fishing license, it

---

[198] Readers should be aware that local governments may enact their own carry or possession restrictions with regard to knives in their jurisdictions. For example, Seattle prohibits carry of any kind, with certain limited exceptions, of any fixed bladed knives, or folding knives with blades greater than three and a half inches. *See*, SEATTLE, WASH., MUNICIPAL CODE § 12A.14.080 (2006).

[199] State law prohibits the furtive carry "with intent to conceal" any dirk, dagger, or "other dangerous weapon." *See*, WASH. REV. CODE § 9.41.250 (2009). State law also prohibits the carry, exhibition, display, or drawing of any knife with intent to intimidate or that "warrants alarm for the safety of" others. *See*, *id.* at § 9.41.270. Cautious travelers would do well to avoid carry of dirks, daggers, or stilettos, especially in urban areas.

is reasonable to conclude that the person is participating in lawful outdoor activities or is traveling to or from a legitimate outdoor recreation area[.]"²⁰⁰ Thus, your visit to Seattle's Space Needle is unlikely to qualify.

Travelers with recognized permits may carry loaded handguns in a vehicle, provided the firearm is carried on the person and not stored, for example, in the glove compartment, center console or other storage container.²⁰¹ A traveler with a recognized permit who wishes to store a loaded handgun in an unattended vehicle must ensure the vehicle is locked and the firearm is concealed from view. Even with a recognized permit, all long guns must be transported unloaded when in a vehicle, as carry permits apply only to handguns in Washington.

Vehicle travelers without recognized permits must transport all firearms in an unloaded and securely cased condition. Firearms are considered unloaded only if both the firing chamber is empty and the gun is devoid of ammunition. For those firearms with detachable magazines, no loaded magazine may be inserted into the firearm.²⁰²

Knife Carry:

Visitors to the Evergreen State will find a moderately permissive legal environment for knife carry. State law permits open or concealed carry of ordinary folding pocket knives. Ordinary fixed bladed knives, as well as dirks, daggers, and stilettos may technically be carried openly under state law, although visitors should be aware that many fixed bladed knives, especially large knives such as bowies, and dirks, daggers, and stilettos, will likely be considered *per se* weapons. Given that state law forbids the carrying, exhibition, display, or drawing of any knife or weapon "in a manner, under circumstances, and at a time and place that either manifests an intent to intimidate another or that warrants alarm for the safety of other persons[,]"²⁰³ visitors should exercise considerable caution whenever openly carrying any fixed blade, especially in urban areas, lest they run afoul of this statute.

There is no statutorily defined blade length limit under state law. Automatic knives, to include switchblades and gravity knives, are prohibited. Balisongs may fall under the switchblade prohibition, as

²⁰⁰ *See*, WASH. REV. CODE § 9.41.060 (2009).
²⁰¹ *See*, WASH. REV. CODE § 9.41.050 (2009).
²⁰² *See*, WASH. REV. CODE § 77.15.460 (2009).
²⁰³ *See*, WASH. REV. CODE § 9.41.270 (2009). Certain exceptions do exist for persons in their homes, or for lawful self-defense. *See, id.*

balisongs do in some states, and several appellate court decisions have referred to balisongs (butterfly knives) as illegal knives.[204]

State law prohibits carry of dangerous weapons on elementary or secondary school premises, including school-provided transportation (e.g., school buses) and other areas or facilities while being used exclusively by such schools. State law also forbids the possession of weapons in the restricted access areas of jails and law enforcement facilities, court facilities, the restricted access areas of mental health facilities for inpatient hospital care and state institutions for the mentally ill, the portions of alcoholic beverage establishments off-limits to persons under twenty-one, and the restricted access areas of airports.

Note that local governments are free to impose their own restrictions or prohibitions on knife carry within their respective jurisdictions, and some, notably Seattle, have done so. Seattle, for example, prohibits the carry, whether open or concealed, of *any* fixed blade, regardless of blade length, or any other knife with a blade greater than three and a half inches, with certain narrow exemptions for bona fide hunting, fishing, or occupational uses.

61.2 Places Off-Limits While Carrying

Firearms Carry:

Washington prohibits carry or possession of firearms on the premises of any elementary or secondary school, school-provided transportation such as school buses, or any areas or facilities while being used exclusively for school functions. *See*, WASH. REV. CODE § 9.41.280 (2009).

State law also prohibits firearms carry in the restricted access areas of jails, law enforcement facilities, detention facilities, courthouses and court rooms. In addition, firearms carry is also prohibited in the restricted access areas of public mental health facilities providing inpatient hospital care, and state institutions for the care of the mentally ill. In general, the restricted areas do not include common areas of ingress and egress to the building that are open to the general public. *See*, WASH. REV. CODE § 9.41.300.

---

[204] *See, e.g., State v. Parr*, 2001 WA 693, slip op. at ¶ 28 (Wash. Ct. App. May 8, 2001) (discussing arrest and referring to knife as "illegal butterfly knife").

Washington prohibits the carrying of weapons, including firearms, in those portions of establishments, e.g. bars, classified by the state liquor control Board as off-limits to persons under twenty-one years of age. *See, id.*

State law prohibits carry in the restricted access areas of commercial service airports, although such areas are already off-limits under federal law. Note that carry is not restricted in the areas of the airport outside the restricted access areas that are normally open to unscreened passengers or visitors to the airport. *See, id.*

Travelers planning on attending any outdoor music festivals in the Evergreen State should be aware that state law prohibits firearms possession or carry at such venues. *See*, WASH. REV. CODE § 70.108.150. The definition of an "outdoor music festival" does not, however, include "any regularly established permanent place of worship, stadium, athletic field, arena, auditorium, coliseum, or other similar permanently established places of assembly for assemblies which do not exceed by more than two hundred fifty people the maximum seating capacity of the structure where the assembly is held", nor to government sponsored fairs held on regularly established fairgrounds. *See*, WASH. REV. CODE § 70.108.020.

Travelers should be aware that carrying firearms on tribal lands and Indian reservations located in the state requires permission of the appropriate tribal official, such as a tribal judge. In addition, visitors should be aware that state agencies may, by administrative rule, prohibit firearms in their facilities.

Knife Carry:

Washington prohibits the carry of dangerous weapons on elementary or secondary school premises, including school-provided transportation (e.g., school buses) and other areas or facilities while being used exclusively by such schools. *See*, WASH. REV. CODE § 9.41.280 (2009).

State law also forbids the possession of weapons in the restricted access areas of jails and law enforcement facilities, court facilities, the restricted access areas of mental health facilities for inpatient hospital care and state institutions for the mentally ill, the portions of alcoholic beverage establishments off-limits to persons under twenty-one, and the restricted access areas of airports. *See, id.* at § 9.41.300.

302 | THE TRAVELER'S GUN & KNIFE LAW BOOK

61.3 Selected City Ordinances

The state legislature has preempted municipalities and other political subdivisions from regulating firearms to any extent greater than state law. Thus, firearms regulation is uniform throughout the state.

The city ordinances below relate to knife carry:

Seattle – "Dangerous knife" includes *any* fixed bladed knife, regardless of blade length, and any other knife with blade greater than three and a half inches long. Carry, whether open or concealed, of dangerous knife prohibited. *See*, SEATTLE, WASH., MUNICIPAL CODE § 12A.14.080 (2010). Exceptions exist for licensed hunters and fishermen while hunting or fishing, and for lawful occupational use if carried openly. *See, id.* at § 12A.14.100.

Cheney – Concealed carry of any dirk, dagger, or other knife, other than ordinary pocket knife, prohibited. *See*, CHENEY, WASH., MUNICIPAL CODE § 9A.07.020 (2008). Exception exists for bona fide hunting, fishing, or camping purposes. *See, id.* at § 9A.07.021.

61.4 State Resources

Washington State Patrol
General Administration Building
P.O. Box 42600
Olympia, WA 98504-2600
Phone: (360) 596-4000
Website: http://www.wsp.wa.gov/

Attorney General of Washington
1125 Washington St. SE
P.O. Box 40100
Olympia, WA 98504-0100
Phone: (360) 753-6200
Website: http://www.atg.wa.gov/

62 West Virginia – The Mountain State

Area: 24,078 sq.mi. (Rank: 41st)   Population: 1,814,468 (Rank: 37th)
Violent Crime Rate (per 100,000 residents): 273.8 (Rank: 15th Safest)
State Motto: *Montani semper liberi (Mountaineers are Always Free)*

Firearms Carry Summary:

Carry considerations	Status
Restaurants and bars	Allowed
Churches / Places of worship	Allowed
State parks / forests	Allowed with permit; may be prohibited in some city parks
Vehicle carry	Loaded handgun allowed with permit, otherwise all firearms must be unloaded and securely cased
LE notification if stopped?	Not required
Retreat requirement for self-defense	Required
Preemption law	Yes, but pre-1999 ordinances grandfathered. *See*, W.VA. CODE § 8-12-5a (2009)
Open Carry	Generally allowed, but some localities prohibit
Military-pattern semi-auto restrictions	Not restricted
NFA weapons	NFA-friendly, compliance with federal law only

Reciprocity / Recognition

West Virginia **recognizes** *permits from the following states:*

Alaska	Arizona	Arkansas	Delaware
Florida	Kentucky	Louisiana	Michigan
Mississippi	Missouri	North Carolina	North Dakota
Ohio	Oklahoma	Pennsylvania	South Carolina
South Dakota	Tennessee	Virginia	Utah

West Virginia permits **are recognized by** *the following states:*

Alaska	Arizona	Arkansas	Delaware
Florida*	Idaho	Indiana	Kansas
Kentucky	Louisiana	Michigan*	Mississippi
Missouri	Montana	North Carolina	North Dakota

Nebraska	Nevada	Ohio	Oklahoma
Pennsylvania	South Carolina*	South Dakota	Tennessee
Utah	Vermont	Virginia	

Note: In the reciprocity / recognition tables above, states with an asterisk (*) require the permit holder to both have a permit from, and be a resident of, the recognized state in order for reciprocity / recognition of the permit.

Knife Carry Summary:

Note: Blade length limits, if any, in parentheses.

Knife Type	Open Carry	Concealed Carry	Notes
Folding	Yes	Yes (≤ 3.5")	
Fixed Blade	Yes	Yes (≤ 3.5")	See note[205]
Dirks, Daggers, Stilettos	Yes	Yes (≤ 3.5")	
Automatics	Yes	No	
Balisongs	Yes	No	

62.1 Discussion

Firearms Carry:

Visitors to the Mountain State will find a somewhat friendly legal environment for firearms carry. West Virginia requires a permit to carry a handgun concealed on one's person, or in a vehicle. Such permits are issued on a "shall issue" basis to qualified residents. West Virginia does not issue permits to nonresidents, although the state will recognize the permits of other states that have signed reciprocity agreements. At this time, West Virginia recognizes the permits of twenty other states.

---

[205] State law allows hunting and fishing knives to be carried for legitimate hunting, fishing, sports or other recreational uses, as well as knives designed as tools or household implements. Such knives are not considered deadly weapons *per se*, unless used or intended to be used as such to inflict serious bodily injury or death. *See*, W. VA. CODE § 61-7-2 (2009).

Open carry of a firearm while on foot is legal without a permit[206], although travelers should be aware that some cities such as Charleston prohibit open carry. Such bans are unfortunately grandfathered and not preempted by the state's preemption law. In addition, those carrying handguns in outdoor areas during hunting season would be well advised to have a recognized permit with them, in case they be mistaken for someone hunting illegally. Carry of a concealed handgun with a recognized permit for self-defense is explicitly permitted while hunting, hiking, or camping. 20-2-6a.

A traveler without a recognized permit may not carry a loaded firearm of any kind while in a vehicle. Such firearms must be unloaded and should be securely cased. Any ammunition should be separately cased and stored apart from the firearms.

A traveler who possesses a recognized permit may carry a loaded handgun openly or concealed on his person in the vehicle. Long guns, however, must be transported in an unloaded condition, regardless of whether one has a carry permit or not, and should be securely cased when in the vehicle, and any ammunition should be separately cased and stored apart from the firearms.

Knife Carry:

Visitors to West Virginia will find a fairly permissive legal environment for knife carry, with a strong legal bias for open, as opposed to concealed, carry. State law allows open carry of a wide variety of knives, including dirks, daggers, stilettos, and automatic knives. As with most states, readers should exercise caution when carrying large knives openly, especially in urban areas, as such carry is likely to attract law enforcement attention.

State law allows concealed carry of pocket knives with blades three and a half inches or less. Fixed bladed knives, including dirks, daggers, and stilettos with blades three and a half inches or less, may also be carried concealed.

---

[206] Travelers should be aware that the West Virginia Attorney General's brochure for concealed carry holders states that "[w]hile West Virginia is an 'Open Carry' state, only residents of West Virginia may do so." *See, On The Mark: A Guide to the Concealed Weapons Laws of West Virginia*, W. Va. Attorney General's office, available at http://wvago.gov/pdf/brochures/2009 gunbrochure.pdf, at 4. The statutory law does not appear to support this statement, however, as the statutes appear to address and prohibit only concealed carry without a recognized permit. The statutes are simply silent on the issue of open carry.

State law prohibits carry of knives, regardless of blade length, in schools and school property, including school buses. In addition, knife carry in courthouses, and in the offices of family law masters, is prohibited.

As is the case in most states, municipalities may enact their own ordinances prohibiting or otherwise restricting knife carry in their jurisdictions.

62.2 Places Off-Limits While Carrying

Firearms Carry:

West Virginia prohibits the carry of firearms in primary and secondary schools and school premises, school buses, although unloaded firearms may be transported or stored in a private motor vehicle; if the vehicle is unattended, then the vehicle must be locked. See, W. VA. CODE § 61-7-11a (2009).

State law also prohibits firearms carry in courts and courthouses, and the offices of family law masters. See, id.

Carry of firearms and other deadly weapons is also prohibited on the grounds of the state capitol complex. See, id. at § 61-6-19.

Note that other government agencies may promulgate rules regarding firearms and weapons carry in their facilities, such as jails, detention and law enforcement facilities.

Knife Carry:

State law prohibits the carry of firearms and other deadly weapons, the definition of which includes knives, in schools, school buses, courthouses, and the offices of family law masters. See, W. VA. CODE § 61-7-11a (2009).

62.3 Selected City Ordinances

The state legislature has preempted municipalities and other political subdivisions from regulating most aspects of firearms possession and carry. Unfortunately, the legislature has grandfathered existing ordinances in effect at the adoption of the state's preemption law (ca.

1999), and thus a number of such ordinances are still in effect. Some selected pre-1999 ordinances still in effect include:

Charleston – Unlawful to carry firearms in municipal buildings. *See*, CHARLESTON, W. VA., CODE OF ORDINANCES § 78-163 (2009). Unlawful to carry firearms without valid carry permit in Sternwheel Regatta area for ten days preceding Labor Day, and including Labor Day. *See, id.*

South Charleston – Unlawful to carry firearms (with or without permit) in or on city-owned building, park or recreational area. *See*, SOUTH CHARLESTON, W. VA. CODE § 545.15 (2009).

The city ordinances below relate to knife carry:

Charleston – Unlawful to carry dirks, bowie knives, razors, "or other dangerous or deadly weapon of like kind or character." *See*, CHARLESTON, W. VA., CODE OF ORDINANCES § 78-163 (2009). Unlawful to carry same in designated Sternwheel Regatta area of Kanawha Boulevard during period ten days before Labor Day, and including Labor Day. *See, id.* § 78-164. Carry of such knives prohibited in or upon city hall, municipal auditorium, civic center, all parks and recreation buildings and facilities, and all other buildings or facilities owned or occupied by the City. *See, id.* at § 78-165. Possession of switchblades prohibited. *See, id.* at § 78-168.

62.4 State Resources

West Virginia State Police
725 Jefferson Road
South Charleston, WV 25309-1698
Phone: (304) 746-2100
Website: http://www.wvstatepolice.com/

Attorney General of West Virginia
State Capitol Complex - Bldg. 1, Room E-26
Charleston, WV 25305
Phone: (304) 558-2021
Fax: (304) 558-0140
Website: http://www.wvago.gov/

63 Wisconsin – The Badger State

Area: 54,310 sq.mi. (Rank: 25th)   Population: 5,627,967 (Rank: 20th)
Violent Crime Rate (per 100,000 residents): 274.0 (Rank: 16th Safest)
State Motto: *Forward!*

Firearms Carry Summary:

Carry considerations	Status
Restaurants and bars	Prohibited
Churches / Places of worship	Open carry required; church can prohibit
State parks / forests	Prohibited
Vehicle carry	All firearms must be unloaded and securely cased
LE notification if stopped?	N/A
Retreat requirement for self-defense	Required
Preemption law	Yes. *See*, WIS. STAT. § 66.0409 (2009).
Open Carry	Allowed, but uncommon
Military-pattern semi-auto restrictions	Not restricted
NFA weapons	Machine gun ownership requires Sheriff / Police Chief authorization, as well as compliance with federal law.

Reciprocity / Recognition

Wisconsin **does _not_ recognize** permits from any other state.

Wisconsin **does not issue** carry permits, and thus there is no permit for another state to recognize. Wisconsin residents who can lawfully possess firearms, however, may carry concealed handguns in Alaska and Vermont, because those states do not require a permit to carry concealed handguns. After July 29, 2010, such residents may also carry concealed handguns without a permit in Arizona.

Knife Carry Summary:

Note: Blade length limits, if any, in parentheses.

Knife Type	Open Carry	Concealed Carry	Notes
Folding	Yes	Yes	
Fixed Blade	Yes	No	

Knife Type	Open Carry	Concealed Carry	Notes
Dirks, Daggers, Stilettos	Yes	No	
Automatics	No	No	
Balisongs	No	No	

63.1 Discussion

Firearms Carry:

Travelers to the Badger State will find a generally unfriendly legal environment for firearms carry. This may seem somewhat surprising, given the state's Midwestern location and farming and hunting heritage. Wisconsin is one of only two states in the nation that does not issue firearms carry permits to "mere" citizens. Naturally, Wisconsin also does not recognize the carry permits of any other state.

State law prohibits the carry of firearms concealed on one's person, or in a vehicle. The only option available to law-abiding citizens who wish to carry a firearm for personal protection, is to do so openly. While technically legal, however, travelers should be aware that open carry is uncommon and will likely draw the attention of law enforcement, particularly in more urban areas.

Even more unfortunate, the open carry option is only available to those on foot, and is not available to those traveling in a vehicle. State law prohibits the carry of loaded firearms of any type while in a vehicle.

All firearms, whether handguns or long guns, transported in a vehicle must be in an unloaded condition, and securely cased in commercial gun cases. Ammunition should be separately cased and stored apart from the weapon. State law defines "unloaded" as meaning that the weapon is completely devoid of ammunition, that is, no ammunition is present in either the firing chamber or in any attached or inserted magazine.[207]

Knife Carry:

Visitors to the Badger State will find a somewhat restrictive legal environment for knife carry. Under state law, ordinary folding pocket

---

[207] *See,* WIS. STAT. §§ 167.31, 941.237 (2009).

knives may be carried openly or concealed. There is no statutorily defined blade length limit under state law, although visitors should be aware that some municipalities do have blade length limits in their jurisdictions.

Wisconsin's broad concealed weapons prohibition strongly cautions against concealed carry of most fixed blades, lest they be deemed a "dangerous weapon" and thus proscribed under state law. Knives such as bowie knives, dirks, daggers, and stilettos are considered *per se* dangerous weapons, and thus may not be carried concealed. State law prohibits mere possession of automatic knives, including switchblades and gravity knives. Balisongs (butterfly knives) fall under the switchblade prohibition, and are thus prohibited as well.

State law prohibits the carry of dangerous weapons on school premises. Local municipal governments may enact their own ordinances prohibiting or otherwise restricting knife carry within their respective municipalities, and a number of municipal governments have done so. For example, Milwaukee has declared that any knife with a blade three inches or longer is *per se* dangerous.

63.2 *Places Off-Limits While Carrying*

Firearms Carry:

Wisconsin prohibits the possession of firearms in so-called "gun free school zones", defined as on the grounds of a school, or within 1000 feet of it. *See*, WIS. STAT. § 648.605 (2009).

State law also prohibits the carry of firearms in any building owned or leased by the state or by a local government. *See*, WIS. STAT. § 941.235.

Carry of firearms is prohibited in establishments that sell or serve alcoholic beverages. *See*, WIS. STAT. § 941.237.

Knife Carry:

Wisconsin prohibits the carry of dangerous weapons on school premises. *See*, WIS. STAT. ANN. § 948.61 (2009).

63.3 Selected City Ordinances

The state legislature has preempted municipalities and other political subdivisions from regulating firearms to any extent greater than state law. Thus, firearms regulation is uniform throughout the state.

The city ordinances below relate to knife carry:

Milwaukee County – Unlawful to go armed with concealed and dangerous weapon, with the following knives declared dangerous *per se*: "bowie knife, dirk knife, dagger, switchblade knife, or any knife which has a blade that is automatically opened by slight pressure on the handle or some other part of the knife, or any other knife having a blade three (3) inches or longer[.]" *See*, MILWAUKEE COUNTY, WIS., CODE OF GEN. ORDINANCES § 63.015 (2009).

Racine – Possession or carry of any dangerous weapon, whether concealed or in "plain view", prohibited. *See*, RACINE, WIS., MUNICIPAL CODE § 66-58 (2010). A separate provision prohibits going armed with a concealed and dangerous weapon. *See, id.* at § 66-57. The definition of dangerous weapon includes any "bowie knife; dirk knife; dirk dagger; any knife which has a blade that may be drawn without the necessity of contact with the blade itself but is instead automatically opened by slight pressure on the handle or some other part of the knife and is commonly known as a switchblade knife, straightedge razor or any knife having a blade three inches or longer[.]" *See, id.* at § 66-56. Carry of firearms, bowie knives, dirks or daggers, or any other dangerous or deadly weapon in properties under the jurisdiction of the Board of Parks, Recreation and Cultural Services prohibited. *See, id.* at § 70-79.

Sheboygan – Concealed carry of bowie knife, dirk or dagger prohibited. *See*, SHEBOYGAN, WIS., MUNICIPAL CODE § 70-253 (2010). Unlawful to be armed with switchblade or any knife with blade exceeding three inches in length, or "[a]ny other dangerous or deadly weapon, whether its purpose is offensive or defensive." *See, id.* at § 70-252. Possession of switchblades and "any other knife having a blade which opens by pressing a button, spring or other device in the handle, or any knife that opens by gravity or by a thrust or movement" prohibited. *See, id.* at § 70-258. Unlawful to board bus with dangerous or deadly weapon concealed upon person or effects. *See, id.* at § 70-218.

63.4 State Resources

Wisconsin State Patrol
Division Headquarters
Hill Farms State Transportation Building
4802 Sheboygan Avenue, Room 551
P.O. Box 7912
Madison, WI 53707-7912
Phone: (608) 266-3212
Fax: (608) 267-4495
Website: http://www.dot.wisconsin.gov/statepatrol/

Attorney General of Wisconsin
P.O. Box 7857
Madison, WI 53707-7857
Phone: (608) 266-1221
Fax: (608) 267-2779
Website: http://www.doj.state.wi.us/

64 Wyoming – The Equality State

Area: 97,100 sq.mi. (Rank: 9th)   Population: 532,668 (Rank: 50th)
Violent Crime Rate (per 100,000 residents): 232.0 (Rank: 8th Safest)
State Motto: *Equal Rights*

Firearms Carry Summary:

Carry considerations	Status
Restaurants and bars	Allowed in restaurants only
Churches / Places of worship	Allowed with written permission of church. *See*, WYO. STAT. § 6-8-104 (2009)
State parks / forests	Allowed
Vehicle carry	Open carry of loaded handguns, or loaded long guns in plain view allowed without permit, otherwise must be securely encased
LE notification if stopped?	Not required
Retreat requirement for self-defense	Required, except in home
Preemption law	Yes. *See*, WYO. STAT. § 6-8-401 (2009)
Open Carry	Allowed, and generally accepted
Military-pattern semi-auto restrictions	Not restricted
NFA weapons	NFA-friendly, compliance with federal law only

Reciprocity / Recognition

Wyoming **recognizes** *permits from the following states:*

Alabama	Alaska	Arizona	Arkansas
Colorado	Florida	Georgia	Idaho
Indiana	Kentucky	Louisiana	Michigan
Minnesota	Mississippi	Missouri	Montana
Nebraska	New Hampshire	New Mexico	North Carolina
North Dakota	Ohio	Oklahoma	Pennsylvania
South Carolina	South Dakota	Tennessee	Texas
Utah	Virginia		

Wyoming permits **are recognized by** *the following states:*

Alabama	Alaska	Arizona	Arkansas
Colorado*	Florida*	Georgia	Idaho
Indiana	Kentucky	Louisiana	Michigan*
Minnesota	Mississippi	Missouri	Montana

Nebraska	New Hampshire*	New Mexico	North Carolina
North Dakota	Ohio	Oklahoma	Pennsylvania
South Carolina*	South Dakota	Tennessee	Texas
Utah	Vermont	Virginia	

Note: In the reciprocity / recognition tables above, states with an asterisk (*) require the permit holder to both have a permit from, and be a resident of, the recognized state in order for reciprocity / recognition of the permit.

Knife Carry Summary:

Note: Blade length limits, if any, in parentheses.

Knife Type	Open Carry	Concealed Carry	Notes
Folding	Yes	Yes	
Fixed Blade	Yes	Yes	
Dirks, Daggers, Stilettos	Yes	No	
Automatics	Yes	No	
Balisongs	Yes	No	

64.1 Discussion

Firearms Carry:

Visitors to the Equality State will find a generally friendly legal environment for firearms carry. Wyoming requires a permit to carry a handgun concealed on one's person. Such permits are issued on a "shall issue" basis to qualified residents. The state does not issue permits to nonresidents, but does recognize the permits of twenty-three other states.

Open carry of a firearm while on foot is legal without a permit, and generally accepted. In addition, travelers without recognized permits may carry loaded handguns while in a vehicle, provided the handguns are carried openly in plain view. Handguns may also be transported unloaded and securely cased anywhere in the vehicle.

Long guns may be transported in a loaded condition in a vehicle so long as they are visible from outside the vehicle, such as secured in a visible gun rack. Otherwise, long guns may be transported unloaded and securely cased anywhere in the vehicle.

Wyoming's strong preemption law prohibits local governments from separately regulating firearms carry or possession. Thus, visitors will find firearms regulation to be uniform throughout the state.

Knife Carry:

Visitors to Wyoming will find a permissive legal environment for knife carry, with a strong bias towards open, versus concealed, carry. Most knives may be carried openly under state law. There is no statutorily defined blade length limit under state law, although some cities impose their own blade length limits for certain knives.

Knives such as ordinary folding pocket knives may be carried concealed. Fixed bladed knives that are not designed as, or otherwise considered *per se* weapons, may be carried concealed so long as the circumstances surrounding their carry do not evince an intent to use such knives unlawfully against others. For example, a hunting or fishing knife, while on a bona fide hunting or fishing trip, and used for legitimate hunting or fishing purposes, would likely meet this standard.

Knives such as dirks, daggers, and stilettos that are considered *per se* deadly weapons, however, may not be carried concealed. Automatic knives such as switchblades, while not specifically enumerated as *per se* weapons under state law, are often considered as such, and so the cautious traveler should avoid concealed carry of such knives. Travelers should also be aware that switchblades are enumerated as *per se* weapons under the municipal codes of some of the state's larger cities, and carry is restricted or banned. Balisongs, which are often associated with, and perceived as, martial arts weapons, should not be carried concealed, lest they be deemed weapons, and hence prohibited from being carried concealed.

Wyoming prohibits the possession of deadly weapons in jails, penal institutions, and other correctional facilities, and the state hospital (mental hospital). Towns and cities may pass their own local ordinances prohibiting or restricting knife carry in other areas or locations within their jurisdictions.

64.2 Places Off-Limits While Carrying

Firearms Carry:

Wyoming prohibits the carrying of concealed firearms, with or without a permit, into a variety of places, including law enforcement facilities (without written permission), detention facilities, prisons or jails, courtrooms, meetings of governmental entities, meetings of the legislature or legislative committees, and at school, college or professional athletic events not related to firearms. *See*, WYO. STAT. § 6-8-104 (2009).

State law also prohibits the carrying of concealed firearms into any portion of an establishment primarily devoted to serving alcoholic beverages for on premises consumption, such as bars and taverns. *See, id.*

Carry of firearms is also prohibited in all elementary and secondary school facilities. Colleges and universities are also off limits, unless written permission has been obtained from the college or university. *See, id.*

State law prohibits firearms carry in churches and other places of public worship without the written consent of the church or place of worship. *See, id.*

In addition, state law makes it a felony to take or pass a deadly weapon into a jail, state penal institution, the Wyoming boys' school, Wyoming girls' school, other correctional facility, or the state hospital (mental hospital). *See*, WYO. STAT. § 6-5-209.

Carry of firearms and other deadly weapons into the State Capitol building is also forbidden. *See*, WYO. STATE BUILDING COMM. R. ch. 6 § 2 (2010).

Knife Carry:

Wyoming prohibits the possession of deadly weapons in jails, penal institutions, and other correctional facilities, and the state hospital (mental hospital). *See*, WYO. STAT. § 6-5-209 (2009).

With regards to schools, no apparent state law limitation exists for non-students. Students who carry or possess deadly weapons on school grounds or school buses may, however, be suspended or expelled. *See*, WYO. STAT. § 21-4-306 (2009).

64.3 Selected City Ordinances

The state legislature has preempted municipalities and other political subdivisions from regulating firearms to any extent greater than state law. Thus, firearms regulation is uniform throughout the state.

The city ordinances below relate to knife carry:

Cheyenne – Unlawful to carry concealed any knife with blade exceeding four inches in length, any dirk, dagger, sword-in-cane, or any other dangerous or deadly weapon. Unlawful to carry openly any such item "with the intent or avowed purpose for injuring any person." See, CHEYENNE, WYO., CITY CODE § 9.24.040 (2009). Possession of switchblades ("switch knives") prohibited. See, id. at § 9.24.050. Carry or possession of deadly weapons on school grounds or school buses prohibited. Exception exists for persons with valid concealed weapons permits. See, id. at § 9.24.090.

Casper – Concealed carry of switchblades, fixed bladed knives of any length, folding knives with blades greater than four inches in length, swords-in-canes, or any other dangerous or deadly weapon, prohibited. See, CASPER, WYO., MUNICIPAL CODE § 9.44.020 (2009). Prohibition does not apply to those with appropriate concealed weapons permits. See, id.

Laramie – Concealed carry of knives with blades over five inches long, or other deadly weapons, prohibited. See, LARAMIE, WYO., MUNICIPAL CODE § 9.28.010 (2009).

64.4 State Resources

Wyoming Highway Patrol
State Headquarters
5300 Bishop Blvd.
Cheyenne, WY 82009-3340
Phone: (307) 777-4301
Website: http://www.whp.dot.state.wy.us/wydot/

Wyoming Attorney General
123 Capitol Building
Cheyenne, WY 82002
Phone: (307) 777-7841
Fax: (307) 777-6869
Website: http://attorneygeneral.state.wy.us/

About the Author

David Wong, an attorney in private practice, has been teaching and training in a variety of self-defense disciplines for many years, from firearms to knives to defensive tactics for high-risk situations, and holds instructor certifications in a variety of disciplines.

David is an NRA Life Member and NRA-certified firearms instructor, and has taught both lawfully-armed civilians and sworn law enforcement officers. He is an adjunct instructor at the Sig Sauer Academy in Epping, NH, where he currently teaches the Self-Defense Law and Basic Threat Management course for armed citizens. David is a member of the International Association of Law Enforcement Firearms Instructors (IALEFI), and is a charter member of the International Law Enforcement Educators and Trainers Association (ILEETA).

This book was inspired by the author's extensive cross-country travels, and the need to have an easy, accurate summary of the gun and knife-related transport and carry laws of each state.

Ordering Information

Need More Copies?

Retail Customers:

Order fast, safe and secure via the web: **SpartanPressOnline.com**

Dealers, Gun Stores, Clubs, Libraries, Organizations, and CCW Instructors and Educators:

We offer quantity discounts!   See our wholesale discount and quantity pricing schedule at **SpartanPressOnline.com**